George Scarbrough,
Appalachian Poet

Contributions to Southern Appalachian Studies

1. *Memoirs of Grassy Creek: Growing Up in the Mountains on the Virginia–North Carolina Line.* Zetta Barker Hamby. 1998

2. *The Pond Mountain Chronicle: Self-Portrait of a Southern Appalachian Community.* Edited by Leland R. Cooper and Mary Lee Cooper. 1998

3. *Traditional Musicians of the Central Blue Ridge: Old Time, Early Country, Folk and Bluegrass Label Recording Artists, with Discographies.* Marty McGee. 2000

4. *W.R. Trivett, Appalachian Pictureman: Photographs of a Bygone Time.* Ralph E. Lentz II. 2001

5. *The People of the New River: Oral Histories from the Ashe, Alleghany and Watauga Counties of North Carolina.* Edited by Leland R. Cooper and Mary Lee Cooper. 2001

6. *John Fox, Jr., Appalachian Author.* Bill York. 2003

7. *The Thistle and the Brier: Historical Links and Cultural Parallels Between Scotland and Appalachia.* Richard Blaustein. 2003

8. *Tales from Sacred Wind: Coming of Age in Appalachia. The Cratis Williams Chronicles.* Cratis D. Williams. Edited by David Cratis Williams and Patricia D. Beaver. 2003

9. *Willard Gayheart, Appalachian Artist.* Willard Gayheart and Donia S. Eley. 2003

10. *The Forest City Lynching of 1900: Populism, Racism, and White Supremacy in Rutherford County, North Carolina.* J. Timothy Cole. 2003

11. *The Brevard Rosenwald School: Black Education and Community Building in a Southern Appalachian Town, 1920–1966.* Betty J. Reed. 2004

12. *The Bristol Sessions: Writings About the Big Bang of Country Music.* Edited by Charles K. Wolfe and Ted Olson. 2005

13. *Community and Change in the North Carolina Mountains: Oral Histories and Profiles of People from Western Watauga County.* Compiled by Nannie Greene and Catherine Stokes Sheppard. 2006

14. *Ashe County: A History; A New Edition.* Arthur Lloyd Fletcher. 2009 [2006]

15. *The New River Controversy; A New Edition.* Thomas J. Schoenbaum. Epilogue by R. Seth Woodard. 2007

16. *The Blue Ridge Parkway by Foot: A Park Ranger's Memoir.* Tim Pegram. 2007

17. *James Still: Critical Essays on the Dean of Appalachian Literature.* Edited by Ted Olson and Kathy H. Olson. 2008

18. *Owsley County, Kentucky, and the Perpetuation of Poverty.* John R. Burch, Jr. 2008

19. *Asheville: A History.* Nan K. Chase. 2007

20. *Southern Appalachian Poetry: An Anthology of Works by 37 Poets.* Edited by Marita Garin. 2008

21. *Ball, Bat and Bitumen: A History of Coalfield Baseball in the Appalachian South.* L.M. Sutter. 2009

22. *The Frontier Nursing Service: America's First Rural Nurse-Midwife Service and School.* Marie Bartlett. 2009

23. *James Still in Interviews, Oral Histories and Memoirs.* Edited by Ted Olson. 2009

24. *The Millstone Quarries of Powell County, Kentucky.* Charles D. Hockensmith. 2009

25. *The Bibliography of Appalachia: More Than 4,700 Books, Articles, Monographs and Dissertations, Topically Arranged and Indexed.* Compiled by John R. Burch, Jr. 2009

26. *Appalachian Children's Literature: An Annotated Bibliography*
Compiled by Roberta T. Herrin and Sheila Quinn Oliver. 2009

27. *Southern Appalachian Storytellers: Interviews with Sixteen Keepers of the Oral Tradition.* Edited by Saundra Gerrell Kelley. 2010

28. *Southern West Virginia and the Struggle for Modernity.* Christopher Dorsey. 2011

29. *George Scarbrough, Appalachian Poet: A Biographical and Literary Study with Unpublished Writings.* Randy Mackin. 2011

30. *The Water-Powered Mills of Floyd County, Virginia: Illustrated Histories, 1770–2010.* Franklin F. Webb and Ricky L. Cox. 2011

31. *School Segregation in Western North Carolina: A History, 1860s–1970s.* Betty Jamerson Reed. 2011

George Scarbrough, Appalachian Poet

A Biographical and Literary Study with Unpublished Writings

RANDY MACKIN

CONTRIBUTIONS TO SOUTHERN APPALACHIAN STUDIES, 29

McFarland & Company, Inc., Publishers
Jefferson, North Carolina, and London

LIBRARY OF CONGRESS CATALOGUING-IN-PUBLICATION DATA

Mackin, Randy, 1958–
    George Scarbrough, Appalachian poet : a biographical and literary study with unpublished writings / Randy Mackin.
        p.   cm. — (Contributions to Southern Appalachian studies ; 29)
    Includes bibliographical references and index.

    ISBN 978-0-7864-6371-8
    softcover : 50# alkaline paper

    1. Scarbrough, George, 1915–[2008]   2. Authors, American — 20th century — Biography.   3. Appalachian Region — In literature.   I. Title.
    PS3537.C18Z78   2011   811'.54 — dc23   [B]   2011022790

BRITISH LIBRARY CATALOGUING DATA ARE AVAILABLE

© 2011 Randy Mackin. All rights reserved

No part of this book may be reproduced or transmitted in any form or by any means, electronic or mechanical, including photocopying or recording, or by any information storage and retrieval system, without permission in writing from the publisher.

On the cover: George Scarbrough in June 2003 (photograph by Dylan Mackin); *inset* the writing corner at Scarbrough's home (photograph courtesy of George Scarbrough)

Manufactured in the United States of America

McFarland & Company, Inc., Publishers
  Box 611, Jefferson, North Carolina 28640
    www.mcfarlandpub.com

For her love, grace, and a lifetime of support,
this book is for Lynda

Table of Contents

Acknowledgments xi

Preface 1

Introduction 9

Part I — Walking the Paths of His Own Premise: The Life and Literature of George Scarbrough

One: Biography   15

Two: Family   51

Three: Songs of Defiance to Death   60

Four: A Small, Comfortable World   69

Five: The Novel   81

Six: Holding Han-Shan's Hand   100

Seven: Myth and Metaphor Out of the Way   111

Eight: Scarbrough's Critics   121

Part II: Selected Unpublished Poems, Letters and Conversations

Nine: A Selection of Previously Unpublished Verse and "Good Friday, New Mexico, 1955"   127

Ten: A Selection of Scarbrough's Letters   148

Eleven: A Selection of Letters to Scarbrough   170

Twelve: "Something of a Bio and an Itinerary"
(by George Scarbrough)   183

Thirteen: An Interview   189

Appendix: Publications and Awards   201

Bibliography   203

Index   207

Acknowledgments

The author wishes to acknowledge the late George Addison Scarbrough for his generous spirit; the poet's literary executor, Rebecca Mobbs, for her invaluable assistance and words of encouragement at a time when they were needed; Jeff Daniel Marion for sharing his letters from George; and Dr. David Lavery and Dr. Will Brantley, Middle Tennessee State University Department of English, for their gentle guidance.

Many of Scarbrough's letters, journals, and papers quoted in this book are housed at Sewanee: University of the South, University Archives Special Collection; the author is grateful for the services provided by archivists Annie Armour and John Tilford.

Preface

The rooms of George Scarbrough's small, well-kept home must have had walls, but I cannot tell you their color, if they were painted or papered, sheetrocked or paneled. Every inch of available space seemed to be taken up with photographs, paintings, his cherished Arthur Rackham prints, and other hanging expressions of a long life spent collecting memories that could be framed and suspended by wire and nail. Nor can I tell you about his floors, if they were hardwood or linoleum, scattered with throw rugs or carpeted. George's house, it seemed, was epitome of the old adage: a place for everything and everything in its place.

But at the same time I cannot in my mind separate the poet from the place he inhabited. When I think of George, he is in the living room cramped with furniture, insulated with books, neatly cluttered with objects that had little value except to him. Or he is in one of that living room's corners, lorded by a Gatlinburg street artist's pastel portrait of George as a young man; there he is flipping through the pages of his beloved dictionary — an ancient edition about a foot thick and clumsy as a sack of grain — searching for the morning's new word. Or he is showing me through the other rooms: tight kitchen, tighter bath, the room where he slept and wrote, the room he called "Mother's." Or he is standing at his dining table, his finger poised above the play button on a cassette recorder, about to say, "Listen to this." Or he is looking out over his postage stamp lawn from the porch where I first had opportunity to spend time with him in the early 1980s. We sat and talked for about three hours, sipping his own concoction of sweet port wine and Southern Comfort as the late summer evening grew closer and cooler at the foot of one of his mountains, and the afternoon light took on a dim slant.

I was a graduate student at Austin Peay State University, interested in the role place played in the work of Southern poets. My mentor, poet

George Scarbrough at his Oak Ridge home, the walls covered with artwork, the shelves stacked with mementoes, ca. 2003 (courtesy of Dylan Mackin).

and professor Malcolm Glass—who had known George for many years and who held great admiration for his work—suggested I reach out to the Oak Ridge poet as part of my studies. Malcolm said George's verse was deeply rooted in Southeastern Tennessee geography and her people, and that any examination of place in Southern poetics would suffer if Scarbrough were omitted.

That same study, which had originally been considered as a master's thesis, also took me to the offices of Frank Steele and Jim Wayne Miller at Western Kentucky University. When they asked about the poets I planned to interview and learned that Scarbrough was on the list, Professors Miller and Steele spent a good deal of the limited time we had together speaking to George's poetry. They were not only fans, but students, and attributed to George credit for the important role he played in Appalachian literature.

Though I completed the master's with course work alone and never finished that thesis on place and poetry, the early fascination with George's writings and his life lingered; interest found permanent lodging in my brain. I continued to read Scarbrough, we kept in touch, and he contributed

The lawn at Scarbrough's home in Oak Ridge, which was always kept immaculate and, whenever possible, blooming with his beloved hollyhocks (courtesy of Dylan Mackin).

a batch of poems to a short-lived literary magazine I tried to foster, *Hogshead Review.*

After a twelve-year detour into fulltime journalism from 1982 to 1994, I decided to go back to school and entered the doctoral program at Middle Tennessee State University. Early on — that first Fall semester — I asked my major advisor, Dr. David Lavery, if a literary biography of Scarbrough would be acceptable as my dissertation. David liked the idea, and so it began, or rather, resumed: this effort to understand how a poet with the talents and abilities of the best American writers had been so overlooked. From the beginning I wanted to connect the poet with his work through literary biography, and perhaps — and I make no apologies for the subversive nature of this statement — shed a brighter light on what I believed then and believe now to be some of the highest quality verse penned in this country in the twentieth century.

The book you hold in your hand already has a history. After completing the doctoral degree, advisors suggested the manuscript be sent out for publication consideration. In fact, this study in another version was accepted by a publishing house several years ago. I called George and told him the news, and we set up a meeting; when I arrived a few weeks later,

George was having second thoughts. References to sexuality caused him some concern, and rightly so. On more than one occasion he had been physically threatened because of his homosexuality; he felt ostracized by society in general and by certain individuals who "moved in darkness," to paraphrase Robert Frost, one of George's favorite poets. Allusions to his sexuality in a dissertation were not as dangerous as they would be in a book. George said at our meeting that we had two options: one, remove all material of a sexual nature, or two — and these are his words, not mine: "Wait until I'm dead and I don't care what is published."

Early in our discussions about the dissertation, George broached the issue in a letter dated 23 September 1994:

> Here is something, Randy, you should know. I am gay. You may have heard as much, since the literati are a bunch of old gossiping women whatever their anatomy says. In the work you are or will be doing, there should be no hitch coming from that fact. J.W. [Williamson] is, of course, issuing the journal as it stands. If you have read John Cheever's journals and were put off by them, you will be put off decuply by mine. I've written very few gay poems, if any, strictly speaking. My writing matter has been family, place, and the establishment of those I've loved as family in a habitation and with a name. Thought you should know about the gay thing.

George again discussed the subject in a letter of 1 November 1996, in response to my question about how to best handle the matter:

> As for the "gay thing," of course it needs to be mentioned ... I'm the aggressor, Randy, and have been almost from infancy, in the wondrous ways of God and man. If you come here, Buddy, you'll be in jeopardy, too! So come along ... I do not consort with gays. I'm uncomfortable with them, unless bisexuals are gay. And most of the men I've ever known are bi's. But that's not here nor there. I like the male world, was born liking it, and have lived passionately in it .... I can't control what you write, Randy. I'm not trying to. I feel (know) that you will treat me — the subject itself — kindly. So far as concealment is concerned, I am not interested in hiding. I'm only waiting for that biographer, gay himself, who will be able to see how, why, and where my young world was. So, I haven't written "gay" poems. Not ostensibly. All my poems are gay poems, all my religion has been gay religion, every breath I've ever drawn has been a gay breath. You see, I understand gayness as genetic in origin. I am that I am. No reviewer of my books has mentioned sexual predilection. I'll be doing that in *Poetry* Chicago soon, with a poem that accepts my "gay connection" in a way I've always understood it. I wear the "coat" with pride, though mostly in hurt because of the world's way.

During the interview, included in this book, George spoke openly about his sexuality. In fact, he answered the phone during our recorded session and told the caller that he felt "light as air," that he had "come clean" in his answers. George seemed honestly relieved to have finally said aloud what he had so long pretended was privy to only a few. Everyone who knew George knew he was gay; the information was not a secret. Perhaps that is why his reluctance at seeing this book's references — and his own comments — in print was a surprise. George made it clear on many occasions that he wanted this book to be published, but he was torn between three poles: the self-protection the book might have compromised, the "light as air" freedom the book might have produced, and the desire for proper attention his work deserved, had it been printed in his lifetime.

As I worked on the dissertation and this book, friends who also knew George asked me what it was like to deal with the poet himself. Some labeled him difficult, self-absorbed, even impossible. I cannot attest to those descriptives. In every moment we pursued this writing project, George was forthcoming and cooperative. As noted elsewhere, George's willingness to give me full access to his papers and journals archived at the University of the South came without hesitation, and was the first of many selfless gestures on his part. He made for me the necessary contacts, secured the required permissions, even wrote a letter of introduction — my "credentials," he called it — for me to present to the Sewanee archivist. George asked only that quotes from the journals be brief, then turned me loose with a caveat in a letter of 3 March 1995: "Have at it, son. May the angels attend you."

Without doubt, and evidenced by his actions, George was one of the most generous people I have ever known. At our first meeting in the 1980s, as our interview drew to a close,

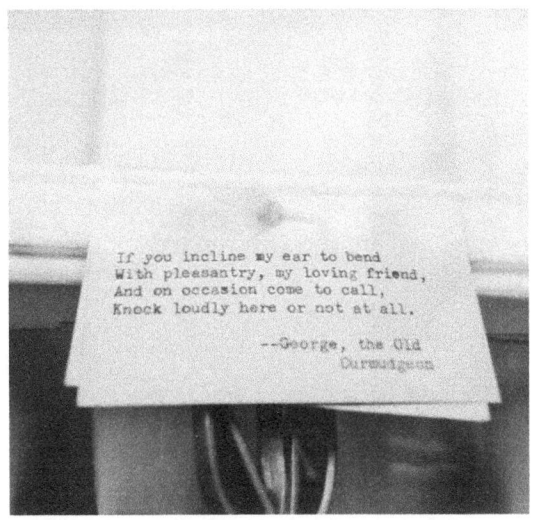

Always the jokester, Scarbrough often kept poetic messages pinned to the back door of his Oak Ridge home (courtesy of Dylan Mackin).

he disappeared into the house and came back bearing gifts: three 1926 editions of "The Pamphlet Poets," a Simon & Schuster effort to promote poetry to the masses through paperback offerings sold for twenty-five cents. The featured poets in my copies are Elinor Wylie, Nathalia Crane, and H. D. These he handed me first, then said, "And I want you to have this." George proffered a June–July 1923 issue of "The Fugitive," which includes poetry by some the literary movement's most influential writers — John Crowe Ransom, Donald Davidson, Allen Tate, Merrill Moore — and "Crusade" by an eighteen-year-old Robert Penn Warren who had entered the poem for The Nashville Prize.

Nearly two decades later on another visit — this one with my oldest son, Dylan Thomas Mackin, George left us in the living room and went

The writing corner at Scarbrough's home, flanked by a photograph of the poet after receiving the honorary Doctor of Letters from Lincoln Memorial, photographs of his mother and father, his beloved dictionary on the nearby stand, and a pastel portrait of Scarbrough as a young man, by a Gatlinburg street artist. This tableau, in honor of a native son, has been recreated at the Polk County Museum, using his desk, typewriter, portrait, and work in progress, which he bequeathed (courtesy of George Scarbrough).

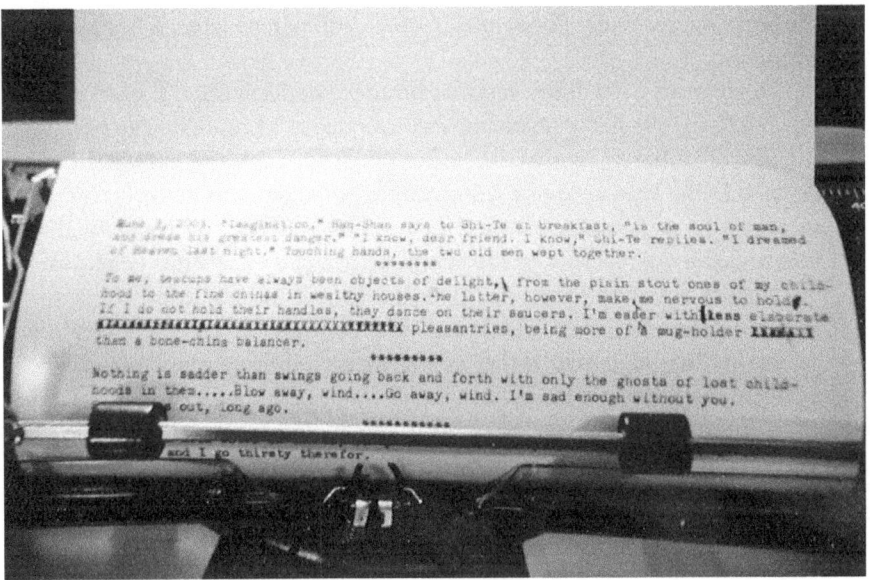

Scarbrough always kept a sheet of paper in his typewriter, where he spent countless hours recording thoughts, playing with words, creating poems (courtesy of Dylan Mackin).

to another part of the house. When he returned, he gave Dylan a 1952 limited edition, pristine, hardback copy of *In Country Sleep* by Welshman Dylan Thomas. The book, published just a year before Thomas' death, contains that immortal poem, "Do Not Go Gentle into that Good Night."

On that same visit George offered me the complete manuscript of *Under the Lemon Tree*, his yet unpublished volume of Han-Shan poems. He said, "Go through these poems, pick out whatever you like, and include them in the book." He also gave me the originals of several other unpublished poems, the prose piece that appears in another chapter, other unpublished materials he thought I might find interesting and useful, and a promise to assist me in every way he could.

The image, however, that remains in my mind and crawls to the forefront every time I think of George is this: we are standing in his kitchen, beside the dining table, the forefinger of his right hand hovering above a button on a battered cassette player. "Listen to this," he says.

From the tiny speaker, a scratchy recording of Bach-Gounod's "Ave Maria," with simple piano accompaniment. The tenor manages well the lower ranges of the composition, but struggles as the octaves climb toward the famous crescendo. The soloist, George will tell me later, is Alessandro Moreschi.

George then sits down, motions for me to do likewise, and in effortless detail tells me the story: Moreschi was castrated as a boy, before he reached the age of puberty, so that his musical talents could be exploited and enjoyed at the Vatican where women were not allowed to perform. It was, George says, a common practice for hundreds of years to create quality tenors in this way, sacrificing the manhood of a chosen few for the pleasure of a chosen few. The recording, George tells me, was made in 1902 at the Sistine Chapel, and that Pope Pius X eventually ruled the castration procedure barbaric and ordered that arrangements requiring soprano and contralto voices be sung by boys. Moreschi, then, became the "last castrato."

The lesson did not click at once, but I came to realize that George felt kinship with Moreschi who, though celebrated for his talent, must also have been an anomaly — the last of his kind — subject to speculation, ridicule, and misunderstanding. Like Moreschi, George's early leanings toward the artistic — as well as the effeminate nature his father despised — set the young man apart from people his age, created a chasm that some family members refused to maneuver, and likely pushed George toward his later-in-life, relatively reclusive existence. Throughout his journals, notes, and scribblings, George returned time and again to that theme of loneliness, of being unlike, and separate from, others. But the similarities with Moreschi end there; unakin to the created, skill-challenged tenor, George's natural literary gifts allowed him to reach the high notes, maintain a steady tempo over more than nine decades of living, and remain in all his remarkable work on key.

Introduction

For many years the poet and novelist George Scarbrough was little known outside the area that literary circles have labeled Appalachia. But from northern Georgia to the reaches of Virginia and all the adjacent area between and alongside, Scarbrough is recognized as a writer of serious intent, a quiet and fiercely private man who, for most of the last century and into the new millennium, tested the limits of verse and produced literature that deserves careful attention. His literary life spanned seven decades of publishing: five books of verse, a novel, and hundreds of poems appearing nationwide in the best magazines.

This study is an attempt to not only examine the work but to connect more than ninety years of an extraordinary life with the writing that Scarbrough produced consistently and with great quality. It focuses, of course, on available primary and secondary material, but Scarbrough's consent to allow the author to read and quote from his personal journals, archived at the University of the South's duPont Library, provided the thread that ties biography to art.

Chapter One is "Biography." While its not presented in chronological order, it relates the important details of Scarbrough's life but diverts to examine experiences that had a lifelong effect on the writer: feelings of rejection, childhood traumas, and a newfound courage on the poet's part to say what he felt needed to be said. The chapter includes information on Scarbrough's final years that were marked by a renewed critical interest in his work.

Subsequent chapters focus on influences that have proven constant in Scarbrough's writing. Chapter Two, "Family," analyzes the importance of kin in the poems, especially those that relate to the writer's father, siblings, and mother. Through poetry Scarbrough tried to reconcile his ambivalence toward his tyrannical father, explain his life and work to his misunderstanding brothers, and celebrate the lessons of his mother.

Scarbrough admits in his journals to having had a love affair with language, and Chapter Three, "Songs of Defiance to Death," is a careful look at the value that he placed on the written and spoken word. The section not only considers poetry but also comments on important prose and an essay that provide pivotal information on how closely — almost at a level of interdependence — his existence was driven by passionate loyalty to language.

It is impossible to read Scarbrough's poetry or fiction without noticing the important role landscape plays in the writing. His devotion to this small world, the southeastern corner of Tennessee called locally the Eastanalle, was unfaltering. While Polk County and environs is an actual place, Scarbrough built a mythical county similar to Faulkner's Yoknapatawpha. He peopled it with interesting characters, created for the region a personal history, and was so closely tied to his county — both emotionally and aesthetically — that landscape became the physical world from which Scarbrough formed his cosmology. This consistent sense of place has on more than one occasion caused critics to label him an Agrarian, or more limiting, regional. Scarbrough had strong feelings about that description, and those viewpoints are included in Chapter Four, "A Small, Comfortable World."

Very little critical attention has been paid to Scarbrough's only novel, *A Summer Ago*. Chapter Five, "The Novel," assesses the value of the book from five perspectives: the use of descriptive and colloquial language; the farm family's specific activities during a six month period, April to September; the often humorous bits of country wisdom that find their way into the book; major themes of the best coming of age stories and the rites of passage that Alan, the protagonist, undergoes in one particular summer; and Scarbrough's use of the novel as a vehicle to romanticize the actual events of his youth.

Chapter Six, "Holding Han-Shan's Hand," focuses on Scarbrough's final work incorporating ancient Chinese poet Han-Shan. Scarbrough admitted that Han-Shan was his alter-ego; the kinship opened new doors for Scarbrough and allowed him to write very personal, autobiographical poems that used Han-Shan as the subject, an effort that was very successful. *Poetry* magazine published a dozen of the poems over a two-year period, and Scarbrough completed a book-length manuscript of Han-Shan poems titled *Under the Lemon Tree*.

"Myth and Metaphor Out of the Way," Chapter Seven, examines poems from several periods of Scarbrough' life, in an attempt to ascertain the poet's views on religion, theology, and mythology. The centerpiece of that chapter is twofold: a rare journal entry in which Scarbrough discusses at length his own views about a poem he considered important, "Good Friday, New Mexico, 1955," and an examination of the poet's ability in that poem to demystify and discount myth — both Christian and Native American — by almost abandoning simile and metaphor, and relying instead on symbolism.

Chapter Eight, titled "Scarbrough's Critics," includes a survey of articles written about the poet's body of work, and addresses an important question: why Scarbrough was not a more widely read poet.

The most important and valuable section of this book is Chapter Nine, a collection of twenty-one previously unpublished poems offered by the poet for inclusion here. The majority of those poems are from Scarbrough's final point of focus: the Han-Shan series. The longest poem in that selection is "Good Friday, New Mexico, 1955," which Scarbrough wanted included in this book.

Chapters Ten through Twelve are composed of many items: letters from Scarbrough, correspondence to the poet from influential writers of the time, and a recollection titled "Something of a Bio and an Itinerary," written by Scarbrough in 1992, and contributed by the poet to this book.

The elder poet, at home in Oak Ridge, with his beloved typewriter, ca. 1993 (courtesy of George Scarbrough).

Also included in Chapter Thirteen is a transcript of an interview conducted at the poet's Oak Ridge home in February of 2000. Scarbrough was frank and honest in his answers. He told stories that have not been published in any other interviews and were not used as subject matter for his poems. Scarbrough was very open about his feelings and beliefs on a number of issues including childhood, religion, the Bible, regrets, poetics, and the future of the written word. The appendix is a list of many of the publications and anthologies in which Scarbrough's work appeared, and a list of awards he received.

At the time of the 2000 interview, Scarbrough was undergoing a physical anomaly, one his doctors could not explain. The poet's hair, which had grown brilliantly white with age, seemed to be reverting to its youthful darkness. The poet parted the hair with his fingertips and the pitch black coloration Scarbrough inherited from his part-Cherokee father was visible at the roots. One might have felt that Scarbrough was getting younger or that he had found some secret that would allow him to live forever. While that fate was greatly to be wished for this Tennessee poet, death finally remembered him. After living at home for most of his later years, Scarbrough finally agreed to enter an elderly care facility because of ongoing health concerns; he died Tuesday, December 2, 2008, at Brakebill Nursing Home, Knoxville.

One truth remains: George Scarbrough, on his own terms and through his exceptional talent, produced literature that is important and valuable and will stand the test of time. Proper recognition for this artist is long overdue.

PART I

*Walking the Paths of
His Own Premise:
The Life and Literature of
George Scarbrough*

ONE

Biography

The First Poem Was About the Orchard

By the time George Addison Scarbrough received his high school diploma in 1935, near age twenty, his family had moved more than a dozen times. His father, William Oscar Scarbrough, was an itinerant sharecropper who was forced, on a regular basis, to load his large clan into a wagon and find farm work on land always owned by someone else. It was a meager existence that demanded great sacrifice from his wife, Louise Anabel McDowell Scarbrough, and their seven children: Lee, Edith, George, Charles (Pete), Bill, Blaine and Kenneth (Kim). They lived in hand-me-down housing that Scarbrough described in his journals as "more shacks than homes, more slatted cribs than shacks," in which there was little or no privacy and certainly not places one could call home (T-40).

While these meanderings must have seemed constant for the Scarbroughs, they really covered very little ground. George was born on October 20, 1915, on the Harrison place, a farm near Patty Station, six miles from the Polk County seat of Benton, Tennessee. The lower end of the Appalachian Mountain range, a permanent fixture that proved constant in Scarbrough's life and his work, is visible in the distance. The rivers that would one day be so influential in Scarbrough's poetry — the Hiwassee and Ocoee — are also nearby. This region of Scarbrough's early life, limited in scope to the counties of Polk and McMinn, eventually became the land he tilled, not only as the son of a sharecropper, but also as a poet.

An interest in the written word came at a very early age for Scarbrough, as did his ability to understand language. The cracks in the walls of his many homes were insulated with old newspapers. From these World War I-era headlines Scarbrough's mother taught him to recognize letters and, eventually, to read before he ever entered grammar school. In an introduction to two of his poems included in *Southern Appalachian Poetry: An Anthology of Works by 37 Poets* (2008), Scarbrough discussed that early love of words fostered by his mother:

> Books, taking me immediately away from locale, influenced me more than terrain, reading having been available to me as long as I can remember. I was born into the alphabet, as it were, though its primary function on those cabin walls was to keep out the wind, I became warm in other ways from headlines that loomed large and gothic black above my bed. My mother's love of reading and her habit of reading aloud engrossed me in the shapes and meanings of words, a temple she lived in which became my one and only house of worship [183–84].

Knowledge proved to be, however, a two-edged sword, severing him from his peers, and alienating him from much of his family, who never understood the little boy who preferred to spend his spare time reading books and writing.

Scarbrough vividly remembered his first effort at poetry. He was in the fifth grade because he recollected showing the finished poem to Ms. Woodson, his beloved teacher, who praised his work. The poem was written in the vacant upstairs of the fourth house that Scarbrough lived in as a boy. Because the room was not being used, Scarbrough's father had moved the family's meat box to the second floor; the young poet turned the empty

Scarbrough described the Oak Grove School in Polk County as "the worst scenario of my non-education," ca. 1920 (courtesy of George Scarbrough).

box on its side, borrowed a straight chair from downstairs, and used the setup for a desk. Scarbrough remembered:

> The first poem was about the orchard. The man [owner] had planted a very fine orchard when we had lived there. I wrote a poem about apricots, and plums, peaches, and apples. I had read an English poem about an apple orchard in the spring. So, I began to measure my lines by, obviously, the only meter English ever had ... iambic [Interview].

Writing his own poetry made Scarbrough even more interested in reading, and he consumed everything available to him. Of course, the Bible was required reading: he did not, however, read it for religious instruction but for the beauty of words which he recognized, for the first time, as poetry that did not rhyme. Outside Ms. Woodson's class, Scarbrough became responsible for his own education, and like the protagonist, Alan, in *A Summer Ago*, the natural world around him became a great source of fascination during his primary and secondary school years.

I'm Going to College

Because of constant moves from one farm to another, and because schools closed down regularly whenever childhood diseases made their rounds through the community, Scarbrough finally finished high school later than most students and began talking of college. It was a subject that his father found repulsive. In a journal entry, Scarbrough wrote:

> "I'm going to college," I declared to my father one day as we hoed along a field of corn. "You're going to shit and fall back in it," he retorted. "You've got as much chance going to college as a one-legged man has in winning a ass-kicking contest." He grinned sourly. "You're going to the poor-house if you don't learn more about farming than you know now. Look at them rows you laid off. Corn's as crooked as a dog's hindleg. The neighbors all a-laughing at me. For why? For having a boy like you, who couldn't stick his finger in his ass iffen you held his shirttail up" [I-55].

Nevertheless, the father's attitude about higher learning did not deter Scarbrough's pursuit. After graduation from high school, Scarbrough borrowed money — from twelve local benefactors — and went to the University of Tennessee. The original pocket notebook sheet on which Scarbrough listed his supporters remains in the archived papers at Sewanee. Those who made the loans, totaling $115, and ensured the young poet's entrance at UT Knoxville were A. J. Anderson, George Norton, Hoyt Lillard, J. C.

McAmis, Red Wilson, C. L. Campbell, L. H. Parks, J. M. Lillard, Mrs. W. J. Smith, J. L. Brewer, L. W. Moore, and F. R. Bradford. Scarbrough also took advantage of the National Youth Administration program and earned $15 per month.

When Scarbrough boarded the Knoxville-bound bus in the Fall of 1935, he was not alone: his longtime friend, Ruth Haskins — the daughter of a sharecropper — took the same, bittersweet journey that left from Red Wilson's Drugstore in Benton. Scarbrough's relationship with Haskins began in childhood. Her family "lived down the road a piece from us," Scarbrough recalled in a journal entry where he described her this way: "Pretty, intelligent, always shining clean, Ruth was a source of inspiration and loveliness in her self-made gingham and voiles and taffetas. A fearless, pink-face 'sister,' of whom I was very proud." Scarbrough wrote about his departure to UT in a contribution to *Knoxville-Bound*, an anthology of remembrances by former students; his essay was dedicated to his friend:

> Unaccustomed to being away from home, both of us were sad as we left our families. Neither of us would be home that fall to help our brothers and sisters pick the boon of scrap cotton, which always had been given to us by the landowners to claim for our very own. We knew we would miss our families, but we knew they were proud, and we were proud of their pride. Ruth loaned me a handkerchief, a small dainty cloth on which her name had been neatly embroidered, to wipe my tears .... She was my source of strength as we began our journey .... Traveling north we crossed our beloved Hiwassee River, which made me most sorrowful .... We went past strange, foreign towns: Etowah, Englewood, Madisonville, Vonore, Maryville, Alcoa: towards the future. I wept again. But Ruth's face was bright with a beautiful smile.

Scarbrough was more than aware that his good fortune, and this opportunity to further his education, had come at a tremendous price to those left behind in "the county." Both his and Ruth's mothers had "spent the summer sewing and patching so we would be warmly outfitted in the northern climate of a strange, great city," Scarbrough wrote (*Knowville-Bound*). His mother, saddled with the knowledge that her son needed five dollars for a deposit on his room at school, sold a double wedding ring quilt — the product of many hours of labor. "I'm thankful," Scarbrough wrote in the same essay, "that half a lifetime later, I was able to buy her the only set of diamond wedding rings she ever possessed in an attempt to express my love and gratitude for her sacrifice."

Following the first semester — in which Scarbrough made good grades — the school moved him to a dormitory that was run by the students themselves. After only a year at UT, Scarbrough was forced by financial difficulties to leave the university and begin farming again. He also began writing for several newspapers in East Tennessee. Gilbert Govan, at the *Chattanooga Times*, became interested in the young poet's work; the newspaper even carried a story, with photograph, on Scarbrough's recent accomplishment:

> George A. Scarbrough, 25 ... has been recognized as a poet of more than usual ability, and nine of his poems are in the current issue of the *Sewanee Review*, published by the University of the South, at Sewanee .... The young poet writes about the things with which he daily comes in contact and of which he knows most. His subjects are confined to rural life, about the soil, nature, his family, farm animals and birds and animals of the forests [11].

While not juvenilia, the first poetry Scarbrough published in the *Sewanee Review* provides a glimpse of a writer who had not yet fully honed his skills and was not, perhaps, courageous enough to tackle the more serious of themes. As Govan noted, the poems are about the environment that Scarbrough knew best, those things close at hand that began to comprise the poet's cosmology. In the poem "Experience" the speaker comes "face / To face with death" (1–2) in the form of a black bull inside a stable. While the speaker keeps assuring himself that he is not afraid, his actions immediately following the encounter reveal the truth: "But when I'd climbed the ladder and come down / Outside again, I knelt and kissed the ground" (13–14). The other of these nine poems, eight of which are sonnets, hint at the same subject matter that filled much of his first book, *Tellico Blue*: a collection of verse told in a strong narrative voice marked by perfect pitch and peopled with the unusual characters of Scarbrough's youth, including family.

The newspaper announcement about Scarbrough's verse being published at Sewanee was followed closely by another: the young poet began writing regular book reviews for the *Times*. Govan introduced Scarbrough by reminding readers that several of his poems had already appeared on the editorial page of that newspaper, and that those lines had sparked Govan's interest:

> It was those poems which caused me first to grow curious about George Scarbrough. They were, I thought, evidence of two things: First, an individual with both the insight and the skill of the real poet; second, and of equal importance, one who realized that true poetic values are to be found in the daily round of living [5].

Govan went on to connect, and then separate, Scarbrough's work from the Agrarian movement. He said that though Scarbrough was agrarian, the poet was writing out of true experience and not because of a sympathetic leaning toward a particular political and economic ideology. Alongside Govan's comments was printed Scarbrough's first review of three books of poetry from now unstudied writers. Interestingly enough, and somewhat telling of Scarbrough's own concerns, the review relied strongly on comments about the sense of place that these three poets exhibited in their work. In one statement, Scarbrough noted that the writer produced poetry of New England people and that "their story is that of the whole American scene in miniature" (5). The poet whose work was being reviewed had something in common with the reviewer: the creation of a microcosm that represents a world much larger than itself, as Scarbrough would later do with his "county." The November 17, 1940, Sunday edition marked the beginning of a regular venue for Scarbrough; he continued writing reviews for the *Times* for several decades.

According to Robert Phillips (419), it was Govan who was instrumental in securing Scarbrough's literary fellowship to the University of the South (the first ever given at Sewanee), an experience that was both positive and negative for the young writer. At the time, Govan was also a member of the *Sewanee Review* advisory board. Out of place among the more aristocratic students, Scarbrough was labeled a "covite," or one who came from the coves of Tennessee. Coupled with the ridicule was deep guilt; for the first time ever, Scarbrough was living in what seemed, at first, ideal conditions: books at his fingertips, learned professors, and no want of necessities such as food. At Sewanee, when Scarbrough was twenty-six years old, he experienced his first traditional Thanksgiving dinner (at home the holiday was greeted only with an ordinary meal and one simple exception, a pumpkin pie). Scarbrough was amazed at the actions of the students who threw raisins, grapes, nuts, and apples at each other in observation of holiday. In Scarbrough's mind it seemed wasteful. In a journal entry, he wrote:

> A way of celebration, I suppose. Nonetheless, it left me bitter and dismayed, considering the prodigious waste and the sacrilege. It was sacrilege to me. In the room fairly whizzing with good things, I sat, hardly touching my food, thinking of my mother at home scraping together the makings of a meal for our family [A-238].

Adding to this feeling of uselessness and waste was the knowledge that Scarbrough's accident-prone father was recuperating from a broken back that he suffered after falling out of the barn, and that his inability to work put an even greater strain on the family's survival.

Also during his two years at the University of the South, the *Sewanee*

Scarbrough as a young man, reading at home, during the Sewanee years, ca. 1941 (courtesy of George Scarbrough).

Review again published a selection of Scarbrough's poetry. In a section titled "Tennessee Tomes," editor William S. Knickerbocker chose an unusually large number of poems — fifteen — as a feature in one of the 1941 issues. While eight are sonnets and all follow traditional form, the poems show an improvement from those published just a year before. The language is tight, the enjambment effective, and the rhyme not so obvious. In terms of theme, the 1941 *Review* poems are not merely images of the farm life that Scarbrough has experienced, but speak to the political as well, especially in terms of the suffering of sharecroppers who work all year, sometimes for nothing in return. These lines from the first of two sonnets, titled "Tenant," provide a perfect example:

> It takes a stout heart to assail the land
> When all a farmer gets is his poor third:
> I've known my men who didn't understand
> How they had nothing after they had bared
> Their sweaty backs to toil the summer long.
> They told their grievances in halting tongue,
> How they had sold their labor for a song,
> How hope was hard for them, no longer young [1–8].

Although Scarbrough had opportunity to learn from outstanding teachers such as Tudor Long and George Baker, and to work for a year as an office boy and proofreader in the *Sewanee Review* office under Andrew Lytle, his departure from the school was not pleasant. Near the end of his junior year, Scarbrough, as he put it, "ran afoul" of Dr. Alexander Guerry, who, said Scarbrough:

> ... harped so much on his "Sewanee gentleman" until I thought I would vomit, and somebody told him that I didn't much care for his southern gentleman. He invited me out to his house. He said, "You say you don't like my Sewanee gentleman?" and I said, "No, Dr. Guerry, because most of them have more damn money than sense." That was not a politic thing to say [Interview].

The statement, of course, put Scarbrough on Dr. Guerry's bad side, and the professor reacted by telling the student that next year he would be working in the kitchen and cafeteria, "waiting on these boys you pretend to despise," or as Scarbrough describes it, become a "boot-lick" (Interview). Scarbrough told Dr. Guerry he would not be a servant, nor would he be back at the school the following term.

Rather than view this setback as a permanent block to his continued pursuit of higher education, Scarbrough remained true to his "religion" of words, and refused to allow his voice to be silenced by the patriarchs at Sewanee. He expressed it in the *Southern Appalachian Poetry* piece:

> As a sharecropper's son, I had a chip on my shoulder which grew to chop block size under the scorn of many men on the Sewanee campus in the early forties. I was a fellowship student at the University of the South and referred to then as a covite. But they did not, to paraphrase William Gass, cut my tongue out, as he says America has done to most of its poor. I won't be allowed, again in Gass' words, a language as "lousy as their lives," meaning the isolated and deprived. From infancy I wanted more than that. The sunflower told me a story about that as did the wandering cosmos, that startling starry flower which strewed its pink and white flowers over an ancient earthen dairy on one of the many farms we were always in transit to or from [184].

In 1947, Scarbrough earned his B.A. degree from Lincoln Memorial University in Harrogate, Tennessee. Seven years later, he earned the M.A. from the University of Tennessee at Knoxville, with a creative thesis. He began pursuing a Ph.D. at UT, but never finished it, a lingering disappointment that was only assuaged late in life.

Scarbrough as a student at Lincoln Memorial University; his companions are unknown, ca. 1945 (courtesy of George Scarbrough).

Looking back on his formal schooling, Scarbrough was dissatisfied with the quality of education he received, and regrets, in a journal entry, of never attending an institution that was "plugged into the circuits of the world mind." In that same entry, Scarbrough expands:

> The University of Tennessee ... was a hick university in a hick town, which for all its age was little better than a freshwater college .... The University of the South ... was plugged in to the past, purely and, I think now, quite simply in spite of the beautiful words some of the professors spoke... . Sewanee was an ivory tower of the worst sort... . Lincoln Memorial University was only a glorified high school, which disturbed and disgusted me... . The smell of cattle barns replaced the hawthorn at Combray... . Alas, for higher education. I never had any, never found any sign of it in any place I went. (H-30–31)

The only high points of those years, according to Scarbrough, were Tudor Long at Sewanee, a Miss Johnston in the undergraduate program at UTK, and Kenneth Knickerbocker, who directed Scarbrough's graduate work. All three were teachers of English, as was Professor Lytle, with whom Scarbrough reconnected by chance many years later. He describes his early and later experiences with Lytle in the following unpublished prose piece, "Portrait of a Fugitive," which Scarbrough provided for this book and asked that it be included. The poem referenced, "Good Friday, New Mexico, 1955," appeared in the *Sewanee Review*, but was never included in any of Scarbrough's subsequent collections; it appears in its entirety in this book's selection of Scarbrough's poetry, and is the focus of a separate chapter.

"Portrait of a Fugitive"

When I first knew Andrew Lytle, he appeared to be a tall man and imperially slim. His physical presence awed me and, along with his literary reputation, kept me silent, for most part, either in the office of *The Sewanee Review* or at evening at his house, when I remember, vividly, visiting him, along with other students, on open house nights. I can't recall that I said much, if anything, beyond greeting and saying goodnight. I sat actually on the floor, at the feet of the master, listening. He seemed truly magnificent towering over me like an impeccable prince. He was the cleanest looking man I'd ever known. Mr. Lytle was beginning to bald, but what of that? Andrew Lytle was Andrew Lytle, smooth or hirsute, so deeply in love I was in those days with the idea of him. I was in the presence of a great Southern American writer. Back home in Polk County, men who could even read were scarcer than hen's teeth. And I had just come from hunting eggs in the haystack.

My devotion to him never faltered. After I left Sewanee I wrote for the *Review*, feeling I was among the privileged of the earth to have something of mine appear in its pages.

Many years later, a man from a long circling line of diners waiting to be seated in the dining room at the Opry Hotel in Nashville, broke line on the other side of the room and ran to me before I could recognize him. It was Andrew Lytle, heavier and shorter than I had ever dreamed he could be. He had settled into age. We had all settled into age. But Mr. Lytle was taller in a fashion than he had seemed at the University. And more famous than ever for his matchless writing. Love lifted him as it had done before. I went breathless. Tears stung my eyes. His cheek against mine was a seal on the scroll of my respect and affection for him. Stepping back, smiling, speaking my name, he raised his hand and went back to his place in line.

I never saw him again. I could tell that he was not feeling well, but never surmised he would be dead so soon thereafter, but not before I had written him a long, heartfelt letter, telling how much I loved him for all the help in becoming a writer he had given me, thanking him for having been a beacon in my life. That he loved and respected me was a revelation that has kept me going all the years thereafter. I'll never forget his saying that my poem, "Good Friday, New Mexico, 1955," was among the great poems of the last half of the century. I've received very little attention, I'm told, as a writer, but that one statement has kept me at my desk, writing away forty years now. Salute, Sir, in loving remembrance.

The War Years

A subject Scarbrough rarely discussed was his service during time of war. Friends agree that his hesitancy was due to a feeling that he did very little for the cause in either World War II or the Korean War. When President Roosevelt signed the Selective Training and Service Act on September 16, 1940, creating the first peacetime draft in the United States, Scarbrough — then one month shy of his twenty-fifth birthday — registered as required of all males ages 18 to 65, with those under age 45 immediately liable for induction. He was denied the opportunity to defend his country through regular military duty because he was so severely underweight. A decade later, however, his skills as a teacher were targeted by the U.S. Air Force, and Scarbrough was sent to Nancy, France, with several other educators, in August of 1952, to help "make a high school," in Scarbrough's words, for the children of Air Force servicemen. For unknown or unexplained reasons, the teachers were never called to teach and spent their time traveling throughout Europe for approximately four months.

A lengthy letter, written by Scarbrough to his mother after he arrived by plane in Europe, discusses the trip in detail, as well as many of his reflections on his first experiences overseas. That dispatch, in its entirety, is included in the collection of letters in this book.

In a March 4, 2007, conversation with Judy Loest — a vital member of the Knoxville Writers' Guild who gave freely of her time to care for and visit George during his two years at Brakebill Nursing Home — Scarbrough recollected those months he spent abroad.

Scarbrough lived on the Rue de Paris in Nancy, and recalled attending a worship service with his teaching companions, Margie and Louise, at the cathedral there, in an attempt to "modify our accents." Among his other scattered memories nearly seven decades later, Scarbrough said he was once almost run over by a taxi, and that he met a young man, Bernard, at a movie theater showing "Redemption." Bernard took George home to meet his family who "practically adopted" him. "They welcomed me like a son," Scarbrough said.

During that half-year in Europe, George and his companions traveled to Holland, Switzerland, Germany and Belgium, and made their way to Paris on numerous occasions. Of all the cities he frequented, Paris was the one he always longed to return to.

In her notes of that conversation, Loest wrote: "He saw the chestnut trees and ate boiled chestnuts at a café on the Rue de Champs-Elysees. He saw the booksellers on the Rue de Seine, old men with 'weathered faces and ragged hats.' He visited Notre Dame, the Rodin museum, the Shakespeare & Co. Bookshop on the Left Bank, saw three Americanized French plays and two German plays, walked through the Tuileries and the Luxembourg Gardens. On a trip to Strasbourg he came very close to being electrocuted when he stepped over the third rail while crossing the

Scarbrough's passport photo, 1951, in preparation for his trip to Europe where he was to "help make a high school" in France for the U.S. Air Force (courtesy of George Scarbrough).

tracks. Only because he was 'fastidious about his luggage,' not wanting to scuff it, that he survived. He said the stationmaster ran toward him yelling, 'Non, Monsieur! Non, Monsieur!'"

To Loest, Scarbrough described the French people as "warm and hospitable," adding, "All the people took trouble to teach you a new word or phrase if they saw that you were interested. I was young and the world was before me, and it wasn't long before it was behind me and kicking my butt."

In another conversation with Loest, Easter Sunday, April 8, 2007, Scarbrough continued his reminisces. On a trip to Holland with French friends, George met Tina, whom he later in life referred to as "My Dutch Girlfriend," and two of her friends. Tina escorted Scarbrough to a famous nightclub where they danced. During the evening — and to George's surprise — Tina arranged for the band to play "The Tennessee Waltz" in his honor.

Scarbrough told Loest that Tina wanted him to marry her and bring her to America, that "America was uppermost in her mind." Scarbrough said he loved Tina but would have hated to see her work like his mother did — and to see their tiny bathroom since she was accustomed to the large, ornate facilities in France. The bathroom at the Scarbrough home was the size of a "telephone booth." George and Tina took a boat ride to an island near Amsterdam where Delft china was manufactured, and Scarbrough bought a piece for his mother.

Upon returning to the states, Scarbrough wrote Tina and her female companion, but received no reply. George was able, however, to stay in touch with fifteen-year-old Bernard.

Though as an adult Scarbrough destroyed most of his earliest journals in a backyard bonfire, he did retain and send for archiving a twenty-eight page prose piece written aboard ship on the way home from Europe, apparently honed and redrafted shortly after his return to the states, and eventually sent home in East Tennessee. Titled "Log: Ship: General LeRoy Eltinge," the essay describes many of the men with whom he shared passage, their conversations, playfulness, attitudes, and day-to-day activities. The USNS Eltinge was a 522-foot, troop transport ship with a complement of 32 officers and 224 crew members. In addition to operational personnel, she could bunk 228 more officers and 3,595 enlisted men, carrying them across the Atlantic Ocean at a top speed of 16.5 knots. While the essay is informative, its true merit lies in passages — like those that follow — in which the voice of the poet took control and Scarbrough described what he saw and felt:

Night, December 11: I walked on deck this evening. Bitter cold and dark and dangerous. Skyward, the stars bloomed large and freshly gold, burgeoning on the sight as if they grew interiorly from some mysterious process of fission, like clouds two miles high in the air, towering and expanding from an inner will, some teleological urge that applies form to mountains as well. These stars and clouds have taken hold on me, and these Atlantic passages, east by plane, west by ship, have cast a teleological spell on me also. And I am returning home shaped, refashioned by this heaving, starry world. A ship crossed our bow, strung with lights, headed for the Old World. Offside, the waves looked white as cotton and as kind, and the thought struck that he who might be tempted to step down into that softness would be welcomed into the warmth of snow and the power and motion of a universe at war [5].

Friday, December 19: Awoke this morning to a good sea, but a light, bitter offshore wind. How beautiful the sea was last night, with streaks of light curveting in the darkness, as if horses were being driven by reins of fire. Disturbed seas during this voyage have kept the phosphorescent planktons down at invisible depths. But last night we had them. And a slowly calming sea. Two nights ago, the waves were battering rams that tried to stave us in, bringing the ship into what seemed a 40 degree list, and us out of our bunks. But at dawn the ocean had been a beauty to see, unleashing the furies and drenching even the bridge. Today, it is calm and almost cottony, inviting a step down and a stroll in the softness! No wonder men have always striven in word and deed with the sea. Only a faint swell heaves the surface, dark glass green in color, shadowed by clouds which today take on the formations peculiar to great land areas and bespeak the coast somewhere near at hand to the west. Perhaps landfall before dark. Somewhere Montauk, Narragansett Light, the Rhode Island Coast. At my house, for a great part of my life, Rhode Island was a chicken. Now it was a shore being approached, a land being lifted. My land. I have forgotten my flag. I never had much use for one before.... I walked on deck. The incurvate moon is like a dark gold slice in the sky, almost the color of blood, accompanied by the whiter glare of the — is it evening, now?— star. Dark water spangled with ships' lights, a ship meeting and going past us now, and dark sky littered with stars. Wind and a rush of seas beneath us, rolling like cold glass, awash, dead, dead; all is dead; even the throbbing ship is without significance in the whispering silence, star-studded and coldly inimical; no warm, no passionate adversary, this world; this sky. But canny voices are flung out on the night from the deck above, men's words, about man's things. It is human speech, and under its influence, at this late hour, the world livens again, lives, is causal again, not unmoved. The magic word has been spoken at the midnight hour, in a casual celebration; no mass of any color; but sound. Word. And the sea turns towards morning, and I sleep again in the snoring cabin [22, 24].

Saturday, December 20: We came into New York Harbor at dawn.

Over Long Island the morning sky held a dawn like nothing I had seen over the damp misery of France. The towers of Manhattan Island in the mist as if the Saint had thrown down a handful of strange seed and reaped a ragged harvest of steel and stone in the heart of the smaller boroughs. But it was beautiful, and it moved me towards tears. But not tears. New York is an artifice to exult over, to be proud of, with a sense of fear and horror lurking in the background of the mind; as Brooklyn Bridge is a thing to sing about, an artifact on which to compose epics and music and long apostrophes, but not to induce any maudlin state of feeling; neither is fit for tears, except to a man starved for a sight of home, an exile returning [24–5].

A Horse of a Different Color

When not attending a university on a regular basis, Scarbrough was still in the classroom as a teacher. His first job at an area high school was in 1937; he earned $55 per month. He lost that job when a grocery store owner, who also happened to be on the Board of Education, had him fired because he was not making any purchases at the man's business (Interview). At another school Scarbrough was charged with teaching "too analytically" and refused tenure. These job losses began a pattern that was to follow for many years, and caused a burden for the young educator when he was asked why he had taught at so many different schools. Scarbrough states:

> Again, the old complaints of being too liberal, being too forward. I taught history and gave them my own interpretations, which didn't often suit with the textbook. I taught in so many places that, toward the last, it alarmed my would-be employer, because I told him why I got shifted, that I was a horse of a different color [Interview].

Of course, those years of teaching — despite the frequent change of venue — had their high moments, and in conversation Scarbrough always remembered his career with fondness. As an educator — and by his own admission — Scarbrough expected a great deal from his students. One pupil recalled the first day of class at Clinton High School in 1964, when Scarbrough's initial words to his neophytes came in the form of a challenge: "Do you have the audacity to doubt my veracity, or to insinuate I would prevaricate? Are you so bombastic and I so illiterate? You will have to illustrate before I can comprehend."

Perhaps students are the most accurate judges of a teacher's influence. When Arlena Coffman learned in 2008 that Scarbrough was still alive, and a resident at Brakebill Nursing Home, she made arrangements to visit,

One of Scarbrough's duties as a teacher at Elnora High, Elnora Township, Washington County, Indiana, from 1953–1954, was directing the cast of *Annie Get Your Gun* (courtesy of George Scarbrough).

and then wrote "A Thank You Long Time Coming," a column for the *Elnora Post*, her hometown newspaper in Indiana. Scarbrough taught at the high school in Elnora in the mid-1950s. Coffman wrote:

> I learned more from him [Scarbrough] in the two years he taught me than from all my other years put together in high school. He knew how to teach and make it interesting.... Sitting on the edge of his desk reciting Shakespeare and poetry, even the farm boys sat up and took notice. He captured us not only with his words, but by explaining in plain English the meaning of what he had just recited. Too many times in literature we are left confused by the strange twist of words, which causes most to lose interest. George lit the fire of inquisitiveness in all of us, making us search on our own for more literary knowledge.... It was through his teaching and encouragement that I learned to write and express myself. Shy about being criticized, I had always written in secret, an outlet for my emotions, but never shown my compositions to anyone. My day of awakening came while George was handing back our graded essays. He lay the paper on my desk and I saw a big, red A+ staring back at me. He leaned down, looked deep into my eyes and said two words, "You're good." ... Often we may feel our lone life is of no

Scarbrough teaching at Clinton High School, 1964; his first words to his students: "Do you have the audacity to doubt my veracity, or to insinuate I would prevaricate? Are you so bombastic and I so illiterate? You will have to illustrate before I can comprehend" (courtesy of George Scarbrough).

importance among so many on this earth. Our words of encouragement may not be enough, our presence in time of need may have no effect, our one vote in an election may not make a difference, but I have learned that one person can change this world. Mine was changed by two words. All I have to do is think of George Scarbrough to be reminded.

As a teacher, Scarbrough felt most comfortable in the college classroom. He taught at Hiwassee College in Madisonville, Tennessee, from 1965 to 1967, and at Chattanooga College during the 1968 academic year. By the end of his career, eighteen years in all, Scarbrough's mother had become ill and needed his attention. He gave up teaching for two reasons: to be with his mother (her son became a constant companion and nurse for the final fifteen years of her life), and because he was tired of being rejected from the teaching profession because of his viewpoints; he could never "knuckle to [the] stupidity" of administrators who were "always the fly in the ointment; unctuous hypocrites" (Journal T-185).

Feelings of rejection, however, were not new for Scarbrough. This emotion haunted him most of his childhood, and continued into adulthood. A pall hung over Scarbrough's outlook once he learned, at a very early age, that he was his parents' first unwanted child. Oscar and Belle Scarbrough had already two children — a boy and girl — and Scarbrough's mother apparently was satisfied with their little family. Oscar was not. In fact, Scarbrough sensed some bitterness from his mother and blame leveled at the father for demoting her to the role of childbearer. Scarbrough remembered it this way in an interview with Jerry Williamson:

> This was the first big trauma that ever happened to me, because my mother hadn't really wanted me. She wanted two children, a boy and a girl, and she had those already. So I'm sure that during the months of her pregnancy, she and Dad had a rather rough time. She blamed him for my being there; he blamed me for her blaming him for my being there [29].

Scarbrough was only three years old when this "first big trauma" occurred. Immediately after the birth of her fourth child, Belle became very ill and George was sent to live with the Harrison brothers on the other side of the river, on the farm where he was born. It was a logical choice, since he was named for two of the brothers, former landlords George and Addison, and a good choice, it turned out, because the oldest brother, John, was very kind to the little boy, as Scarbrough recalls in the same interview:

> Daddy liked the Harrison brothers, but it was John ... who took me in, attended to my needs, bathed me, slept with me, dressed me in one of his big blue shirts, and held me while I cried myself to sleep. I resented being separated from my mother, but John was one of the stable points in my life, one of the kind people I knew, and that made a terrible impression on me in one way, because it made me more dependent on my mother for everything I learned [31].

The hiatus in "Brother John's" care finally ended when Scarbrough's mother told her husband to go and bring George home because she did not feel it was right for the Harrisons to be taking care of her son any longer. Even though the boy was reunited with his mother — whom he had been forbidden by Oscar to see during those months because he said George would have cried to stay at home after visiting — the feeling of being unwanted was firmly established, as are so many negative childhood experiences. Scarbrough stated:

Rejection, the feeling, the sense, the knowledge of rejection, began to sink in then. And I guess, forever after; I still feel rejected. I don't know why. I have all these friends. I feel like the boy in the coat of many colors [Interview].

Scarbrough returned to those feelings of abandonment, coupled at age seventy-eight with loss and, still, a palpable uncertainty, in an unpublished poem found among his papers after his death. The poem is titled "The Gift":

> Unwanted, I was orphaned at birth.
> At three, I was offered to neighbors,
> A gift my mother prevented, crying
> "Shame!" to my generous father.
>
> At thirty-five, I held my dying
> Father in my arms. At sixty-eight,
> Holding my mother, I was further
> Abandoned. Now a decade later,
> Having planted my own cabbages for
> Fifty-three years altogether,
> I still hold my parents in my arms.
>
> How much abandonment must occur
> Before a man's arms give way
> And are truly empty?

Stained to Perfection

The second great traumatic experience in Scarbrough's life occurred only a few years after his family's "rejection." Though mentioned sparingly in the journals — and even less in his poetry — rape robbed Scarbrough of his childhood and innocence, and propelled the young boy into what Scarbrough calls "the world of overt sexuality" (Journal Q-123). In a very brief entry, Scarbrough writes, "To be raped in a cottonshed by a hardfisted farmhand when I was six years old was one way of being 'stained to perfection'" (A-231). The later journal entries are very revealing of Scarbrough's gay identity and his relationships, areas with which he is most comfortable, but he could not help but wonder if this childhood violation was the catalyst of his sexuality as an adult. In another journal entry, Scarbrough contends:

> Sexually precocious I may have been. I don't know. I think we are or become what our very first encounters make of us, willynilly. I was

> forced to become much in advance of my years sexually; as a result of which ... I continually yearn backward to the infancy I lost [Q-123].

Through a pattern of memory in which it appears more details become vivid, Scarbrough offered another telling of the story:

> There was always that business in the cottonshed to be kept in mind. I was a pretty child and men wanted me. I stirred them without knowing it, until I became a more knowledgeable stirrer and sought revenge. Perhaps my father understood more of this than I gave him credit for. Perhaps he knew about, or suspected, the farmhand's assault, and perhaps he more carefully assigned the blame. He detested me no less for my childish part in it. I crept away afterwards and picked an armful of those April-sky-blue chicory flowers and carried them home to my beloved mother, safe for the moment from the world of men [R-75].

In his poetry Scarbrough broached this subject from behind a veil. Even after a series of abdominal surgeries took him to the brink of death, and he felt a newfound conviction to say what needed to be said, the rape itself was relived with a certain vagueness. "Room With A View," from *New and Selected Poems*, describes a young boy's desire to make for himself a "picture" to hang on the barren wall of his room. The child plans to create a mosaic of a combed cotton boll pressed beneath a square of glass. While stealing a dirty and unused window pane from the crawl space of his landlord's home, the boy is caught by the man and accosted:

> Behind the toolshed, the landlord's pale
> prick lanky as a severed vine in the shaking
> afterthought of my bloody fright,
> I hawked and spat and polished the grimy pane
> on my shirt-tail, being a juicy and
> resourceful boy. "Better a slimy ass
> than a room without a view," I opined,
> to the goddam yammering jay who kept
> announcing my whereabouts to an
> interfering world [38–47].

The child's reactions are mixed between shame — the fear that he might be caught — and acceptance; he did indeed achieve what he wanted, even though the cost was great. The final lines of the poem, in which the child is removed from the exacting horror of the experience itself, are equally troubling for the reader. In an effort to harm as helpless a creature as himself and draw an accurate analogy of how lowly the violation made him feel, the boy places a "fat tabby-black slug / on the hot sand of the garden path / to see if he could oil his way out of that" (87–90). The slug suffers a "sizzled" death, and is transformed into a "smelly / ghost like a black tarry henturd / on the baking sand" (91–93). Once the torturing is complete — the punishment exacted and relief gained — the poet finalizes:

> In the middle of the afternoon,
> goddam dopey time when all skill of hope,
> and all hope of skill, has gone out of the mind,
> I stretched myself out on the back porch
> and, fool that I am, had me this
> beautiful dream [95–100].

Speaking to the long-term effects of the early sexual experience, Scarbrough wrote in "Of Classrooms," also from *New and Selected Poems*, that his "epiphany was in a cottonshed." The concluding lines of that poem are as graphic as Scarbrough ever came in verse to describing the rape itself:

> For on that autumn day of brown clouds
> streaked in wind like finally combed hair,
> the full, strong odor of man was on him
> when, in raised cloths, he showed me first
> the strong, full value of man [41–5].

The early journal entries are marked by a noticeable avoidance of sexual issues, though later the subject is discussed openly. The journals provided a private medium through which Scarbrough could deal with these issues without airing them openly for all to read — at least during his lifetime — and, perhaps, miscomprehend. Following is another excerpt from the journals:

> "What do you do for a living," I am often asked. I reply, "Nothing. I keep a journal to live." The questioner does not understand. Nor would I, in his position. How could he know that a day's journey ... could be accomplished by writing in a book? [H-73].

Adding to this fear of being misunderstood was another: that of being misjudged and dismissed simply became of his sexual orientation. Scarbrough had real concerns that if the journals were published, people would remember only that he was gay, not that he wrote literature of merit. Speaking of Walt Whitman, Scarbrough revealed this concern, "People attacked him, some still do, because he was gay, but that's the absolute lowest of points to say about a man of his stature" (Interview). When asked about regrets, Scarbrough alluded to his secretive nature in dealing with sexual issues:

> I wish I hadn't tried to conceal things. I felt so low, so cheap, that I used a woman's name in a poem that was addressed to a man.... That's cheap. I was taught to be honest, but I have found that lies can be a man's chief support.... A lot of people would try to hold me accountable even when I was trying to avoid unpleasantness, and one time, possibly even death [Interview].

Rejection was reinforced by the way other children in the family treated Scarbrough for what his father called his "sissy" ways. Scarbrough said, "But most of the sissiness, so-called, came in the charge of my cousins, who were really root-hoggers" (Williamson 31). Taking cue from their father, even some of Scarbrough's siblings were cruel toward him. At Polk County High School, the slight young man weighed only 105 pounds and was tormented by bullies, one of whom was the son of the local undertaker and openly poked fun at Scarbrough. He was, however, popular with the girls in at least one setting — just before French class — when the female students would gather around Scarbrough so he could read the day's assignment to them. As soon as that task was completed, Scarbrough remembered that the girls would always find an excuse to move closer to some other boy, usually a handsome football player. Scarbrough was amused later in life when that same bully — the undertaker's son — sent a letter requesting an autographed copy of *Tellico Blue*. Scarbrough sent the book, uninscribed, and then received another letter from the man, requesting that the poet sign a sheet of paper that he could paste in the book. In the Williamson interview, Scarbrough said:

> Well, I autographed a little note for him that said, "In memory of the bad old days at PCHS." Incidentally, the initials PCHS meant to us students, "Poland China Hog Shit." That's what we boys chanted under our breath in the back of the auditorium [32].

During his junior year at PCHS, Scarbrough entered a national reading race and won second place. He read sixty-five books and commented on each in twenty-five words or less. The winner, Benny Baker — Scarbrough still remembered his name — was from a northern state; he read and reported on 115 books during the same period. For a moment, Scarbrough was the school hero, the "prize rooster" who was put on stage before the student body with his award — a collection of Modern Library books — and praised by the principal. His fellow students were not impressed. Scarbrough said, "My friends among the males couldn't give a damn how many books I read. They didn't read books; they got their girlfriends to read them" (Interview).

The Polk County High School Class of 1935. Scarbrough is pictured kneeling in the second row, second from the right, beside a female teacher. The poet's lifelong friend, Ruth Haskins, is the first girl sitting in the first row on the left, and her future husband, James Passmore, is kneeling directly behind her (courtesy of George Scarbrough).

Say What You Want To

Scarbrough left the confusing years of his formal training with an even greater desire to write — a longing that led him to the Writers' Workshop at the State University of Iowa in 1957. Still trying to find quality in the educational system, Scarbrough was again disappointed and simply completed the program without any real investment on his part. He took courses in both poetry and fiction, using the same short story over and over to fulfill the professors' requirements. Scarbrough stated:

> I can't say I studied. I just sat there gasping in amazement at what Paul Engle called teaching. He had long, dark, greasy hair which came way back and he would sit on the desk and his hair would fall forward and he would sling it back. He preened a little for the *Times* photographer who seemed always to be coming to the Writers' Workshop in those days [Interview].

Disgusted, for the most part, with the time wasted trying to learn at centers of higher education, Scarbrough began an intensive personal effort to become a better writer. By the time he attended the Iowa Writers' Workshop, Scarbrough was already an established poet with three books to his credit: *Tellico Blue* in 1949, *The Course Is Upward* in 1951, and, in 1956, *Summer So-Called*, which was mentioned in the 1957 *Encyclopædia Britannica Book of the Year*. Harrison Hayford wrote: "The year 1956 brought no flood tide of poetic creation, even though the work of many younger poets was marked by keen insight and technical competence;" Hayford then named, in addition to Scarbrough's book, John Ashberry's *Some Trees*, Donald Hall's *Exiles and Marriages*, and Adrienne Rich's *The Diamond Cutters*. The notation was the first in which Scarbrough was mentioned with well-known poets of his day.

A trio of books in less than a decade by a nationally-known publisher, E. P. Dutton, was quite an accomplishment, but it was twenty-one years before Scarbrough's fourth book, *New and Selected Poems*, was published. That long break between volumes was not idle time. Scarbrough published widely in literary magazines and wrote reviews which revealed the essayist exploring his own ideas about poetry by examining the work of others. In "One Flew East, One Flew West, One Flew Over the Cuckoo's Nest," a review of ten books for the *Sewanee Review*, Scarbrough celebrated the variousness of American poetry. In a statement of his own views on the verse of the day, Scarbrough was setting the stage for his next book, which was more diverse than any of the previous three. He used as metaphor the childhood song that describes a place, the cuckoo's nest, the location of which is a mystery, but must be in "any direction, at all or all directions at the same time" (138). Scarbrough then made

Scarbrough with tulips, at age 30, before the publication of *Tellico Blue* (courtesy of George Scarbrough).

the following commentary, connecting poetry with that concept from his youth:

> American poetry is the cuckoo's nest! Qualifying on every score, as I had imagined that fabulous place. Put together piecemeal of ends and oddments, of bricks and straws and bits of ocean foam. Diversity was all that I could find, and the unity that good poetry, if and when it occurs, achieves through the diversity that it makes is good [139].

Not only was Scarbrough's own poetry becoming more diverse in relation to subject matter and ideas, the next book also marked a change in Scarbrough's style. While the first three books were somewhat dependent on established, traditional forms, the new poems in *New and Selected* are predominantly free verse. The recurrent attention to place and family is present, but the poems in his fourth collection are more deeply personal and, in some ways, more honest than work that came earlier. This change in approach and willingness to take more risks was due in part to health problems Scarbrough encountered during that twenty-year period. After surviving three colon surgeries, and the attending, later unfounded fear of doctors finding a malignancy, Scarbrough decided to throw caution to the wind in terms of subject matter for his poems. That fresh attitude is evident in *New and Selected*; Scarbrough explains it this way:

> I always tried to be invisible because I didn't think I was anybody ... that I was nobody and I was pleased when somebody spoke to me. But after the great illnesses, smelling myself rotting, I realized that it was time to throw some of that junk away, stand up in the world, say what you want to [Interview].

Following publication of *New and Selected*, Scarbrough's next venture was the release of his only novel, *A Summer Ago*, which is discussed at length in another chapter. His last volume of poetry, *Invitation to Kim* (1989), garnered Scarbrough a nomination for the 1990 Pulitzer Prize, a flirt with national recognition that left the poet with mixed emotions. After the announcement that he had not won (in fact, he was not a finalist), Scarbrough again felt that familiar rejection that had long plagued his self-prescribed tentative position in the world of letters. These feelings, both of disappointment and then resolve, are mentioned in a journal entry:

> Many are nominated but few are chosen, I say to my congratulators on being nominated for the Pulitzer Prize in poetry. I had not expected to win but the fact is I felt rejected. To paraphrase Browning, another rejection, "the worst and the last." It would be easy to mean by that "last" not only the most recent but the final one, *finis*. But that would only be pain speaking, a momentary failure of being. I shall try again:

Scarbrough showing his mother, at the nursing home where she resided, the just released *New and Selected Poems*, ca. 1977 (courtesy of George Scarbrough).

that's what I'm best at, trying. I put my book *Invitation to Kim* on the shelf. I shall not look at it again for a while [gg6].

Despite Scarbrough's feeling of once again being overlooked, the Pulitzer nomination actually capped a career marked by recognition. Scarbrough received two Carnegie Fund Grants in 1956 and 1975; the Borestone Mountain Award in 1961; the Mary Rugeley Ferguson Poetry Award from the *Sewanee Review* in 1964 for his poem, "Return: August Afternoon"; a P.E.N. American Branch Grant in 1975; an Authors' League Fund Grant in 1976; the Sheena Albanese Memorial Prize by *Spirit* magazine and the Governor's Outstanding Tennessean Award in Literature, both in 1978.

Even in his young adulthood and middle-age years, Scarbrough did not venture far from the Eastanalle corner of Tennessee—and the family's departure from native soil was a forced evacuation, prompted by political upheaval and violence. Polk County, in the 1930s, became a dangerous place, prompting Oscar Scarbrough to one day announce to his family,

"It's time for us to leave"; and the clan that remained at home vacated to McMinn County.

The politics of Polk County continued to worsen, and those who remained became pawns in a sometimes lethal game between warring parties. The Scarbroughs, with no political clout at all and having expatriated by choice, avoided the ugliest of those times — but many of their friends, neighbors, and acquaintances were not so lucky. Ruth Haskins, married to James Passmore, and their children, experienced the turmoil firsthand. That strength and resolve that Ruth emanated on the bus ride to Knoxville served her well later in life.

In a lecture presented to the Southern Women Writers Conference at Berry College, Rebecca Mobbs — daughter of Ruth Passmore — and now Scarbrough's literary executor, recalled those tumultuous times. Following is an excerpt from her paper, "Is This My Home?":

> The safe and bucolic world of my childhood soon collapsed. My parents became involved in a political reform movement in Polk County that began in 1948 and continued until 1964. My life during all that time was filled with fear — fear for the safety of my parents, fear that our house would be burned, fear that our friends would become our enemies. The events of those sixteen years can be compared to a civil war: families torn apart, churches split, innocent children the victims.
>
> In August of 1948, the election campaign turned violent. Returning Veterans having fought against the evils of a one-party system in Europe would not accept being governed by the same in this country. The dissenting Democrats and the Republicans formed a political coalition which took the form of a new political party, called The Good Government League, or GGL. Tensions were high. My parents took me to political rallies at the courthouse where, in the heat, women fanned and babies cried. Mother, an outspoken critic of the governing party, stood in front of the hot, sweaty people and shook her fist. "This is the United States of America," she cried, "and Polk County is our home. We have the right to vote just like every other American citizen does." Daddy was never very articulate nor did he have a fiery personality like Mother, but he was a master tactician. He worked behind the scenes and was fearless. ...The violence escalated and the governor sent the National Guard into the county to keep order. My parents sent me, alone, by Tennessee Coach Company bus up the valley to an aunt's home for safety...
>
> On the night of the election, no one went to bed. People stood outside looking in the open window of the courthouse and squeezed inside to ensure the safety of the ballot boxes and to guarantee that all the ballots were correctly counted. My parents took me, so I could remember all my life what happened there. The Good Government League won

Scarbrough on the steps of his Oak Ridge Home, 100 Darwin Lane, ca. 1989 (courtesy of George Scarbrough).

every office, and my parents celebrated the election. Finally, they said, the citizens of Polk County, Tennessee could enjoy the political freedoms guaranteed to every American, and thank God, voter fraud was over. Sadly, this did not happen. For the next sixteen years, every election was contested, people were ambushed, machine guns were mounted on tops of roofs near polling places, and our barn was burned.... Someone, we never found out who, came across the pasture, hit the dog over the head, and burned the barn with all the cattle and equipment ...

Mother was so afraid the house would be burned that she divided all the family pictures among family members. For years, when I returned home, I would drive over the hill and look toward the mountain to see if the house was still there. Those years of struggle gradually weakened my parents. Mother, physically strong, was emotionally fragile. My father, physically weak, was emotionally strong. Mother suffered bouts of clinical depression, and eventually became a bitter, silent, old woman. At the end of her life she suffered from dementia. My father suffered for many years with stomach ulcers and died from stomach cancer.

After Oscar Scarbrough's death, George and his mother resided for a short time in nearby Anderson County, and they eventually settled, in 1963, at 100 Darwin Lane, Oak Ridge. They never returned physically to live in southeastern-most corner of Tennessee after their departure—but Scarbrough, at least figuratively and imaginatively, never really left "the county." He once told Rebecca Mobbs that he always dreamed in black and white, unless his dreams were set in Polk County, and then they appeared to his subconscious mind in full color.

In a moving journal entry, Scarbrough explains why he was compelled to stay so close to this region of East Tennessee:

> One thought that remained this morning was that of having a gravesite of one's own in a family cemetery somewhere, waiting. I had remarked that were I living in New York at my age, I would be frantic to get home, to find the county again and the yard at Friendship Church in Polk County where my plot is next to my mother's and father's grave. Being home means everything to me. I can understand that it does not mean so much to many people, home being wherever they happen to be. But with me it is a matter almost of breath to be within an hour's drive of my boyhood mountain, the High Top in the home county, in whose shade virtually I will ultimately rest [O-78].

Final Years

Scarbrough's final years were marked by a renewed scholarly interest in his work and important recognitions. The accolades came in various

Scarbrough autographing copies of *Invitation to Kim* at a book event, ca. 2004. The child is the poet's nephew, Will Lauver (courtesy of George Scarbrough).

forms, including regular appearances in top journals, such as *Poetry, The Southern Review, Shenandoah,* and *Virginia Quarterly.* The annual Literary Festival, held on campus at Emory and Henry College, Emory, Virginia, October 21–22, 1999, was in his honor, and the resulting Spring 2000 *Iron Mountain Review* was dedicated to Scarbrough's work. *Asheville Poetry Review* editor Keith Flynn chose Scarbrough for inclusion in the special millennial Spring–Summer 2000 issue, which focused on "Ten Great Neglected Poets of the Twentieth Century." The section devoted to Scarbrough contained a sampling of his work, an interview, and selected criticism. Of the ten poets chosen for this honor, Scarbrough was the only one still living. In April of 2001, Scarbrough was recognized by The Fellowship of Southern Writers at the biennial Arts and Education Council Conference on Southern Literature in Chattanooga and received the prestigious James Still Award for Writing of the Appalachian South, earned previously by Charles Frazier in 1999 and originally by James Still in 1997. Also in 2001, Scarbrough received the Bess Hokin Prize from *Poetry* magazine for his group of three Han-Shan poems that appeared in the July 2000 issue of that publication.

Scarbrough giving a public reading of his work, ca. 2004 (courtesy of George Scarbrough).

The Emory and Henry Literary Festival marked the first time that Scarbrough's poetry has received comprehensive study from a group of scholars. The official publication of the festival, the *Iron Mountain Review*, carried a sampling of Scarbrough's poetry — seven selections — and essays presented at the festival by Bill Brown, Connie Green, Edward Francisco, and the author of this critical biography (the paper presented by the author appears, in edited form, as a chapter in this book). The *Review* also included an interview between Scarbrough and Jerry Williamson, editor of *The Appalachian Journal*.

Bill Brown, long-time Metro Nashville educator at Hume-Fogg Magnet School and student of the poet's work, focused on the element of light in Scarbrough's poetry. Brown noted examples of how Scarbrough's poetry relies on light and dark, colors and shades, to create varying moods, and how the poet is consistent in the use of certain colors in relation to particular members of his family. For example, Brown found that Scarbrough regularly associates his father with a "shadowy, winter landscape" (12), matching the man's darker character. However, his mother is revealed in a different light, according to Brown: the landscape is the same, but it is more illuminated by brightness. Brown refers to Scarbrough's poem,

"County Lullabye" as "a true gathering of light in a lyric gift of landscape" (13).

Connie Green, who teaches at the University of Tennessee at Knoxville and directs the Creative Writing Program there, chose as her topic the close relationship between Scarbrough's poetry and his family. Green not only provides excellent examples of familial ties, she establishes Scarbrough as an Appalachian poet because of this connection: "Because family and place have always been important to the inhabitants of this region ... and they are central to George's poetry..." (20). Green finds that family is the subject to which Scarbrough returns again and again because there he finds stability but not necessarily always comfort. Green writes:

> No matter how bitter the memory, the poet is bound ineluctably to family, and thoughts of being loosened from such bindings, even metaphorically loosened, terrify [21].

Green concludes by naming the common force in most of Scarbrough's family poems: love, even though that emotion is sometimes difficult to bear, and can prove dangerous. In the most important passage of the essay, Green alludes to one of Scarbrough's poems, the sonnet "Experience," in which the young boy finds himself face-to-face with a large black bull inside the barn. Green writes:

> The poem, though naming neither father, brother, nor any other relative, expresses the danger to be found close to home, the chancy sort of existence that shadows a life lived close to the land, a life for Scarbrough inextricably bound up in family [24].

Likewise, Edward Francisco of Pellissippi State College notes the family and geographical connections evident in Scarbrough's poetry, but uses them to develop a deeper point: that the poet's spirituality is a product of that environment. Francisco states:

> If geography defined the terms of Scarbrough's early spiritual awareness — making him, in his own words, "a worshipper of place, a devotee of boundary and landmark" — family offered both dispensations of love and a harsh reminder of the inherited disappointments we equate with the effects of the Fall [26].

Francisco finds that Scarbrough struggles with a God that will place a human being, especially a child, in this world and then abandon him. According to Francisco, this question keeps Scarbrough from accepting faith on faith's terms and leads to his resistance of "the age's temptation to believe too easily in what it fails to comprehend" (29). This notion connects the poet with Flannery O'Connor's theory of the "Christhaunted"

South. Francisco also suggests that Scarbrough's vision of heaven may simply be home, or a "dream of home" (30), which takes the divine out of the equation and attributes to the poet a very pragmatic spirituality.

The literary festival was a very trying weekend for Scarbrough. He was obviously weak upon arrival the first day, and suffered through an afternoon of over-attention and exhaustion. After the evening meal, he was scheduled to give a poetry reading in the impressive chapel on the Emory and Henry campus. Scarbrough said later that he had no memory of the reading, which did not go well; the ailing poet became disoriented during the event and had to retire early. The following day began with a luncheon, at which Scarbrough collapsed and had to be taken by ambulance to a nearby hospital. Doctors discovered that he had a severe infection, and upon returning home, spent several more days in the hospital before recovering. An interview which was to be held publicly after lunch was canceled, and Scarbrough and Jerry Williamson sat down together months later and completed the session.

By the time Scarbrough was invited by the Fellowship of Southern Writers to participate in their conference, he was back in good health and tremendous spirits. Scarbrough participated in a panel discussion, titled "New Southern Writers," with Rodney Jones, Hal Crowther, John McManus, and Mary Hood, and charmed the crowd as the oldest panelist, at age eighty-five. He talked of his childhood, his work, and Southern literature in general. Scarbrough said he felt a fundamental background in all Southern writing, "from Gaines to Welty to McCullers," was the religious problem. The crowd enjoyed his comments about motivation, which he summed up in one word, "revenge," and then read an older poem, "Victory Song," about facing nature at its worst, "flickering wasps / with red-earth bodies / and amber isin- / glass wings / and death in their asses" (*New and Selected* 210–211). The poem ends with these lines:

> What can I do but laugh?
> To kill one's enemies
> is a joyful exercise:
> how else can one keep
> the whole sweet problem
> of deliverance alive?

Following the morning panel discussion, Scarbrough conducted a workshop with students at Red Bank High School. He was surprised at the honesty of their questions and enjoyed the opportunity to be back in a classroom, since teaching was one of his first occupations.

On Saturday evening, at the final convocation of the Fellowship and the concluding session of the conference, Scarbrough was honored with the James Still Award for his depictions the Appalachian South. The award statement said of Scarbrough: "He limns his land with the exact and keen eye of the landscape painter" and "records its distinctive idiom with an uncanny use of the language." The plaque was presented by Fellowship member and novelist Lee Smith.

In his ninth decade of life, Scarbrough was still experiencing firsts: three of his poems were featured on the internet site, "Poetry Daily." Scarbrough completed a book of Han-Shan poems, tentatively titled *Under the Lemon Tree*, and another collection, *On a Blue Theme*. Scarbrough had additional poems accepted for publication in *Poetry*, and appeared as a panelist and gave a reading at the 2001 Southern Festival of Books in Nashville. More recent honors included the Knoxville Writers' Guild Career Achievement Award in 2003, and a feature story with the *Knoxville News-Sentinel*, in response to the Guild's action. Scarbrough told interviewer Fred Brown, "I'm an old leaf, a-tremble on a twig in fall," and showed his fingertips, devoid of prints from years spent at the typewriter. Scarbrough said, "I have no fingerprints left. I have no feeling in my hands. I'm as polished as a wild onion."

Honoring their native son, the Polk County Commission declared October 23, 2005, as "George Scarbrough Day," for his "lifetime of literary accomplishment as teacher, author, critic, and most of all, distinguished poet, whose work is now recognized and acclaimed not only in our region, but throughout the nation." Scarbrough's final accolade came less than two months before his death with his induction into the East Tennessee Writers Hall of Fame in October 2008.

But perhaps two recognitions later in life meant most to Scarbrough. *Poetry* magazine assembled *The Poetry Anthology: 1912–2002*, and chose one of Scarbrough's poems for inclusion in a book designed to celebrate the best selections appearing in the ninety years of the magazine's existence. "Han-Shan Fashions a Myth" shares pages with the work of the greatest poetic names of the twentieth century, including T. S. Eliot, Robert Frost, Marianne Moore, Ezra Pound, Carl Sandburg, and Wallace Stevens. In an interview with the *Oak Ridger* newspaper, Scarbrough said, "I am where I always wanted to be — considered among the major American poets" (Senn).

And that doctorate that eluded Scarbrough in his youth was finally realized; Lincoln Memorial University — the school where the poet earned his undergraduate degree — conferred upon Scarbrough in 2005 an honorary Doctor of Letters.

Dr. George Scarbrough, immediately after receiving the honorary degree in 2005 from his undergraduate alma mater, Lincoln Memorial University (courtesy of George Scarbrough).

Judy Loest recalls in the following comments Scarbrough's last days:

> George, until a few days before his passing, was his usual charming, delightful self. I think this temperament, the ability to delight others and to be delighted by life was part of the reason why George was able to transcend the meager boundaries of his childhood. People loved being in his company, he made you feel good. He was always happy about something, and it was infectious. He had an unusual way with words which, I think, captivated those around him. "I'm whitewashed today," he would say when he was tired. He once described a thin person as a "meerish twig, as thin as a sparrow's toe."
>
> The staff at Brakebill Nursing Home loved George. I think he may have been the most literary resident they ever had. He was gracious and entertaining and always solicitous of others' comments. For a long time after moving to the nursing home, he was troubled about not being able to pay — he couldn't believe he was getting so much care and three hot meals a day. He said he was fortunate to have a place in which to "live in comfort and radiance for another six months."

The two or three different male roommates he had were mostly silent (I think from strokes), but George always spoke about them with the same generosity and respect he would have shown academic colleagues.

There was nothing he loved more than talking about poetry, about metaphor-making, and a favorite word of his, "seeming." He was continually fascinated with the materiality of the world and the illusion he felt we often see, the "seeming," and poetry was a tool he used to explore that mystery. A good poet, he said, is a "shadow shaker." "I shake the trees I pass to see what flies forth." One very wise thing he told me is that "we have to follow reality, but we don't have to ape it."

He could always quote a line or two to enrich the conversation. He didn't write anything during those last couple of years, nor did he watch television or read much other than greeting cards. But he loved company and, as one nurse told me, he had frequent visitors.

It was my deepest pleasure to have gotten to know George at the end of his life. He was one or those rare figures who enlarge your sense of the world.

Scarbrough, at age 88 (courtesy of George Scarbrough).

Also found among the papers he left behind, the poet made clear his final wishes in the following note, titled "Last Request," and summed up his life's work and hopes for remembrance:

> Please gather my ashes and scatter them privately on the grave of my parents in Friendship Cemetery in Polk County, Tennessee. Inscribe, please, these words on a small brass plate and attach the plate to the base of my parents' gravestone:
> American Writer
> George Addison Scarbrough
> Son of Oscar and Belle
> October 20, 1915–
> His mission was to teach the world to read.

Two

Family

Father-Made Harm

As the title poem of *Invitation to Kim* makes clear, Scarbrough's relationship with family was both troubling and beneficial. Ambivalent offspring of a tyrannical father, grateful child of an overly-attentive mother, and misunderstood sibling in a large family, the poet used words to come to terms with his role as son and brother. A portion of this poetic effort focuses on family history, an apparent attempt to understand the present by learning the past; a much larger selection of poems deals directly with particular family members — the father, especially. Also present, and important, are poems about Scarbrough's beloved mother and two brothers, Lee and Kim.

In a revealing essay published by *Touchstone,* the magazine of the Tennessee Humanities Council, Scarbrough discussed at length the effect of family relationships and the manner in which a positive, or negative, familial environment ultimately shapes the person one becomes:

> I'm not condemning family. We have all suffered, and sometimes benefited, from family, and are all members of a family of some kind. I am only saying that from family come the really telling outcomes [7].

For Scarbrough those "outcomes" evolved into a lifelong effort to reconcile his existence with what he thought his family expected and demanded of him. Unfortunately, as with many sons of overbearing fathers, Scarbrough never had the opportunity to resolve the conflict. Instead, his memories of his father, William Oscar Scarbrough, were, for the most part, dark and unpleasurable. In the same essay, Scarbrough wrote:

> As a result of his attitude, and mine, we never had a conversation in all our lives together. Talk always lapsed when he entered the room. The

other children grew silent, and I drifted away as soon as I, unnoticed, could.... He knew only to be rough with us and to keep us always subordinate and at a distance. This attitude persisted with him to his deathbed, from which he gave peremptory orders not to leave him, commanding what would have been, and was, willingly given. He died a hard death, and it fell to me to cradle him in my arms during his last moments, the others having fled the room [7–8].

While the father-son relationship was barely amiable and produced horrid recollections for Scarbrough, it proved rich ground for poetry. Scarbrough's second book of poems, *The Course Is Upward,* Is dedicated to his father, who died May 10, 1950, the previous year. The first five poems are sincere efforts to come to grips with that death, and to deal with the void left behind as the son considers what the man meant to him. In the first of the dedicatory poems, a sonnet, "Death is a Creek, Backward Flowing," the father figure retreats toward his beginnings as part of the stream, passing in his journey all that made him what he was in a "change of time" (14). The second in the group of poems, "Death is a Short Word," equates the father's death with language; the speaker's words are reduced "in exact proportion to how much he died" (3), devolving in both tone and substance until "only the monosyllable [is] finally valid" (20). And in the final poem of the first section, the poet deals with the feeling that the father is becoming more important

The poet's father, William Oscar Scarbrough, whose close Cherokee ancestry is evident in the high cheek bones; Scarbrough described his father's complexion as "raw tomato red," ca. 1910 (courtesy of George Scarbrough).

in death than he was in life. The son feels, perhaps for the first time, the impact that his father had on him and is reminded that he, as creation of the man, must carry on, however burdened by an "elided story" and "elliptic laws" (23–24). It is necessary to note that these poems were written immediately following the father's death and lack some of the bitterness that is evident in mid-career and later poetry.

From *New and Selected,* the poem "Impasse" is a retelling of the father's death in a "room too small / to heave a bed in, / A window too high / to let the yard in, / but perfect for the exit of souls" (3–8). The speaker is trying, again, to reconcile the father-son relationship in a number of ways. The most effective is by repeating the word, father, thus rendering it powerless, at least momentarily. Having returned to the room of his father's death, the speaker remembers the event and, even though removed physically and, somewhat, emotionally, responds in childlike fear: "And my stomach crawls / like a bucketful of live / crabs shaking hands" (XII 19–21).

The most ambivalent of the father poems is "The Christmas Dance," also from *New and Selected.* In a dream-like sequence the son visits his father's grave, paying close attention to the setting in the cemetery (complete with contrasting imagery of doves and crows) and remembers the pain of being beaten by the man who is now dead: "He whaled me until / I pissed my pants / because I tarried with a terrapin / and would not scythe briars" (88–91). The son, justifiably, finds some relief by denying identification of the father's name, forcing the dead man to wait for recognition while the speaker adheres to an old ritual, molesting the stone angel on the tombstone: "Before addressing the name, / I finger, as always, / the angel's stony robes / to make the flier masculine" (45–48). At the end of the poem the son chides his father into action: "I list his cruel debits / like a long litany never heard in the church" (141–42), and the dead father responds by rising from his grave and the two join in a Christmas dance "ringed by soft, bowing doves, / wreathed by stiff, stepping crows" (151–52).

One of the most disturbing poems in *Invitation to Kim,* "Leathers," recounts a whipping delivered on the son by a razor strap-wielding father who is honing his child to a "fine edge" (5). While suffering this beating, the son drifts off into an ethereal realm where he contemplates the leather being used, not the beating itself. The speaker has the "wonderful thought / That I love leathers: straps, thongs, / Rawhides to tie with, up, down, and / Together" (6–9). He looks forward to the day when the leather strap of his father will be replaced by other objects made of the same material: a valise, a coat, or a book of poems bound in leather. The pain and sound of the strap as it makes a "wish swish wish swish" audible pattern in the air bring the speaker back to reality. The father's face has become leather, and the boy, obviously accustomed to these beatings, is content as "Excitement gathers in my loins" (18–20).

"Daddy, You Bastard," also examines the love-hate relationship that the child speaker has with his father. The adult, when angry, is described as having dark eyebrows that "dived together / like two hawks swooping down / on the same prey: poor, whimpering rabbit-boy" (3–6). The speaker says he "grew up in a striped suit," his skin permanently scarred from the many beatings (52). The poem also speaks to the enduring effects of suffering at the father's hands and mental cruelty: "Too short on love too long, / I am still short on love. / It would please you to know, / Daddy, you bastard, / That I never exceeded / The cut of my clothes" (55–60).

Also from *Invitation to Kim*, "Poem for William Oscar," begins on a positive note as the child speaker is waked by the father who tells him his breakfast is ready and waiting. The tone of the poem changes, however, when the father is described as having a "salad face — / retinal image in russet / ... and raw tomato red," a vision the speaker retains when he closes his eyes (10–12). What appears to be an act of kindness on the part of the father is shrouded by what the boy knows to be true: the caring man who prepared the meal is an illusion, and the violent nature of the father may soon be exposed as the boy eats in "hesitant breakfast joy" (36).

And, finally, a more recent poem exhibits empathy and offers explanation about why William Oscar Scarbrough was such a rough character. In "Ice Storm," a poem dedicated to his father, Scarbrough presents a worn and broken man, beaten into submission by a world that is "still too icy in the old, / Aristocratic way" (14–15). The father is reduced to a "Serf with his feet wrapped / ... In tow like mauls / To bear witness to the invariable / Command" (9–12). As a sharecropper always dependent on others for work, the male subject of the poem is allowed to do only what those in charge tell him to do. He cannot even express his anger in the open, cold air of the ice storm but must wait until he reaches the shed, safe from the ears of others, before "muttering hate / In vulgar verbs / ... While his pointed nose / Drips drops of brilliant phlegm / Against the world's orders" (20–24).

Sibling-Sized Obloquy

Sibling poems are also present throughout Scarbrough's long career. Little mention is made of the only sister and three of his brothers — Edith,

Pete, Bill, and Blaine — but Lee and Kim are often the subject matter, or audience, for poetry. Lee was the childhood companion and playful tormentor of George, but the great love the poet felt for him is evident. Kim, the youngest of the children, held a very special place in the writer's heart; Scarbrough readily admitted that he tried to be a father figure for the baby of the family.

While a more complete description of Lee appears in Scarbrough's novel, *A Summer Ago,* the feelings that the writer had for this older and wiser sibling are most evident in the poetry. "Sonnet for My Brother Lee," in *Invitation to Kim,* provides not only a tender account of brotherly love but also displays Scarbrough's sense of humor. In the poem, Lee, the prankster figure in the poet's work, cajoles the speaker into performing stupid acts, all for his own amusement: sitting atop a gate for Lee to practice his aim with a slingshot, or jumping a fence into a "heap of dung / He knew was there for me to land in" (8–9). In each instance the younger boy runs home to tell his mother and makes promises that Lee reminds him are "made to be broken" (12), vows that the speaker will not allow Lee to manipulate him again into activities that are demeaning and dangerous. Or, as mother says in the poem, "He makes a dunce of you, / That brother of yours. Why will you play his fool?" (1–2). But because of the great admiration the younger child feels for his elder sibling, he will do whatever Lee suggests in order to be close to him. Scarbrough writes, "I never learned to distrust him wholly. / Loving him, I loved being his fool" (13–14). Again on the subject of Lee, in an uncharacteristically short poem, "Lee's Funeral," Scarbrough related his feelings at the time of his brother's death. The four-line poem reveals in final terms why the speaker of both poems — one a child, the other an adult — came to love Lee so deeply:

> His hands were small and brown and quick as wrens.
> All I could think, seeing them stacked thick
> As boxing-gloves on the thin breast,
> Was that they never struck me [198].

A Summer Ago makes clear a very pertinent point: George was his mother's child, and Lee was the father's. But, unlike the aggressive father, Lee's often painful adventures were never out of spite or contempt. In the end the speaker of the poem is struck almost speechless, and the quiet hands, once active and alive, were never raised in anger toward his younger brother.

In what may be one of Scarbrough's best poems, the title piece of *Invitation to Kim* is revealing and poignant. The poem is used as a thread that weaves its way throughout the entire book, with sections repeated in the publication at the beginning of each section. The poem is, indeed, an invitation that serves to welcome the youngest member of the Scarbrough family into George's home, both literally and figuratively. While the words might be read as an apology, a more careful interpretation shows that the long poem serves as an extended explanation of who the older brother really is and what factors made him become the misunderstood black sheep of the family.

Kim is invited into the "house / That George built / Of fetched-together / Fragments of father- / Made harm, mother- / Minded weal, sibling- / Sized obloquy, cousin- / Crossed odium, and / All the kudos of / The great-aunt kind" (1–10). Kim is asked to try and understand that the speaker of the poem was forced to find a substitute for the love he was denied as a child. In place of spirit and affection, the speaker has turned to words and knowledge, "the other / Name I chose for love" (79–80). The poet pleads with Kim not to be put off by a certain "Effeminacy of manner" (37) the father had so despised and made point of in the past, but to understand that each person — the speaker included — is unique and peculiar to a certain setting and set of circumstances over which he has no control. The speaker explains the strange decor — peacock feathers' eyes, narrow paths between stacks of books, watercolors, mementos, a house built of metaphor — as being carefully arranged so that the house is indicative of the inhabitant: "such interiors as / Mine are not as accidental / As they seem" (235–238). The poet states, emphatically:

> Come in, Brother. Because
> I love you, I have spent my
> Life trying to teach you
> Two things: How to let a
> Brother live as he will
> And die his own way:
> Two things which are only
> One in the end [238–245].

The final lines are a plea for acceptance, and invitation to once again "share the thin gleanings" that their common family history allows (248). Highly autobiographical, *Invitation to Kim* is an honest effort to find a connection, once again, with the younger brother. Scarbrough tried to be for Kim what his mother had been for him as a boy: the person who points out the smaller and subtler things in life and peaks an interest in self-expression. It was a mission he viewed as a failure. Scarbrough explained, "I tried to do the same with Kim. And I awakened a spark in Kim that was artistic. He was a very gifted man, but he had to feed his family. He had no choice" (Interview). The poem is also a sincere request of the younger brother to accept the poet in all his diversity, particularly his sexuality. Scarbrough stated, "My brother, Kim, never forgave me for being gay. I found out later that he criticized me sharply to people who knew both of us. He had no capacity to understand the variousness of nature" (Interview).

Mother-Minded Weal

The one true human love of Scarbrough's life was his mother. Oddly enough, the poet chose not to write about his mother in the earlier years, likely due to the fact that she lived long after the death of his father, and the mother-son relationship was very strong. Scarbrough was his mother's caregiver for the last fifteen years of her life, even after she required the full-time attention of a nursing facility where the son traveled daily to feed and comfort her. Scarbrough held her in his arms as she breathed her last breaths. In the later work, however, the strength of Louise Anabel McDowell Scarbrough exerts itself in a number of poems, none of which deal specifically with her life or passing but with the lessons she passed on to her son and their long-lasting influence.

An early photo of the poet's mother, Louise Anabel McDowell Scarbrough, who taught her son to read before he entered grammar school, using World War I headlines from newspapers that filled the cracks of one of many sharecropper shacks, ca. 1910 (courtesy of George Scarbrough).

In "Monday," the speaker uses floor scrubbing as the controlling metaphor. It is a skill he learned from his mother, passed down to her from her mother: how to "sand a floor / For scouring but to disdain / The crunch underfoot" (2–4). These lessons go on forever for the speaker, who notes, "Old preachments keep sermonizing" (4), and spill over into other godly qualities, such as cleanliness. Even though the speaker will "scrub my own pits raw" (9), he never feels he reaches the "godliness / She subscribed to" (11–12) and will never be part of the trinity of family: grandmother, mother, and son.

The poem "Direction" is also about lessons learned and their far-reaching result. The speaker appears as both child and adult in this memory of a correction by the mother to a son who took a book from the neighbor's home without permission. The boy is chastised by the mother who demands that he return the book at once, admonishing him with this line, "When have I taught you to break in and steal?" (2). As an adult, thinking of doing something forbidden, the speaker remembers the comment from the mother and is instantly reminded of "the way / My relucting feet must go" (14–15).

Always the protector, Scarbrough remembered his mother in a later poem published in a 2001 issue of *Poetry*. The piece deals with cause and effect, advice and results, and "The Good Mother" whose wisdom is tested and admired by the son. In very musical writing, the speaker remembers the way his mother, by creative means, kept her son safe. To divert him from crawling under the house, she tells him trolls and thieves live there and he could avoid the danger by staying upstairs. When childhood curiosity takes the boy to the edge of a dark and mysterious well, the mother tells him that "an ancient salamander / Folk lived in the depths ... / waiting for such innocents as / Me to come and look down ..." (11–15), and to stay away from "deep- / Down water" (20–21). In every instance the boy obeys and learns through his own actions that he will be safe as long as he follows his mother's advice: "I did. And nothing did" (8, 22, 33). In the final two stanzas, the mother has passed into that world that is both marvelous and strange, and the son waits patiently for her to return. The adult voice, however, knows that she will not be back from her berry-picking for the evening meal, and he must wait with great uncertainty for his own death so that he can be once again reunited with the good mother in "the purple glens / I am not yet allowed to enter" (53–54).

In his final years Scarbrough wrote verse that brought together the father and mother into the same poem. "Lesson" explores the differences between the two central characters of the poet's life. The overbearing father figure is present, and the mother is, once again, kind, nurturing, and edifying. The father tells the six-year-old boy, "You know nothing. / Nothing at all" (2–3) as he urges him to get ready for the first day of school. The father's words, "blows to the head" (6), spurn the boy into thinking about what he does know, all "(thanks to my mother)" (11). The child realizes that he knows much more than his father gives him credit for, such as which paths to follow when the wind "blew in the wrong direction" (23), and that the "moon rose over the dark mountain / When mother put out the light" (24–25). The boy, in his mind's voice, could tell the father that "darkness / Does not fall but swoops up from / The ground, overwhelming late travelers" (26–28), but does not. Instead, the father's influence proves to be the stronger, and when the child is asked in class what he wants to be as an adult, the speaker answers, "Nothing. Nothing at all" (40).

The voice of "Friendship Cemetery in Summer" is that of a mature and experienced adult who visits the side-by-side graves of his parents, a plot that shares a single headstone in Polk County, Tennessee. All around the speaker is the beauty of nature: "wild rose, the blue pine, / The blackberry, the purple alum" (1–2). These plants "flourish" in the "scented silence" of the graveyard (3–4). To honor his parents, the speaker brings his poetic ability, a product of their influence, to "test the strength of paradigm, / To chase verbs like rabbits" (7–8), but finds that words fail "in an earth / Without grammar: / Where all sentences end / In the same parsing" (10–13). The son's hope, to express through words what he feels, is powerless in the presence of the life of the cemetery. Verbs that he could once chase like rabbits are now replaced with real rabbits, and the natural processes of life and death are "all present and accounted for / In the wordless wind" (19–20).

Three

Songs of Defiance to Death

Scarbrough turned to language, out of necessity, at an early age. His first memories were of words because they were recognized and appreciated as the tools with which the world around him could be explained, described, and deciphered. That purpose was the most elementary for Scarbrough, and it was an attitude about language that served its user in the first years of life. As a maturing poet, Scarbrough took language to another level and recognized that for him words were more than communication. By his own admission, words formed the parameters of his life; they became the medium through which he understood everything. Scarbrough wrote in a journal entry:

> Words give us the only order we have: the only forms — social, political, religious, et cetera — we know anything about. There are no systems outside language.... The only world I have ever known is a world of words, a world I can make disappear by repeating words over and over until all meaning escapes them. That is, I have only a verbal version of things, and as its creator I have the power of its destruction [I-159].

Because words were so vital to him, Scarbrough attempted to shape the language of his poems in ways that are unique and, often, extraordinary. In the same way that Scarbrough was not a poet of place but *was* the place about which he wrote, he also became emotionally invested in the words he chose to use in his work. Or, as Forrest Gander has noted, "Scarbrough discovered that language itself was freedom" (112).

In "County Lullabye," this close association is made through the purest of metaphor, the combination of two words into one that speaks with even more clarity than mere association allows. The poem is a strenuous exercise in creation, the welding together of words to give each more meaning and make the new compound unique. Consider these single words made of two: *bonelight, treechange, grassemerald, stumpdark, housedark, calmlight.* Each new word not only has the meanings of its parts but also suggests a deeper meaning that must be gleaned from the forceful application of the two original roots. Scarbrough jams the words together, and this process is not unlike the country habit of making our own jams and jellies by combining essential elements to produce a desirable mixture. A jar of pure blackberry jam contains fruit and sugar. The finished product of boiling these two items together and reducing them to their real essence is identical to what Scarbrough does in "County Lullabye" with two words. The jam is still only blackberries and sugar, but it is more than that now: it also represents the best of what both have to offer. Likewise, Scarbrough's jam of words —*stumpdark* is a perfect example — produces an amalgam that combines a common object, the tree stump, with light, or the lack of it. The condition created yields a different kind of darkness, an elemental blackness of the sort described in the poem, "My Grandfather Said," (in *Invitation to Kim*) where the poet records what he discovered as a child trapped in a tree at night.

> All I learned is
> that night doesn't fall.
> It comes from the ground
> like black smoke rising.
> And there I sat,
> thinking to follow
> the last light down
> from the other direction! [20–21].

The child stranded in the top of that tree as shadows rise from the ground is experiencing, firsthand, *stumpdark*.

In dozens of entries the journals confirm how important language was to Scarbrough, who placed a value on words that is at once common and extraordinary. Of course, words were essential because he was a poet, but they also represented his connection to the world around him, the people with whom he coexisted, his past and present, and his memories. Scarbrough explains in his journal:

> Only one thing in my life has been constant: my interest in words. I should say "devotion" to words — for it has been a devotion, rarely known, I suspect, except among the more megalomaniacally linguistic lovers who have always come to people by way of words rather than the reverse [2:270].

And in another entry, Scarbrough equates words with survival, especially during those dark times after health problems or when, as Frost wrote in "Birches," we are "weary of considerations." Scarbrough had a long-standing habit of learning a new word every day. While most people were eating breakfast or commuting to work, Scarbrough immersed in a dictionary, fonund his new word, pored over its possible meanings, and discovered that through this process of constant edification, he pushed death away from the door. From the journal: "Each time I meet a new word, I feel alive again. Looking it up is like a song of defiance to death" (H-6).

These new words, these "songs of defiance to death," of course made their way into the poetry. But it is in their usage that one finds another unique quality of Scarbrough's poetry — a facet of his work that has drawn some negative criticism. While saluting Scarbrough at the beginning of his literary career, and finding much more right than wrong with his first book, *Tellico Blue,* Sara Henderson Hay did point out in *The Saturday Review,* "Sometimes his work is marred, I think, by a sort of studied intellectualism, that modern tendency to be impressively oblique or obscure." (38). Robert Phillips also mentions this criticism but explains it away:

> Most reviewers have thought well of Scarbrough's accomplishment. The only complaint with any consistency is that the erudition of the language seems not to fit with the rural imagery and the emphasis on family. Scarbrough apparently recognizes that, but for him language is what enables the poet to find or achieve order [422].

While this may be true, the critics who fault Scarbrough only see him as a poet and not as a linguist. Scarbrough attempted, especially in description, to find the perfect word, not simply a word that would do. This loyalty to what language is in its truest form produced poetry not unlike that of Emily Dickinson, who worked from imagery and then sought the consummate words for her description. Wallace Stevens is also strict in his usage and devotion to language that challenges the reader as well as the poet.

Most critics considered this wordplay a strength in Scarbrough's poetry. In his essay "Poets After Midcentury," James Justus equates Scarbrough's word choice with the experimental and recognizes this quality as a technique that removes the poet from the "bucolics of Jesse Stuart or the more skewed pastorals of Robert Frost, a tradition in which earlier readers were content to place him" (552). Justus finds the intricacies of Scarbrough's language to be part of the poet's maturation process. He writes:

> Yet the poetic style that gradually evolves ... is one that comes from the caressing cultivation of words for their own value and the sheer joy of indulgence in exotic diction, an indulgence that can make *intrados, wiffle,* and *riverine* as domesticated as *mule* and *plough* [552].

Edward Francisco views the use of formal language to describe the ordinary as one more of Scarbrough's particular talents that serve to add another dimension to his poems:

> I know of no living poet, and certainly no poet since Allen Tate, able to use the vernacular and the formal to more heightened effect than Scarbrough. Sometimes the combination creates a necessary distance between the poet and the experience being described. Each utterance is taut but elastic like a fish line subtending a current [922].

And with same obvious appreciation for what Scarbrough is attempting to do, Gander comments:

> However various their forms, Scarbrough's poems are all remarkable for a vocabulary so richly sonorous, so elegant and exact, they have few contemporary equals. What he is after, he says, is a language "the size of life" [110].

As evidence of this sonorous vocabulary, consider these obscure but lyrical words that are contained within the pages of the Pulitzer Prize nominated book, *Invitation to Kim: pejorative, askance, plangency, gravid, consanguineous, lepidopterist, blandished, decrescent, starveling, chaffy, indurated, cozens, fricative, stithy, manumitted, lambrequin, palinged, exudation, hawsered, gaumed, contemn, trivium,* and *bivium.* Reading Scarbrough requires one to have a dictionary close at hand, and to make of the margins a personal slate where extended definitions of certain words may be half as long as the poem itself. Such study is not an easy task, but it is a rewarding one. To further challenge the reader, Scarbrough does not always use the most obvious definition but opts instead for a subtle application that serves to make even richer the texture of his verse. An extension of his self-described "devotion" to words, Scarbrough approaches his work like a lover who wants to know every sensual detail about the body of the poem, and he appeals to the reader through every sensuous possibility.

How does a poet make the transition from being in love with language to having a love affair with the written and spoken word? This development process was often the subject of Scarbrough's writing. In "Several Scenes from Act One," a prose piece in *New and Selected Poems,* Scarbrough explains how language was integral to his earliest memories. In the following passage, the poet remembers his father delivering to him a child's bucket and spade, gifts from a neighbor. There apparently was, however, no explanation from the father, just a handing over of the playthings. Scarbrough went to his mother to receive the words that explained the gift:

> I felt uncomfortable under his (the father's) dark gaze and went immediately to my mother who found words to describe the miracle of spade and bucket; and I trusted in words. I lived words for the first time then, I believe, for previously I do not remember speech of any kind. I loved my mother because of her words. I did not understand my father

because he had none, or did not use any I could at the time comprehend [15].

From "Several More Scenes," also prose from *New and Selected Poems*, Scarbrough explains how words began to set this young poet apart from the people around him. Words were soon to become, by his very devotion to them, the quality that made him different. The people around him did not always understand this love of language because for most of them words were a hindrance; country folk found other ways to express themselves. And understandably, many of those people with whom Scarbrough associated could not fathom how a young mountain child could have come so early to be enamored of words. Scarbrough writes:

> Words helped to make me a loner, from the start. The daily rhymes of a mountain child became the lever that prised me apart from the common round of talk and half-realized association, into no talk at all, or as little as I could afford, and association meriting the name only because I came and went, shy and vexed, among the larger figures in my home [19].

This obsession with words kept getting in the way of his relationships with family members, especially his father, and even caused him to fail at manual tasks because Scarbrough's mind was often consumed with whatever he happened to be reading at the time. In his essay, "My Mother Language, My Father Tongue," Scarbrough writes:

> I recall once riding the cultivator up and down the river bottom half a morning without letting the gangs down, my thoughts tending towards home where a battered old copy of *The Scottish Chiefs* was waiting for me at the noon hour. Suddenly a clod whizzed past my head and my father bellowed, "Get your ass off of that cultivator and get to the house. You ain't worth your weight in cold dog manure. Hell's bells, what have I done to deserve this?" [28–29].

Scarbrough's father, a man's man who used language like a cattle prod, immediately deemed his son's seeming lack of interest in physical labor to be a sign of femininity. As Scarbrough remembers, his father said, adding insult to injury, "'Put your apron on, and help get dinner. You ain't fit fer anything else?'" (29).

Despite the harshness of his father's words, which were juxtaposed with his mother's calmer, soothing expressions, Scarbrough did gain from his parents the primary tools necessary to become a poet, and from an early age he recognized that words could serve at least two purposes. In the same essay Scarbrough describes his mother as a "realist" who was "gestaltic by nature" and taught him how to recognize color, shape, and form. Yet it was from his father that Scarbrough learned metaphor:

> From my part–Indian father, whose cheekbones crowded his eyes almost out of sight, I learned a stock of descriptions which fitted all these things but seldom told me anything but poetry about them.... I surmise, my penchant for poetry may have had its beginning with him rather than with my mother, for I wanted a whole set of replacements for his expressions and so turned early to a study of words.... So, in the beginning was indeed the word, her word and his, or his before hers, and tied to both words, my own [29].

In Scarbrough's novel *A Summer Ago,* words also are given a place of prominence and serve as the tool in this coming-of-age story by which we can judge certain aspects of the protagonist's maturity. When, near the end of the book, Alan recognizes that his pet bull will, by necessity, have to be sold at the auction in town, he accepts the fact and finds comfort in the knowledge that money from the sale will be given him to purchase a complete set of books for the coming school year, a luxury Alan has never before enjoyed. In a literal sense, Alan chooses words — the words in his new textbooks — over the farm life; he decides that books are more important to him than Buckeye, the young bull he loved and fed to near maturity. When he returns home from town, books in hand, Alan is ecstatic; the scene is perhaps the happiest in the novel — at least for the boy who has come of age through his giving up the beloved animal in exchange for his already recognized passion, words:

> "Mom!" he shouted, bursting into the frontroom. "Mom! I got all my books and Lee got all his books and you got a new dress with blue ribbons in it!" [214].

At this point, with Alan's exclamation of delight that both he and his brother have books instead of Buckeye, the novel ends.

Just as explanation for his love of words found its way into the prose, the poetry is also inundated with references to language and how vital it was to Scarbrough's existence and work as a poet. Later in life Scarbrough would write again about ploughing, this time a breaking plough, not a cultivator. But the more mature poet (in *Invitation to Kim*) does not forget to let down the plough point as he compares writing to the springtime ritual of turning over the ground in the poem "Ploughing." The earth becomes his own personal history of language from which the poet must roll "grubs of poems out / to the lank / light." The language of earth is made up of "tattered dictions," "the roughest usage of tongues," "the serf's sniffle of verbs," and the "rottenest eggs of words," all gathered together in an attempt to describe the "stooping killdeer's / withering cry" (55–56).

Another poem, "Summer Revival: Brush Arbor" in *Invitation to Kim*, recounts a childhood memory, that of attending a church service. In the same way that the young man's fascination with his parents' language helps him understand the inherent power of words, so does the preacher's "wild and wonderful" sermon: "His word's improbable beauty brought us down / To wallow gorgeously before him in the brown / Brush of his summer church" (39). The young listener experiences the omnipotent nature of words as the sermon makes the surroundings pale by comparison, even though there is beauty everywhere. The churchgoer learns that "Being a soul is also beautiful," but that is through the words of the minister that this notion becomes real, imaginable, and important.

In another childhood memory poem, this one, too, from *Invitation to Kim*, the experience of finding a prehistoric relic becomes real only through its connection to words. In "Implication," Scarbrough perceives language in every object, from the most common to, in this case, the most rare:

> ... I found
> A trilobitic stone with the look
> Of language on it, and in a dry
> Biblical county stood like a man
> With a slab ordained to be interpreted
> To a beleaguered people, but covered
> It back with red leaves for safe—
> Keeping on the mountain [50].

The allusion to Moses is a fitting one, but here the speaker does not take it upon himself to deliver the word to the displaced Israelites; instead he leaves the message on the mountain to be found later by some other prophet. This is the true mission of the poet as Scarbrough saw it: not to be a prophet who interprets the implications of what is written, but to be someone who writes the words and leaves them behind for others to find— or who stands admonished by the fear of what his father has taught him about the power of words. Later in the poem, the young man dismisses an opportunity to speak with a local hermit, who is also a lover of words, as the speaker learns by spying through a window and seeing the lonely old man reading a favorite book. Just as the speaker, a failed Moses, leaves the trilobitic stone on the mountain top, he refrains from using words because of what his father said: "'Keep your mouth shut, boy. / We have no portion here'" (51).

The title poem in *Invitation to Kim* offers in purest form a glimpse of Scarbrough as apologist. Just as the poem attempts to reconcile the brother to the life of the poet, it also offers further insight into the role language plays in Scarbrough's life. The poet tells Kim:

> Put the books on the floor,
> These chairs are never
> Sat in. Clear a place
> On the table for the prized
> Cup, and take care when
> You walk the narrow paths
> Of this house. Reading
> Was the rede I followed,
> Finding in the letter
> The spirit that escapes
> The law [3–4].

Only a few lines later we learn that, for Scarbrough, reading equals knowledge, and knowledge equals love. How can one have a more intimate relationship with language?

Another important aspect of Scarbrough's relationship with words was that they connected him directly with the past, particularly with his own ancestors. In "Calligraphy" (from *Invitation to Kim*) Scarbrough laments the lack of physical contact he had with the maternal grandfather whom he never knew but can only imagine through scraps of words left behind. In this case, the clue is his grandfather's name, written in his own hand in calligraphy inside a blue velvet box that contains the deceased doctor's stethoscope. Scarbrough, while he is pleased to have these items in his possession, is still not satisfied and thus inquires, who was this man? The speaker says:

> These were my progenitor's.
> That should be satisfying enough. But it is
> Not. I need more than a ticked box from a man who
> Swam leagues of mountain inland from the Cape
>
> To reach me but did not arrive, drowning before
> In some interim valley, the letter unwritten,
> The poem I am told he was capable of, unpenned [107].

The grandson needs more and admits to having tried to compensate for the absence of a personal relationship with his grandfather by writing of him in his own words, using language he felt his grandfather might have chosen. Scarbrough refers to an earlier piece, "The Private Papers of J. L. McDowell," as the poem in which he "cheated." In the end, the only tie Scarbrough has with Dr. McDowell is the written word, this time the signature in calligraphy that his grandfather penned, three words—*Joseph*

The poet's maternal grandparents, Dr. and Mrs. McDowell; the grandfather was the subject of one of Scarbrough's most noted poems, "The Private Papers of J. L. McDowell," date unknown (courtesy of George Scarbrough).

Leander McDowell— that stand symbolically in place of the man, and in response to which the poet comments on his own advancing age. Scarbrough writes, "An artful script then is all / I have to speak to — beside which my own crabbed hand / Is mazed as sparrow tracks in smudged snow" (108). The grandson-poet needs to make a deeper connection and refers, finally, to the grandfather as "metaphor man."

Just as words linked Scarbrough to his own past, language also offered a tangible possibility of eternal life, a link with the future. Scarbrough plays with this idea in "Small Poem," from *Invitation to Kim*. In this work the poet realizes that the daily struggles of writing are worth the effort or, as Faulkner said, "worth the agony and the sweat." If the poet can, through his own efforts — "fixing the right word / daily nail-like into / its post" — leave something behind of merit, then he has cheated death; or as Scarbrough writes, "a man could / eventually go away / without leaving" (118). Since Scarbrough had no biological offspring, the poems became his children, the next generation that carries with it the genes of the past. And in this case, the genetic makeup is the word.

Four

A Small, Comfortable World

"To make an art for a county on the rim of a rock has been all my intent" (P-84). Scarbrough recorded this thought, one of many about why he is a writer, in the pages of his journal. From the outset of his literary life, which he said began at age twelve and continued daily since, Scarbrough had a larger purpose in mind than being merely viewed as a regional writer. Art is a higher calling than simple recollection through description, an aim never satisfying to Scarbrough. The art he was so intent on creating is made clear in another journal entry:

> My friend insists that art imitates life. I tell him No. That art imitates nothing. Art is. Is itself. A moment of evanescence caught from the midst of the grim, bloody mess life is. A sudden scintillate light on a leaf, under which a battle to the death is closed. What shines on the leaf is art; what happens underneath is life.... The artist catches this over and above the ordinary and preserves it for us in words, in paint, in metal, in whatever his medium is [I-44].

Scarbrough's work can be gauged using his own definition. Does it have the qualities of artistic endeavor? Does it have longevity? Does it have the capabilities of producing in the reader a universal response, regardless of how tiny the poet's world may seem to be? If so, then Scarbrough was an artist, and with that title came the responsibility of being more than regional, more than just another poet rooted deeply in a specific landscape.

Early attempts to establish Scarbrough as simply a regional writer have long been forgotten. Most later critics recognize that Scarbrough is a poet whose work is dependent on place, but also give him credit as being capable of great range in terms of what he is able to do with this small plot of ground. Scarbrough's work is much larger than an actual place alone will allow, so he has created, for the sake of art, a mythical county,

Picturesque Polk County, a photo provided by Scarbrough as an example of the way his county appeared in his earliest recollections (author's collection).

much like Faulkner's Yoknapatawpha County of northern Mississippi, from which he could examine human nature and trace the roots that make everyone part of this common species. Yes, Scarbrough, especially in his fiction and poetry through *Invitation to Kim*, wrote almost exclusively about this area of Tennessee, the southeastern-most corner, commonly called Eastanalle. But, again, like Faulkner, this county may or may not be real in all its details; it serves not as a region, but as a microcosm of all humankind. With this notion in mind, Scarbrough's work must be approached with more latitude than simple regionalism allows. In a later, undated, and not yet catalogued journal entry, Scarbrough discussed this matter:

> My poems are and were products of cottage industry, made at home but not for home consumption, alone. The County was small but contained within the same scope a number of venues: of hills and flats, of ridges and rivers, whose very names were venues in themselves, of corn-land, hill-land, and valleys. High blue days and low-clouded morning and evening. I knew instinctively that earth was only an extension of one place into another, smallness into largeness, a hill-spring into a seat of water. That one man, or woman, was only an extension into a further

range of humanity, with all hopes and expectations, loves and detestations, hopes and expectations, the sum and totality of aspirations, disappointments, accomplishments and failures.... Extend a radius and you get a diameter, close a half circle and you get a dome.... What is pertinent at this moment is that one travels to see and describe. One comes home to think and feel. Not only to seem but to be, as bell. Being is most important. If I have one stratagem left, it is that of being myself.

In a scene from *A Summer Ago*, Scarbrough's only novel, the writer firmly establishes that his sense of place has boundaries but, at the same time, asserts the idea that any place can be examined from all angles and that an area, real or mythic, can be viewed as a small world inside a bottle. While traveling with his brother, Lee, to pick muscadines from an old vine tangled in a large tree, Alan, the protagonist and Scarbrough's persona in the novel, makes a discovery:

> Not far from the tree, Alan stopped to examine a bottle lying in the ditch. Pointing upward, so that its mouth had received a small portion of washing earth, the greenish-clear glass had become a miniature garden. Inside it Alan could see a small expanse of moss, with its scarlet-headed beards, a tiny fern, perfectly formed, beautiful as its adult kind, a white fragment of pebble, and most interesting of all, a young snail, whose white limy casing gleamed against the darker background. It was a perfect world, he thought, for the snail; a small, comfortable world, like the walls of a beloved room close around and protecting [200].

The world created inside that bottle is, in many ways, identical to the world Scarbrough created for his readers. It is complete, it is varied, and it is, at least in one sense, inclusive. Once formed, this accidental terrarium can survive on its own merits, create its own oxygen and moisture in quantities sufficient to maintain life. Scarbrough's mythic county, located somewhere in the Eastanalle, is a microcosm replete with life and the often unusual people who inhabit it. The landscape, a veritable breeding ground of images and symbols, is omnipresent. Scarbrough notes in the journal, "The natural symbol is an outgrowth of place" (K-21). Because it is a symbol, natural or otherwise, it must carry with it qualities of universality. It is in the choice of his images and symbols that Scarbrough moved beyond the limitations of regionalism — and its dreaded stepbrother, local color — to create literature that can appeal to anyone, not simply those peculiar to Tennessee, or even the South.

In an apparent attempt to define place as a factor in writing, the Southern Appalachian Writers Cooperative submitted a short essay to the *Appalachian Journal* in 1976. Oddly enough, the statement appears immediately following an essay by Scarbrough in the same issue, and reads:

> "The connection to place" is *not* synonymous with provincialism, nor with local color. Great writing has always had its roots in the concrete reality of place — from Troy through Dublin and Yoknapatawpha to Tamalpais. The universal significance of man's experience is communicable only through the localized utterance [34].

This mission statement is central to what Scarbrough did as a writer: he saw within the geographical limits of his world all the major subjects that are so prominent in literature — love, death, nature, struggle, loss, defeat, happiness, victory, religion — the list is endless. Place, then, served as the backdrop, while the great dance of humanity went on in the foreground. This is one quality that makes Scarbrough's work universal.

Forrest Gander recognizes the universality of Scarbrough's poetry. While the landscape "infuses his writing," Gander sees that it could be any landscape, for Scarbrough is simply using his place as a post from which he examines all humankind (109). The inhabitants of this world are so closely connected to place that they become "neither more nor less than / a walking berry," as Scarbrough described them in the "Dedication to the Book" at the beginning of *New and Selected Poems*. Speaking of the poet's epistemology, Gander writes:

> The natural world is the first order from which the merely human devolves. Both the world of human relationships and the domain of memory are fixed, for him, in a landscape of wild upland groves, vine and stalk, bastard figs, gooseberries and muscadines, a world of "almost / pure chlorophyl" [109–110].

Adding to this idea of place as the beginning of humankind's lessening, Gander states emphatically that Scarbrough "believes ... as the poet Frank Stanford once said, the way a field is planted matters less than the quality of the yield" (111). This quality of yield is another of the factors that make Scarbrough's poetry universal: any rich soil, properly cared for, will produce a favorable and substantial crop that anyone can enjoy.

In that vein, Scarbrough's first published efforts received similar criticism. Sara Henderson Hay, in her *Saturday Review* commentary on *Tellico Blue*, made it clear that the young poet, then only in his thirties, was more than a regionalist. While granting that Scarbrough wrote out of a specific place, Hay added that the poems are not simple objective lyrics about a locality and its people, however; like Frost, "Mr. Scarbrough gives a deeper significance to a familiar landscape or fact, a double meaning to what seems on the surface a single observation" [38].

Dan Leidig draws connections between Scarbrough's place, and the images that resonate from it, in his review of *A Summer Ago*, pointing out that the writing is also larger than the landscape, even when the genre is fiction. Addressing the universal nature of the novel's setting, Leidig equates the fictional county with the Biblical garden from which all life was supposed to have sprung. He writes:

> The imagery that graces the world of *A Summer Ago* and extends into the poetry is alive with import. No garden is more prominent in Scarbrough country than is Eden. These persistent thematic patterns forever preclude definitions of Scarbrough in terms of regionalism only. His perceptive distinctions and connections between garden and flight, pride and love, sign and symbol, gesture and act, word and Word ought not be omitted from a serious reading of his work [388].

Scarbrough dismissed the idea that he was another of the regional writers in his "Sidelights" comments for the *Contemporary Authors* series. It is clear in his statements that he hoped for something larger than regional attention, and suggested that his role as writer was to take what he was given in terms of place in order to offer it to the reader as a small piece of something much larger:

> I am a kind of writing spider that catches only what his net is capable of catching — which means, only, that I am limited in my own time, place, and my sense of values of these. I am not a regional writer. I am a southern writer, with a difference: that difference being that I was born north of the majority of slavery, in the shadow of the southern Appalachians, not of the mountains but nurtured by them. I wish to write out for America what it meant to be such an individual in such a time and in such a place [474].

Central to this effort to establish Scarbrough as a poet of place have been suggestions that he was a member of the Agrarian group. It is a term often mentioned when Scarbrough's work is being discussed, but there are more elements to his poetry that separate it from the Agrarian movement than connect it, not to mention the fact that Scarbrough is much younger than most original Agrarians. Perhaps Charles Edward Eaton said it best, "Enough affinities with Ransom, Tate, and Warren may indeed be buried in the poems so that a case might be made for Scarbrough's being the 'last of the Agrarians,' or perhaps the *latest* would be better, since we hope for the best" (xx). Eaton suggests that Scarbrough is on the outer edge of the Agrarian movement, not actually a part of it.

In fact, Scarbrough found himself at the edge of many movements. His earliest poetry, which was imitative in style and took the shape of accepted forms such as the sonnet, was published just as the country saw new directions in verse. During the period when Scarbrough's first three books were published, America was reading Robert Frost, William Carlos Williams, e e cummings, and Wallace Stevens, writers who favored innovation over convention. Scarbrough's style placed him at the edge of the modern movement in American letters. When the U.S. was producing poets of the sixties and seventies whose work was highly introspective and deeply personal, Scarbrough was just beginning to take a more casual stance; *New and Selected Poems* contains verse written without paying homage to traditional forms. The problem with placing Scarbrough in a box is that he does not fit, and that is due to the fact that his career was so long — half a century — and he did not feel a need to acknowledge an alliance with any recognized movement. He even shunned being called an Appalachian poet since he grew up and has lived in the shadow of the mountains rather than in the hills, hollows, and highlands commonly associated with those writers.

As to being an Agrarian, Scarbrough admitted that he was agrarian, but not in the sense that the word is used in various criticism. Scarbrough had agrarian concerns, but the difference between him and the group that wrote *I'll Take My Stand*, published in 1930 when Scarbrough was only fifteen years old, is one of principle and purpose. The Agrarian movement, according to Lloyd Davis, had "become increasingly concerned with social developments in the South, chiefly the incursion of the idea of 'progress' pushed by the encroachment of the industrial complex and the business community" (27). Davis sees the thrust of the movement, and especially the essays of their treatise as much philosophical and political as artistic, with a concerted effort to establish the Southern lifestyle as preferable over what the immigrating North had to offer. That was never Scarbrough's aim. In another journal entry, he addressed this label:

> I may be the last of the Agrarians, as some have said. I wouldn't know about that. I am, so far as I am able to gauge, the first true Agrarian, knowing whereof I speak, having been there, naked to mine enemies, on the land.... I would not want readers to think I imagined myself heir to the *I'll Take My Stand* authors. If others choose to think so, it is all right with me. But the stand I have taken is purely private in nature: not to let the lives of my family go for nothing [Z-95].

Scarbrough also illustrated what he felt was his relationship with the aristocracy of the South, which he saw as the breeding ground for the Agrarian movement. In the *Contemporary Authors* comments, Scarbrough said, "As a born dirt farmer, I have dirt, soil, under my nails" (474). He equated that image with the Agrarians, asserting instead that writers like Warren, Ransom, and Tate were the wealthy landowners whose households

A very thin Scarbrough outside a barn at the home in Etowah, ca. 1954.

he served as the son of an itinerant sharecropper. In another journal entry, he writes:

> I was the other side of the agrarian south as exemplified by most of the members of that group. I was the cabin in the field side, the sharecropper side, not the big house, the manorial side. I could see the white building on the hill, and now and then, selling blackberries at backdoors, see through white-curtained windows the shining world within, which I supported, I and my kind, by backbreaking labor in hot and cold fields of the seasons [Z-93].

With this almost rebellious attitude, it is easy to see why Scarbrough wanted to distance himself from the Agrarians of Nashville. He felt he had nothing in common with them, except in a role of servitude. Scarbrough's poetry does not endeavor to establish the poverty-stricken lifestyle of Polk County as an example of the South at its best, but instead — as an observer and recorder — struggles to capture in words the people and their region. This is especially true of his early poetry, which alternates between lyric expressions of nature, and the poet's fascination with the unique, and often peculiar, people of his county.

In the author's preface to the second edition of *Tellico Blue*, re-released by Iris Press in 1999 to mark the book's fiftieth anniversary, Scarbrough turned his immediate attention to place and, in one sentence, re-established his cosmos:

> After fifty years the mountains are still in place, still blue with distance, peaked and ridged, rivered, still rife with memory, still the habitation of wild boars, bears, deer.... The earth remained dearer to some of us because of its remoteness. During the war years, those of us who for one reason or another never left the county ... grew even closer to the old landscapes.... Polk County remained off the beaten path, becoming even more isolated as the interstate highways by-passed it on their way south [xi].

Tellico Blue is a celebration of this landscape and its inhabitants, and its animals, both human and otherwise, are the subject matter of the poems. With the publication of the first edition in 1949, Scarbrough firmly established himself as a poet of place. Two poems from the text provide perfect examples.

In "Eastward in Eastanalle," Scarbrough refers to his landscape as the "heart's world," a land "of the spirit" (1–2). In the tradition of American poetry begun by Whitman in the previous century, Scarbrough becomes the namer, and by so doing, attempts to establish the importance of the objects he finds around him: "cedar-colored skies," "clouds as white as skulls," the "tender land," the "indiscriminate land," which claims each inhabitant as its own, as its "children." Scarbrough states that the region "deals impartially in indistinctions, / And is kind and open to interpretations / Various as men who love it." Because the land is open for interpretation, the poet takes advantage of the landscape in his efforts to describe it and, like Whitman, finds meaning in the descriptions in his understanding of the world through image.

In "The Lark," a lyrical poem about the everpresence of nature, Scarbrough further establishes the importance of place by allowing days and events to pass in relation to what is going on in the world around him. The natural progression becomes, then, his calendar by which he marks memory, particularly the death of a childhood friend Reuben. The wandering boy comes upon a group of men under a grove of sycamore trees, who understand, momentarily, the loss the boy has suffered. The speaker of the poem is then swept up in the world around him, oblivious to the men, and remarks on the passage of time in a sudden realization:

> Suddenly blazing against the sides of a wondrously
> Green valley, the Eastanalle sycamores
> Have numbered seven springs since Reuben died;

> And rivers breaking on this tilted world
> Have poured their April waters seven times
> Into our valley; and bright-green cedars
> Darkened seven times to ancient blue.
> Yet they, the elders, are not much misled.
> Spring never changes, only the face of spring [58–66].

By paying such close attention to the landscape, the speaker comes to understand that everyday occurrences — even death — are simply part of a larger, more worldly picture. While changes are sure to happen again and again in the human realm, nature will remain constant; Spring will forever come and go in the great cycle of the natural world.

People, too, become inextricably bound to a place to such a degree that it becomes impossible to separate one from the other. The characters that earn Scarbrough's attention are those who are slightly left of center, eccentrics who seem to be a by-product of the region. Their qualities are shaped from having lived in the same area all their lives, and this influence sometimes presents itself in the most peculiar of ways. In "Story," the poet introduces an unnamed character who lies in bed and shoots his gun "with small direction at the sky" (4). The man is under the control of place, labeling with bullet holes all four compass directions while "lying toes-up the total length of summer" (11). Because the man is believed dangerous — and because walking near his home is, indeed, risky — the community avoids him, reducing him to fodder for gossip. Only when the shooting stops for more than a week do the neighbors, referred to in the poem as a "posse," venture close and then inside the "sieved room freckled with sun" (16).

And in another poem from *Tellico Blue*, man and landscape become caught in a struggle of control. Mr. Wyatt, from "The Creek," is a local who forbids the children to swim in a stream on his property. The poem sets up an interesting conflict between the young boys and the landowner who, in his carelessness, falls victim to his own design and is killed by his own bull. In his efforts to control nature — access to the creek and the powerful bull — the man fails and the boys are triumphant. Following Mr. Wyatt's death, the wife buries her husband and sells the bull, making it possible once again for the youths to enjoy the cool water of the stream. Wyatt's death, and his failure to manipulate surroundings to his own purpose, opens a door to the natural world which is rife with imagery for both the swimmers and the poet. The boys can once again "climb in the beeches / Or wade the creek to its source in the iris, / Pale and palpitant under the wild green willows.... (10–12).

The poet at the Etowah home, where his first three books—*Tellico Blue, The Course Is Upward,* and *Summer So-Called*—were written, ca. 1954 (courtesy of George Scarbrough).

The poetry from *New and Selected Poems* offers a more mature look at place. In one of the longer poems, "The House Where Rivers Join: Confluence of Ocoee and Hiwassee," the controlling image is the structure itself; but in a more philosophical mode, Scarbrough comes to terms with his own idea of place. The poem establishes the region, Eastanalle, not only in terms of particulars such as "Pancake hills, earth droplets, / cones, quartz-glittering knolls / are fringing landscape," but as part of a much larger picture, the world as a whole (I 26–28). The microcosm, the mythical county, becomes the universe for the poet: "Then, the greater room I / lived in, all unknowing, was / the green-walled room / of a county's limitations" (III 76–79). The confluence of two rivers, which creates a mystical

Scarbrough by the mailbox of his home in Oak Ridge, ca. 1970 (courtesy of George Scarbrough).

coloring when the waters meet, is simply one of the "limitations," a boundary by which the poet can delineate one edge of place. The county is a source of comfort for the speaker of the poem because he can firmly establish its boundaries and accept all of its vastness as home. The final lines of the poem speak to this level of acceptance and to the satisfaction of being a willing participant: "I have drawn the breath / of a mazed, enraptured anchorite, / couched in the elegant cave / of my county mind" (IX 54–57).

Scarbrough later revisits this idea in "Tenantry" from *Invitation to Kim*. The poem focuses on the life of an itinerant farm family that is constantly moving from one house to another, never staying long enough at any one site to truly make it a home. Instead, the county in which all these houses are located becomes home, or in other words, the world becomes home for a family eternally in motion: "It was the measurable / pleasurable earth / that was home" (17–19). The speaker of the poem, a youth with the convenience of omniscient experience, can look back and see that "where it stood, / it stood in earth, / and the earth welcomed us, / open, / gateless, / one place as another" (34–38). Making use of a Biblical allusion to Christ's promise that he would go ahead to make ready a place in God's house of many rooms, Scarbrough writes, "because the county / was only a mansion / kind of dwelling / in which there were many rooms. / We only moved from one / room to another, / getting acquainted / with the whole house" (43–51).

Scarbrough made several points about the importance of place in his writing. By creating this county as his own personal cosmos, Scarbrough provided himself a vast source of images and interesting characters. Because the "county" was symbolic of the larger world, the poet invited readers to recollect their own experiences by sharing his as both participant and observer. The emotional investment Scarbrough placed in the poems is universal, since humanity, as a whole, harbors the same feelings. The ubiquitous nature of a mythical location provides the common ground on which Scarbrough could successfully "make an art for a county on the rim of a rock."

Five

The Novel

Scarbrough's only novel, *A Summer Ago*, has received the least critical analysis of any of his work, due to the fact that Scarbrough spent his career establishing himself as a poet, with three volumes published by the time *A Summer Ago* was released by St. Luke's Press in 1986. The book followed *New and Selected Poems* by almost a decade, and students of Scarbrough's work expected another collection of recent poems, not a prose recollection of childhood. But, in many ways, the novel is not simply prose. The same immaculate attention to language is evident in this book as well, and those critics who did review the novel were quick to make that observation.

In what may be the most careful of critical analyses on Scarbrough to date, Dan Leidig had both favorable and unfavorable comments about the novel. He recognizes what Scarbrough was attempting to do: re-create a more innocent time of youthful amazement and coming-of-age. Leidig does not fault the writer on these endeavors; he finds problems only in certain technical aspects of the book, which he refers to as more an "all-encompassing prose memory from which — for half a century — his poems have been departing and returning" (384). In other words, a reader could approach the novel as an extended prose poem written by a "senior and established poet" (384). According to Leidig:

> It should be said that beneath the metaphorical and linguistic brilliance of *A Summer Ago* there is a less-seasoned methodology than is to be found in the deft, crafted poems. The uneven omniscience, the tendency to transpose to a lad the seasoned conceptualizations of an adult, and the use of transparent devices to account for the boy's wide knowledge present some problems. Scarbrough's dramatic sense is better realized in his imagery than in the advancement of narrative, and the book's "enduring sense of the earth" may well identify also its limitations as "fiction" [388].

Robert L. Phillips makes similar statements in his comments on the novel, suggesting that the book is more akin to a collection of memories from childhood and relies on the remembered events more than it does on generally accepted rules of narrative. Phillips writes:

> *A Summer Ago* is an autobiographical episodic novel, more a series of sketches than a narrative.... Time — the passing of summer and the growth of the calf that will be sold in the fall for school books — provides the the narrative framework. Typical activities of the children of farmers ... are the acts that tie the narrator — an agrarian — to the living, reproducing earth. He, time, and the physical world make a harmonious whole [421].

In a journal entry Scarbrough wrote his own criticism of *A Summer Ago* which sounds strangely familiar to the comments made by Phillips and Leidig. The journal entry, however, establishes the novel as an experiment, a conscious leap from poetry to prose in order to achieve a desired effect by creating independent episodes that are connected but not dependent on each other. Scarbrough writes:

> I wrote each episode so that it was complete in itself as it might be, without impinging on what had gone before or what would come after. In a sense there is very little, or almost no, plot present in the book. There is a kind of plot that overshadows the story, or stories, but it is a plot of place and time and not of event: the geography of space and of location bind together what otherwise might appear to be short stories threaded on an apparent rather than a real thread [A-255].

Regardless of how one approaches the novel, it has value on a number of levels. First and foremost is the use of language to re-create the world of Scarbrough's youth, complete with all the humor and pain of his own family's, and other families,' dependence on subsistent farming. Second, the novel offers clear details about the activities which fill the months from April to September: berry picking, apple harvesting, crop tending, church revivals, skinny-dipping at the local swimming hole, and caring for farm animals. Third, the book is a collection of country knowledge: remedies, humor, stories, sayings, preparation of food stuffs for the coming winter. If Scarbrough is regional in any sense, it is through the observations and re-telling of these acts peculiar to that region of Appalachia. While the novel is not (ala the *Foxfire* books) a how-to guide for making molasses or kraut, it does offer enough information to allow the reader to understand such processes, at least as far as the protagonist, twelve-year-old Alan, can comprehend. Fourth, the novel has the strong underlying themes of the best coming-of-age stories. Alan is, at times, simply amazed at how his world works, how it is forever changing, while concurrently dealing with his own burgeoning sexuality and curiosity about life and death questions, particularly "the serpent principle." Fifth, and most interesting of all the elements to be found in *A Summer Ago*, the novel offers Scarbrough an invitation, which he accepts, to romanticize his youth. The demanding but pastoral life on the McDowell farm of the novel is a pleasant contrast to the real-life experiences of Scarbrough as a boy.

Language

The same richness of language that has become a benchmark of Scarbrough's poetry is also at work in *A Summer Ago*. The linguistic achievement of the novel indicates that it was written by an adult looking back at childhood through the senses of a practiced poet with a polished vocabulary. Consider these lines from a scene in which Alan has taken a cotton sack of corn to the mill for grinding:

> Alan wandered about in the cool, dusky light of the building, seeing, high up, the small-paned, cobwebby windows through which the daylight came softened, almost drained of the sun blazing outside. Brown beams, ancient and shaped by the wielder of some long since dulled axe, were strung above him, showing the strength of mortice and tenon and here and there the square heads of the iron nails used to hold the building together. There was the smell of cornshucks and cobs everywhere he went in the dim interior, as well as the faint ammoniac odor of urine. He recognized rats, seeing their gnawed holes everywhere in the planking of the floor and the lower walls. A few of the larger holes had been boarded up with tin bucket lids; others, smaller, had pieces of tough corncobs stuck into them, like so many corked, flat-topped jugs, stoppered and containing the furtive, whiskered lives of the animals trapped behind the panels [12–13].

No matter how precocious the child, these are not the spoken aloud memories and observations of Alan as a near teenager but the constructed recollection of an older, ominiscient narrator.

In an interview with Jerry Williamson, Scarbrough said of the novel, "*A Summer Ago* was an honest-to-God attempt to reconstruct a sort of coming-of-age tale of a boy twelve years old growing up in the Eastanalle Valley" (35). Scarbrough suggests that the novel was carefully crafted, "an honest-to-God" effort. What the poet did not tell Williamson was this information, recorded in his journal, which makes the quality of language in *A Summer Ago* even more amazing: "I wrote my novel, *A Summer Ago*, straight through in two weeks, and never re-read it nor changed a word." The process of composing this near one hundred thousand word book must have been exhausting, because Scarbrough adds, "I do not wish to write 'novels' anymore" (I-113). In another entry Scarbrough claims that he never read the book after publication — that he does not "know what is in the book. But that is all right," since *A Summer Ago* is a "closed account" (A-255). In fact, because of his refusal to rewrite the novel, at the behest of Houghton-Mifflin, to make it more salable, Scarbrough turned down the opportunity to have the novel released by a major publisher. St. Luke's Press published the book ten years after it was written, apparently in its original form.

As David Rogers mentions in his review of the novel, language is key to Alan's discoveries. He is clearly a budding poet, and it is in this summer, in particular, that language becomes most important to the twelve-year-old boy. Rogers explains:

> "The growth of a poet's mind" is so implied in every scene it scarcely needs to be stated. But as well as the unfolding of the poet's consciousness, *being* itself is the subject, for the world the poet awakes to is alive with ontological electricity [1].

The source of this electrical charge of knowledge is due not only to the myriad occurrences during the six months of the book but to the realization that the way to comprehend these happenings is through words, both those spoken in description and those spoken as way of explanation. Alan, like Scarbrough, learns to appreciate language by hearing the words of his mother and father. Almost verbatim from an earlier essay by Scarbrough, "My Mother Language, My Father Tongue," Alan "believed he loved his mother because of her words and that he did not understand his father because his father had none." (54). Scarbrough explains further in this same passage:

> Alan's mother might with words make color drip and cry; his father could with words make, not only color, but the forces of darkness and evil as well, appear and disappear in a chameleon world like a magician practicing a sleight of hands [54].

As an addendum to the power of his parents' words, Alan listens and absorbs the words of those other people in the community, particularly the minister, and neighbor John Wade. While both men espouse their ideas the way preachers sometimes do, the revival speaker delivers his message from the pulpit and John Wade on horseback when he takes Alan home early from the revival service. The Reverend Musgrove's words are powerful because they speak of things to come, terrible things for those who are not ready for the afterlife. Scarbrough captures the flavor of a real fire-and-brimstone sermon:

> "Neighbors," he shouted, "on that great and awful day what will your answers be? What will you say then to the questions of salvation and eternity? Nothing, my friends. For it will be too late. The old account will have long been settled, and you will be divided, to the left, to the right, some into eternal morning, some into the blackness of hell and utter despair. Will you be on the right hand of the King coming in glory? Decide my friends. The Judgment Day is coming. The time is at hand. Make ye straight the pathway of the Lord. Be ready! O be ready!" he repeated, his voice rising until it filled the room with a terrifying roar [176].

Neighbor Wade, also in attendance at the heated revival, decides it is time to go home and offers Alan a horseback ride to his house. On the way, Wade's words juxtapose the minister's in terms of time but offer an almost opposite, pleasing alternative to the preacher's apocalyptic view. Wade's sermon from the mount, which Alan finds powerful, perhaps even more so than the minister's, is also fashioned with words:

> "I'd tell the people that every day is judgment day, so far as we are concerned. Every sundown is the ending of the world and every morning is a new creation, with a new chance for us to make seven new and better worlds in a week, with the best perhaps on Sunday when we could just sit and think about the worlds we had made, and pick the best from all of them to make the last world in the week. And then, when we got to heaven, that last world of all, we could just sit and make it from our memory of the best of all the worlds we had made on earth" [177–78].

Having received two sermons in one evening, Alan is left to choose which best suits his view of this world and the next. He clearly prefers the message of John Wade; it is more comforting and places more emphasis on Alan's immediate environment. In terms of the boy's exposure, the important lesson is that not only worlds can be created through language; so can eternity. Alan interprets this insight as the poet should: words are the medium through which everything is described and understood.

Not all of Scarbrough's attention to language in *A Summer Ago* is dedicated to the examples already offered. The novelist collects and allows his characters to use a vast assortment of country sayings, many of which are as figurative as poetry itself. Scarbrough's personal journals are filled with little rhymes, often bawdy, that reduce a situation to its most basic elements in an effort to entertain. *A Summer Ago* also is quite unique because of the author's ability to use the phrases at just the right moment.

By including these "one-liners" in the novel, Scarbrough re-creates even more accurately the vernacular of his family and friends, offering a humorous glimpse at how the local language was sometimes twisted for the sake of embellishment.

Some of the sayings are responses or admonitions, most often delivered by the father or Lee, Alan's country-wise brother who is three years his senior. When Alan asks his father if Buckeye, his pet bull, is growing horns, Oscar McDowell does not just answer yes but says instead, "Chickens have feathers, don't they?" (9). And when Alan is caught daydreaming instead of removing the choke of dodder from a crop of lespedeza, Lee says, "Snap out of it. Any jackass can go to sleep standing up. It's going to be dark before we get this danged dodder done"; then adding as a tease, because he knew Alan's teacher, Miss Woodson, had praised a recent poem by the younger brother, "How's that for poetry, son?" (24). Another example from Lee is offered when Alan is again caught thinking instead of doing and has left his brother waiting impatiently. Lee says, "Come on.... Get your clothes on.... Stop standing there naked as a jaybird, and hop to it. Boy, you're slower than the seven-year itch" (84).

Supporting Scarbrough's statement in "My Mother Language, My Father Tongue" that he learned metaphor from his father, the patriarchal figure Oscar McDowell also uses colorful, descriptive phrases as a natural part of his speech patterns. When describing the aggressive billy goat, Can-Can, Oscar says, "That goat butts coming and going, hind part and fore, and wrong side out" (37). When Alan, during another mental wandering, considers the sillyness of hens and compares them to a hog that will "charge back and forth all morning right past the hole where he got out, and never think of returning to the pen," his own thoughts are replaced by the word memory of his father's expression: "'A hog,' said Oscar, 'doesn't have the sense of a last year's bird's nest'" (84). And out of the oral tradition of tall tales, Oscar is even more descriptive when he explains to a neighbor that Alan is not a good shot with a pistol and recounts an episode in which Alan was trying to kill a snake in the spring. Alan had missed so badly that Oscar had to exaggerate to explain: "About knocked the spring dry.... If the snake died, I suspect he starved for water" (42).

Finally, the phrases associated with country folk are often used to express one's philosophy. An example of this usage is found in the passage when Alan takes a sack of corn to Mr. Wyatt, a shade tree philosopher who offers the boy bits of wisdom. After he has ground the corn into meal, Mr. Wyatt says, "The staff of life, son.... Man's history is a long breadline"

(14). Before Alan leaves the mill he visits the upstairs room to view stacks of old coffins that the miller once built for local families. Sensing Alan's fear in the semidarkness, Mr. Wyatt uses his apron to wipe the dust off the window and says, "You see, boy.... Things are mostly what you make them. Light is a marvelous thing for cleaning up the corners of a dark room, or of a man's mind, for that matter" (15). And from John Wade, Alan overhears another statement of philosophy: "You can't teach an old dog new tricks.... We bark the way we were raised to bark" (43). Just as Scarbrough has, for many years, catalogued these expressions in his journals, Alan does much the same, storing the figurative language in the mind of a young poet learning the mechanics and limitless capabilities of words.

April to September

As stated earlier, *A Summer Ago* is not a *Foxfire* book written for those without a real experience of the country life. What the novel offers in terms of importance is an accurate portrayal of the activities engaged by a farm family that was trying to eke out an existence with what they had at hand. More valuable is that the reader sees these events through Alan's eyes; by experiencing via a twelve year old boy, the mundane becomes extraordinary. Even though Alan has apparently been depended upon for chores and for a helping hand when, for instance, the staples for winter had been prepared and preserved, this summer is different. Because Alan is coming-of-age, the acts carry more meaning than ever before. It is as if Alan sees through new eyes, and the excitement is passed on vividly through Scarbrough's attention to detail and clear description. All of this is an effort on the part of the author to re-create the lifestyle of his youth and to assign some import to the fascinating, though simple, East Tennessee farmstead.

Equally significant is what Alan learns from being around the people involved in the activities. When his family, and all of the neighboring families, spend a week at John Wade's to make molasses, the community takes on a holiday atmosphere, even though the work is difficult and painstaking. Alan is more caught up in the stories that the men tell than he is in the slow process of cooking down the sorghum cane juice from one vat to another until the sweet thick liquid is seined into bright silver buckets to be stored for the winter table. Likewise, when Alan and Lee help their mother Belle shred cabbage for the gray crock that would pickle the kraut, Alan's real pleasure is in watching his mother's skilled hands layer the cabbage with just the right amount salt, or in studying the cabbage itself and its "arrangement of leaves about the central spine, finding the formation curiously like that in a section of sea shell he had seen in a book at school" (103). Also tied into these practices is the overshadow of tradition. John Wade always makes molasses for the community for he is the recognized master. Likewise, Alan is sent to wash the large white rock that his mother has used year after year to weigh down the pickling kraut. These self-sustaining preparations are part of a ritual that has been practiced for generations, and for the first time, the maturing Alan recognizes this importance.

Not all of the chores are pleasant, but all seem rewarding. Alan is amazed by his mother's skill at stuffing a tick mattress. An annual event, usually in July, the process receives a great deal of attention by Scarbrough for one simple reason: he sees it as an act of love, which is more important to Alan than necessity. After freeing the ticks of clinging straw, Belle boils them in an outdoor washkettle and then hangs them on the clothesline to dry. Later, in the cool of the evening, Belle would stuff them with clean straw to make the beds the best they could be. Scarbrough writes:

> Her beds were the objects almost of devotion. They must be evenly packed in the beginning, and carefully, evenly re-arranged each morning of the year. It was also her proud belief that she kept the cleanest beds in the valley. To that end, between the washing of the ticks and the filling, the wooden bedsteads had been scalded with a strong solution of the lye water, and stood now drying in the sun against the side of the house [76].

Most of Belle's actions, like this one involving the annual and daily care of the straw mattresses, are viewed as indicative of the care she took to provide for her family, a dedication not easily realized but one that Scarbrough admires through the reactions of Alan.

These farm concerns also provide a sense of continuity in the novel. The reader realizes that one act follows another, that everything is a means to an end, and each subsequent activity depends on some other that has occurred previously. In this example, the washing of ticks and beds was made possible only because the family had already produced its lye soap. This astringent requires the attention of everyone; Alan and Lee care for the ash hopper, through which water is drained and from which the odorous leachate is collected. (As presented in the novel, lye was just as important as food because it had sundry uses. Not only is it mixed with melted lard to make soap, but in various compounds could be used to tan leather, and Oscar is quick to note that lye is good for hogs: "Keeps them from being wormy" [74].) The fascination for Alan is that his family is practicing chemistry on an elemental scale. He knows that later in life this will be another discipline which he can learn, but for now:

> He was still rather baffled by the undercover world of chemistry, and feeling that he had more to unlearn than learn, he stooped and thrust a finger into the lye, running richer now that the ashes were becoming saturated in the lower half of the barrel. His finger burned. Whatever it was, the power of the stuff was not to be doubted [74].

Country Knowledge

Another unusual offering in the novel is the use of home remedies. Alan and his brother are so familiar with this part of farm life that they even play a game in which one of them names an ailment and the other names the cure. (Most cures come from the wild plants of the hillside.) When the flora fail to produce the needed effect, it would appear that country folk used whatever was at hand, including kerosene, or "coal-oil" as it is called in the novel, which works as a universal agent to clean wounds or repel chiggers. And when these cures are ineffective, there is always folklore to provide imaginary relief. On one of their outings, this time to pick blackberries on the Fourth of July, the boys have a conversation that is both informative and funny. Alan is clearly the more knowledgeable of the two, having gained his information about the healing power of plants from his mother. He shows off for Lee, having for once the upper hand, and tells his brother that calamus root soaked in whiskey will cure a bellyache and that Jerusalem Oak seeds in molasses will get rid of worms. Then Alan asks:

> "Suppose you had the piles, what would you do?"
> "I'd carry a rotten buckeye in my pocket," Lee said. "And I wear a rabbit's foot around my neck, and I hide a horsehair under a rock in the creek. That's what I'd do. And any other slaphappy thing I could think of. Come on!"
> "No, you wouldn't," Alan said, walking rapidly along behind him. "You'd carry a buckeye. The rabbit's foot is only for luck, and the horsehair would turn into a snake."
> "Says you," Lee retorted. "And all the other old witches!" [100–101].

The shift, at the end of the passage, into folklore is not a great leap. The novel is filled with examples of ancient practices that were supposed to have proven results. Lee, feeling for the first time an attraction to members of the opposite sex, is versed in matters of love. For example, he reminds

Alan that if you want to know your girlfriend's feelings toward you, "put a piece of lovevine on a fencepost and [if] it grows, your girl loves you. It's better than mullein for truth" (22). The McDowell boys are, obviously, as aware of the hand-me-down legends as they are the true medicinal qualities of the plants growing around them.

Coming of Age

Scarbrough examines a number of themes in the novel, and it is through a thematic approach that the reader sees how much maturity Alan gains during this one summer. Alan is more than usually curious about why the world is the way it is. In *A Summer Ago* the twelve-year-old boy tries to come to terms with several issues that have apparently been of concern for some time. Among these are the "serpent principle," death, religion, and the interconnectedness of life, and his own beginning sexuality. These problems for Alan are often exposed through the action of the novel, but the subconscious is at work, too, as Alan has disturbing dream sequences that are, to say the least, confusing to his young mind.

Alan learns of the "serpent principle" from his mother. After one of their afternoon walks, Alan and Belle came upon a family; the man stood in the road in a fit of near panic, all because of a snake. The unnamed individual asks Alan to kill the snake and he does, whipping it to death with a cane. Afterwards, Alan asks Belle why the people were so alarmed, and Belle answers, "Their whole lives ... are bound up in the serpent principle" (23). In this summer of many snakes, more in number than usual according to Oscar, the image of serpents abounds in the novel. Alan comes to realize the connection between the human race and snakes, stretching back to the Old Testament account of Adam and Eve, in which Satan appeared first to them in form of a serpent. This new knowledge makes clear to Alan why human beings are so typically afraid of snakes, but he still sees them as beautiful creatures, not to be feared, but respected. As a symbol in the novel the snake is ever present. Warnings to the boys are issued by both mother and father to be careful when afield because of the danger that an abundance of reptiles presents. Lee has matured to the point that he fears snakes because of their potential threat, but Alan, still a boy, is fascinated not only with the fanged possibilities but, as a young poet, sees their symbolic value as well: "Obviously there was a great deal more to snakes than just the snakes themselves. He tried to fit the pieces of the snake puzzle together" (23). The symbol becomes very real when

Alan sees a traveling preacher in town, a snake handler, a "ragged, wild-eyed man" who has a "rattlesnake wound about his extended arm"; in the other hand he holds a Bible. The scene continues:

> As the preacher exhorted the crowd, the snake moved with the motion of his arm, licking out its tongue above the heads of the crowd, whose faces were turned upward shining with an exuberant, glorious horror, mingled with dread and fear. On them all was the look of a terrible happiness [24].

Later that day, when Alan asks his mother about the spectacle, she replies, "The snake is still the symbol of man's lost glory.... So he is taken up as an act of faith. For by faith, evil may be embraced without harm" (24). All this information is puzzling to Alan, but the boy begins to realize that the serpent is central to human fear because it dates back to the beginning of time.

When Alan and Lee are gathering muscadines, Alan climbs a large tree to shake the berries to the ground and "something heavy, like a part of the vine itself, came loose and warped the ground," landing half in and half out of the basket that Lee was using to gather the fruit (201). It is a large black racer that was more afraid of the boys than the boys were of the snake, and Lee chased it unsuccessfully with a stick. Because the boys are still partially unaware of the fear that grips most people when they see a snake, he and Lee reject the serpent. In doing so the snake is just a snake, not a dark, foreboding symbol of man's fall. Scarbrough includes this scene to show the innocence of youth not yet corrupted by the sins of the world.

Tied closely with the "serpent principle" and the age of innocence is, of course, religion. Much of what Alan learns during the summer about religion comes from the church he attends regularly, the minister's message at the funeral of a cousin, and the revival service. What is evident in Alan's thoughts is an unconscious movement toward a view not necessarily consistent with his Bible teachings but in line with what Alan has witnessed in his father's belief system. Quoting the following passage from the novel, David Rogers writes that it could be "used as the source of a new humanism, for it places humanity at the center of things" (5):

> That these forces were in and of his father's own nature, Alan seemed to recognize; the world, for him as for most of us, centered in the light and darkness of the human beings that surrounded him.... The boy finds in his father his beginning and periphery, and in his mother his center and circumference; and these dimensions from point to outpost, are the universe. And so become, through the personal characteristics of those who furnish them, the universal attitude towards the living mote

named the human mind. The universe, as such, does not and will never count. Only sons and daughters, and their sons and daughters, furnish the sky with any place to fall [54–55].

While these are clearly more Scarbrough's thoughts than Alan's, it is an expanded view of what the boy is becoming, again spoken through the voice of a later, mature, and skeptical adult. It is, Scarbrough suggests, a more logical approach to the world and one in line with the outlook of Oscar McDowell, and perhaps, even Alan.

Death becomes very real in this summer life of Alan McDowell. A cousin, Reuben, who is also one of Alan's closest friends and favored playmates, dies suddenly of summer dysentery; "He wasted to death through his bowels," Belle explains (69). The boys are about the same age and had been together only a few days before Reuben's death. As was the custom, the family attends the wake, and while Alan has most likely been around death and dying on the farm, the loss of Reuben has a profound effect on the boy. It causes indescribable emotions in him, but they are something short of grief. He does not want to see his dead cousin and finds the entire situation very uncomfortable, but he is shoved into the room by his father who insists that Alan pay his respects:

> In the room, full of the sounds of summer flies and bad colds, shouldered by clutches of ornamental grasses come from God knows where, Alan viewed his cousin, the small, pale master, opulent-eyed, who seemed with silver stare to be assaying the live boy, looking him up and down, until Alan could no longer bear it. He looked away, through the window, into the bare yard, where a tuft of grass helped him to stature in this new community. The dime in his pocket scalded his thigh [57].

Shortly after what must be Alan's first real experience of the death of someone close to him, the reader learns that Belle is pregnant. While the boys are never told they are to expect a sibling, it becomes evident when the mother's belly begins to swell and she has more and more difficulty performing her daily duties. In this way the death of Reuben and the life of the new baby become for Alan the completion of the cycle: Reuben's death is counterbalanced with the birth of a new brother. The realization is another element in this coming-of-age story.

With almost every passing occurrence, Alan has fitful nights of dreams, all connected somehow to the train that screams its way through the Eastanalle. The train is presented as a symbol in the novel's prologue, when Alan and Lee walk a great distance to watch the train enter Walden Valley. Its presence and power have an unnerving effect on Alan, who is seeing the locomotive for the first time. As a young boy whose entire existence has been linked to his small corner of the world, the train represents everything foreign to this safe microcosm, or as Scarbrough writes, "Something from out there was coming in" (7). Alan does not know how to react; his response is completely the opposite of Lee's — Lee has seen the train before and does not feel any fear associated with its presence. But, for Alan, the train will become the vehicle of his dreams, the first of which occurs the same evening: "That night he woke screaming from his sleep, cowering down in his bed, hiding under the quilts. No one had any notion why he kept repeating, 'The train! The train! The train!'" (8). The catalyst of the fear is in the train's omnipotence. While watching the engine and its cars move into the valley, Alan cannot explain why he wants to lash out at the train and prove that he is stronger than this intruder in an effort to protect not only himself but his world:

> He was sick with fright, wanting for some terrible reason to run forward shouting and fling himself under the swift-pistoning wheels of the train, to beat upon the great black engine with his hands. The huge walk and stride of the train compelled him. Perhaps he could turn it over with one strong, upsurging heave of his shoulders. Shuddering, he turned his eyes against the gray planks of the shack that served as station, sick with a fear that he might obey his impulse, white and weak with a fear that beat its dusty wings over his trembling body and told him not to be afraid [8].

Scarbrough uses this symbol in an extremely effective way, allowing the train to become more real in Alan's imagination by taking on various forms synonymous with the boy's most recent experiences. For instance, following Reuben's funeral the train comes to Alan in a nightmare and its boxcars have become plain pine coffins like those he saw at Mr. Wyatt's mill and the double engines at the front were "shaped like a human body, head and shoulders approaching first" (59).

The train, however, is not always associated with the terrible. After Alan's initial fear has abated — after the boy has matured to the point that the engine's power is understood — he allows the train to become a present reminder that a world exists outside his own. This acceptance is part of Alan's maturation process, and near the end of the summer he sees the train as a source of potential rather than intrusion; in other words, the train, Alan comprehends, really is not a threat to his security:

> Not only had the train dominated the days; time and time again it had crept into the valley dreams, bringing with it, especially to the young, visions of the great journeys youth dreams of taking. To some, it was a reminder of a journey taken and gladly done with, a going in earlier

> years that had been bitterly disappointing and a return, secretly glad and determined, to the valley to resume old ties, old ways. To Alan, somehow, the train became commingled with all the events of his life, as a herald announcing and as a goad to remembrance. The lonely sound of the train gave him an indefinable heartache [133–134].

Innocence is again key to Scarbrough's treatment of Alan's awareness of sex. The episodes are usually underlined with humor or involve animals, since Alan, like most farmboys, learns about sex by watching the antics of the livestock. In one example, Alan throws a stick of firewood at Clockwork, the rooster, because he has been terrorizing the family puppy, Pretty Boy. Belle corrects Alan and warns him to be careful not to kill the rooster. Alan responds, "What difference would it make? He doesn't lay eggs." Belle explains clinically, "The eggs wouldn't hatch. There has to be one good rooster in every flock to fertilize the eggs" (91). Alan's gradual introduction to sexuality is still in its genesis; because none of the adults really talk about sex, he has more questions than answers, but does realize one basic truth:

> It was a male and female world, Alan knew. Rooster and hen, bull and cow, horse and mare, man and woman. He had learned this much from the baby calves and pigs, and pups and chickens and kittens. His own mother was going to have a baby brother, he hoped. But there were still a good many things he didn't understand. So far as Lee and Ira Wade were concerned, what they said in his presence only confused and shamed him, they made their talk so secretive and dark and forbidden. If sex was so wrong, he wondered, why were his own parents involved? [91–92].

From Lee and his best friend, Ira, then, Alan is receiving mixed messages; the older boys offer hints about sex but due to their own lack of knowledge cannot really help clear up Alan's confusion. When the boys are together at the local swimming hole, the subject of conversation always turns to sex and is supported by the presence of the skinny-dipping youngsters. As Alan and Lee arrive at the pool, they notice Ira's pants hanging from a plum tree. The fly, which is open, is framing a trumpet vine. Ira remarks, "The tree of life, buddy...! The real, living vine!" (80). But Ira's discourses on sex are more embarrassing for Alan than they are informative:

> Ira had been a point in Alan's education, a pivot on which his summer world had turned, the larger boy furnishing some items in particular thinking for which Alan was not yet completely ready. Ira himself was a comprehensive lecture in the subject he was most physically demonstrative of. So Alan, engulfed in shame, ran with the body he was criminal

with, being no nakeder than he thought, shielding himself with territorial hands when a finger would have done, against Ira's soaring laughter. The allusions to his body were intolerable to Alan [80].

While it is clear that Alan is innocent in his shame, the allusion to the Garden of Eden is important. Alan stands naked before Ira, the local god of all things sexual, and must endure the wrath that boys inflict on one another. The awareness that his own body is, somehow, sexual is the source of the shame, for Alan is becoming a sexual creature, too, though he does not understand the process.

Romanticizing His Youth

Unfortunately, the events of *A Summer Ago* are quite a bit more idyllic than the actualities of Scarbrough's own youth. It might be said that Alan's childhood is perhaps what Scarbrough wished his childhood had been. The reader may see the circumstances of the novel as demanding, both in terms of physical labor and the slight callousness to which Alan is oftentimes subjected. But these episodes in the novel are romanticized; the equivalent real events were much more brutal, especially when they concerned Scarbrough's real life father, Oscar. The same cannot be said about the mother-son relationship. Belle is clearly patterned after the author's mother, Louise Anabel McDowell Scarbrough, complete with the caring attention she paid to her son, George. Just as Alan has the closer relationship with his mother in the novel, Scarbrough saw himself as his mother's child, while Lee, the name of the brother in both the book and in real life, is the son of the father.

This dichotomy is most evident in a disturbing scene from the novel. It is reminiscent of several journal accounts that recall Oscar Scarbrough's refusal to accept George as his own, and the gloating Oscar exhibited in praise of Lee. In this scene, John Wade's rooster has come into the McDowell yard one too many times to lure the chickens to another location, away from their own nests, which will result in a loss of valuable egg production. When Old Shag struts onto the McDowell property, Oscar becomes enraged, picks up a hoe, and strikes "across the red-gold feathers of the rooster's neck, hushing his invitation" (69). Oscar calls Lee, not Alan, to dispose of the rooster's carcass. A couple of days later, while the family is at breakfast, they hear the familiar gobbling sound of Old Shag and realize that Oscar's attempt to kill the bird had only addled him. This time, Oscar sends Lee not to dispose of the remains, but kill the rooster outright—

"properly this time," Oscar instructs — and also orders Alan to go with Lee to "help him" (70). This event must be immediate, or the McDowells run the risk of having John Wade discover that his prize rooster has been killed. Alan stands by and watches:

> But Lee did not hesitate, being the child of his father. He crashed into the rooster with his young hands, fighting the thresh and beat of the bird until he found the feet, and then, sitting almost on the golden spread of the wing, like a gnome squatting on a golden pallet, with a field stone he beat the head into silence and blood.
>
> Alan, his mother's child, fled downhill, seeing around him in the trees and over and under him in the sky and in the grass, a terrible mosaic of flaring neck feathers and a crooked, bleeding beak. Never again, he felt would he feel exactly related to his obedient brother [70].

The most painful encounters between Scarbrough and his father are transmuted in the novel. When Buckeye, Alan's pet bull that will be sold at the end of summer so Alan can purchase books for school, begins showing signs of horn growth and exhibits aggression only towards Oscar, the father announces that the horns will have to be sawed. When Oscar's ineptness almost kills the young bull, Alan is disgusted at his father's inability to do anything right. Instead of using a dehorning saw, Oscar uses a handsaw, simply because it is available and because he does not want to borrow the proper instrument from his neighbor: "I'm tired of asking John Wade to borrow something every time I turn around.... This will do. It'll have to" (105). Oscar then catches Buckeye quickly, throws him to the ground so that Lee can tie his feet, and instructs Alan to put his knees on the calf's neck to hold the head steady. Scarbrough describes the scene:

> Oscar must have disliked his part of the job, too, for he grew hurried and cross. He cut into the quick of Buckeye's head and blood rose like a small fountain, spraying him and Alan. Lee, holding Buckeye's hind feet, and leaning forward also had blood on his face. He had begun to look worried. Oscar swore, flinging the severed horn away, and began to cut the other, getting too close to the forehead again. Swearing violently and bemoaning the luck of a poor man who had poor ways, he untied the suffering Buckeye, and the calf got to his feet and staggered, bleeding, around the barnyard, his forelegs wet and shining with blood [105].

Oscar's inability to do the procedure properly almost kills the animal. Belle, the mother with a vast knowledge of country first aid, sends Alan to the fields to find devil's snuffboxes that she uses to stop the bleeding:

> Belle dusted the rich brown dust into the red cavities on each side of Buckeye's head, and it was wonderful to see how the blood slowed

down in its pour and came to a small, diminishing drip under her wise hands [106].

Alan, his mother's child, sees his father as handicapped by ignorance, always causing harm, even in his best intentions. But Belle is there; when Oscar wounds, Belle cures.

The phrase "a poor man has poor ways" is echoed in the journals. However, it is not related to the dehorning of a bull. In this example from real life, a young Scarbrough falls under the rough handling of his father who explains his actions in much the same way:

A middle-aged Scarbrough reading at home, ca. 1965 (courtesy of George Scarbrough).

> I can hear my skull bones creak as they creaked the morning, screaming with toothache, I fled and was pursued and cast down on the floor by my angry father, who put his knee on my head and held me down with his whole weight while he extracted a side tooth with wire-pliers, destroying the one next to it.... He often remarked that a poor man had poor ways. I understand that now. I did not understand it then [DD-15].

The pain Alan feels is real while he watches his pet bull come so near death under his father's unskilled hands; young George's pain was actual. The parallel can be drawn that Oscar Scarbrough's assault on his son was demeaning and without emotion, that he viewed his children as another of the farm's livestock that had to be cared for the best way he could, but definitely without human compassion. When Alan screams at his father, "He'll bleed to death like that...! I told you, Dad! I told you!" Oscar McDowell answers, "Well then, by god, you do something! I've done all I know how!" (105).

Perhaps the most poignant of all examples in this coming-of-age story also has origins in real life and finds its way, again in a transmuted form, to the novel. The thread that connects the novel throughout is the young bull, Buckeye, and Alan's devotion to it. The boy's careful attention to the animal is twofold. First, the calf belongs to him and him alone and has since birth. The parents have no time for raising an animal that cannot produce milk, so it is offered to the boy. To make his interest more keen they tell him that at the end of summer he can sell the bull and use the money to purchase all of his school books for the coming year, a treat that Alan has never before enjoyed, having been forced each school term to borrow the needed texts, study with someone else, or do without. Of course Alan becomes attached to the animal as the summer progresses; he marks his own growth with that of Buckeye and dreads the day that the mature bull will have to be taken to town and sold at auction. Still, the promise of his own set of schoolbooks looms large in his mind, and there is little doubt as the novel progresses that Buckeye will, indeed, be sold. Oscar will require it. That does not, however, make the future separation of boy and pet any less painful, but Alan sees it as a means to a very desirable end.

The tension for the reader is that this animal that has received the tenderness of the boy may be slaughtered. But by a twist of good fortune for both Alan and Buckeye, a kind, older gentleman sees in the bull the careful attention that Alan has given and makes his purchase before Buckeye can be placed on the auction block, probably resulting in a higher price for Alan, eighteen dollars, and the assurance that the pet will have a good home and be used for breeding purposes. Seeing Alan's eyes "stung with tears," the old farmer says, "Don't worry. I'll take good care of him" (211). With money in hand, Alan is sad to lose Buckeye, but ecstatic at the prospect of books. In one symbolic swing, Alan — the young poet — has chosen books over farming, making it clear that he prefers a life devoted to words. Alan then performs a selfless act, making sure that his eighteen dollars will buy not only his books for the fall but also Lee's. Oscar steps in and allows Alan to pay for only half of Lee's eighth grade books, leaving the boy a full six dollars that he has already decided to spend on a lunchbox and satchel and a "good supply of pencils and paper"; he will have all the necessities of a writer (213).

In a similar incident Scarbrough related in his journals another selfless act. As a student on a literary fellowship at University of the South, a magazine purchased the first three poems that Scarbrough ever sold. Feeling guilty because he was living in what seemed luxury while his family struggled back home, Scarbrough did not keep any of the money; he remembers:

> With the money from the first poems I ever sold, I bought my youngest brother a pair of shoes. It was the fall of 1941.... The *Atlantic* bought three sonnets, sending me a generous check, which I sent on to my

mother in McMinn County, knowing how straitened the family circumstance was.... I felt guilty because I was at Sewanee, well-housed, well-fed. But it was not guilt that sent that check home: it was love: the greatest love I've ever known: for my mother and Kenneth. He walked not on but because of my poems [T-84].

Just as Alan put his best efforts into raising Buckeye and then spent a portion of his earnings on his brother, out of love, Scarbrough wanted to help his family back home, especially his brother, Kim, who benefited because of Scarbrough's best efforts to write poetry. Both Alan and Scarbrough could have easily squandered the money; it was theirs to spend. Instead, both cared for a brother who needed material things that could be purchased with the well-earned funds.

Six

Holding Han-Shan's Hand

Following the publication of his last book of poems, *Invitation to Kim*, Scarbrough experimented with new directions in his work. His most recent endeavors proved that he was breaking fresh ground with the help of the ancient Chinese poet, Han-Shan. Using the poet as vehicle, Scarbrough did not examine exclusively the life of Han-Shan, but drawing from what little is known about the Cold Mountain poet, wrote provocative and deeply personal poems about himself. Han-Shan became for Scarbrough an outlet. He felt safe writing verse that utilized Han-Shan as the central character while, in actuality, dealt with matters that had been elusive in his own work: sexuality, loneliness, even isolation. Han-Shan, then, mapped an escape route for Scarbrough because he felt that he could be more revealing about himself by standing behind a character, allowing this ancient to feel and say comfortably what Scarbrough found uncomfortable writing in first person:

> He is my alter ego and I'm finding that I can be, well perhaps, more truthful, hiding behind Han-Shan.... I'm using him to cover a lot of things that are written under first person. I get so tired of "I." I get tired of "me," but I get *tireder* of "I." I love old Han-Shan.... [He] has come in very handy. Han-Shan, bless his old heart, has stood me in good stead. In that way, he has become a good companion, but I don't talk to Han-Shan because I'd be afraid he would answer [Interview].

To fully understand the connection between Scarbrough and Han-Shan, it is important to know some of the generally accepted facts about the Cold Mountain poet, who is, by all accounts, difficult to identify. Because of the references to particular religious texts and the mini-sermons that appear in the poems, there is little doubt that Han-Shan was Buddhist. Most attempts to describe Han-Shan also agree that his religious leanings probably led him to Cold Mountain, the reclusive place where he lived as a hermit and from which he drew inspiration for his writing. The name, Han-Shan, is a direct translation of the name of the mountain where he chose to live in his later years. In this remote location, Han-Shan formed a simple cosmology; his images are taken almost exclusively from the natural world that he finds in immediate proximity.

According to "The Story of Han-shan and Shi-te," the hermit poet was often in the company of Shi-te, a male whose name means "foundling." As a child, Shi-te was discovered by monks at the Kuo-ch'ing-ssu monastery and reared among the brothers. He worked at the monastery in the dining hall and kitchen. Han-Shan would visit regularly, often to receive table scraps that were saved for him by Shi-te. The legend says the two men would entertain themselves in the evening hours by reading poetry and watching the heavens.

Beat Generation writer Gary Snyder discovered Han-Shan when he traveled to the Orient to study and translate Chinese and Japanese poetry. For Snyder, Han-Shan was a symbol of Buddhist thought and place, not necessarily an actual person. Snyder writes of Han-Shan and Shi-te, "They became Immortals and you sometimes run onto them today in the skidrows, orchards, hobo jungles, and logging camps of America" (35). What is important for Snyder in his work is the satisfaction of translating not words but ideas that promote Buddhist thinking and the Zen search for "the Way." For purposes of connecting Han-Shan and Scarbrough, it is also essential to note that Snyder views the Cold Mountain poet as Taoist. Han-Shan, if he did in fact exist, chose Cold Mountain as his home, and according to some legends, turned his back on society, his wife, and children and dedicated his final years to enlightenment by observing the common world and living as simply as possible; or, as Snyder writes, "Unformed people delight in the gaudy, and in novelty. Cooked people delight in the ordinary" (67).

Approximately three hundred surviving poems are associated with the name of Han-Shan. Burton Watson says that most of the poems are attributed to Han-Shan but that some critics claim Shi-te composed fifty of the poems, and a few were actually written by the Buddhist monk Feng-kan. In the section of his book on major T'ang poets, Watson acknowledges:

> Some scholars even claim, on the basis of a study of the rhymes, that the poems attributed to him (Han-Shan) range in date over a period of several centuries, though this assertion has been contested. In any event, no way has so far been discovered to ascertain the exact date of the poems, though the late eighth and early ninth centuries is suggested as the most likely possibility [259].

Concerning the themes and subjects of Cold Mountain poems, Watson describes them as sometimes happy and carefree, but also notes:

> The poems themselves, however, are by no means uniformly jolly in tone. Rather they reveal a man at times deeply contented, even rapturous with the delights of his mountain retreat, at other times troubled by privation and nagging loneliness. Underlying them throughout is the Zen ... conviction that these very experiences of daily life, painful or peaceful, harsh or serene, are the stuff that enlightenment is made of. There is ... no Way outside of the way of everyday life [260].

Regardless of which scholar's ideas one finds acceptable, all make significant points that can be used to explain why Scarbrough has found a "companion" in Han-Shan. Also meaningful is the fact that so little is really known about Han-Shan, which allowed Scarbrough poetic license to re-create the Cold Mountain poet to suit his own designs. This license opens the door even wider for Scarbrough to write personal poems about himself that use Han-Shan as a mirrored substitute.

Scarbrough apparently also felt the freedom to supplement what little is known about Han-Shan and Shi-te. In what may have been a rough draft of an introduction to his unpublished collection of Han-Shan poems, *Under the Lemon Tree*, Scarbrough created his version of the Chinese poet myth in an undated journal entry. He explains in that entry that his earliest interest was sparked by a childhood fascination with his mother's keepsake, a China cup which represented origins belonging to a land far away. Curiosity led the boy to books where he learned of a "great land across the waters, where, if you journeyed there, West and farther West, you came home, the book said, by way of the East." Scarbrough's foray into learning about the Orient led him eventually to Watson's translations of Han-Shan in his pocket classic, *Cold Mountain*, and then to Scarbrough picking up the story and offering his own expansion:

> Whatever the facts are, or may have been, in my book *Under the Lemon Tree*, I've dealt largely with states of mind, since nothing much is known about the two old master Chinese poets. I wrote the collection of poems at various times and in various states of mind of my own. I've given the two fabled old men a life of their own, mostly on a mountain called Exile, concentrating on the poetry possible in such a locative insulation. Shit-e, the abandoned one, is found crying in the deep forest, left there by his poverty-stricken parents who are unable to feed a large family, and in the hope of someone more able will find the boy and rear him. He is found by Shen-Fang, a giant who lives in a nearby monastery.... On the day Shen-Fang brings him to the monastery, Han-Shan happens to have come from the Capital to listen to the monks

Another photo of Scarbrough, in his later years, at home in Oak Ridge, ca. 1995 (courtesy of George Scarbrough).

sing and make music. Shi-te inquired of his companion the name of the young man and is told about Han-Shan and his relationship with the royal family. Han-Shan is the young prince's companion, and goes daily to the Royal Gardens to play with and watch over his royal charge. He is spied by the Emperor's sentinel who informs his employer of the incident of Han-Shan's kiss on the cheek of his young playmate. Han-Shan is banned from the court and is sent away to live on Exile Mountain in what might be termed a penal colony and which he refuses to leave after his term of exile is spent. There he is joined by Shi-te, and the old poets live together until Shi-te's death, in a small, long house. Life goes on. For Han-Shan, alone now, until his death in a snow storm. The writer's intent in *Under the Lemon Tree* was to give an imaginary life to two great ancient poets who left behind them only specimens of their art. The rest is silence, except for the noises my effort has made.

Both Han-Shan and Scarbrough chose to lead solitary lives, Han-Shan on Cold Mountain, Scarbrough in a small home on a corner lot in Oak Ridge, Tennessee, only a short drive from the area that he called "my personal Mesopotamia," the valley that lies in the shadow of the mountains, between the Hiwassee and Ocoee Rivers (Interview). As Watson noted, Han-Shan's poems celebrate both the delight of being alone and the torment of loneliness. In the following untitled poem by Han-Shan, a Watson translation, the poet seems happy to have chosen Cold Mountain as his permanent retreat, but after a visit with family, he finds himself painfully alone the following morning:

> I came once to sit on Cold Mountain
> and lingered here for thirty years.
> Yesterday I went to see relatives and friends —
> over half had gone to the Yellow Springs.
> Bit by bit life fades like a guttering lamp,
> passes on like a river that never rests.
> This morning I face my lonely shadow
> and before I know it tears stream down [266].

Juxtaposed against the isolation examined in this poem, the reader also finds verse that celebrates the joys of leading a solitary existence. In the following Han-Shan poem, this one a Snyder translation, the old poet views his existence as the end result of following his predestined path:

> If I hide out at Cold Mountain
> Living off mountain plants and berries —
> All my lifetime, why worry?
> One follows his karma through.
> Days and months slip by like water,
> Time is like sparks knocked off flint.
> Go ahead and let the world change —
> I'm happy to sit among the cliffs [55].

These same sentiments are expressed repeatedly in Scarbrough's journal. One example is a single line, very atypical of most of the entries, "God, I wish I had someone to talk with this evening" (I-44). Then, in another section of the journal, Scarbrough detailed the previous evening's visit from a student who came to conduct an interview and take photos: "I enjoyed the evening with the young man, but this morning I am talked out, exhausted, very nearly witless. The one good matter is that it will be months before someone else comes along" (O-78).

In "Anachronisms," a poem of Scarbrough's published recently in *Poetry*, Han-Shan is pleased to have company, but a bit disappointed that they fail to recognize what the poet has to offer, even folding and putting away a gift poem on "fine rice paper," while complaining constantly about the trouble they had in arriving at Han-Shan's remote home. After the visitors leave, "Still talking and waving back to him" (14), Han-Shan, or in reality, Scarbrough, returns to his happy solitude:

> The good agrarian poet drinks tea from
> His blue cup and stands at the South
> Window, sniffing the scent of warm
> Roses wafted from beyond the plantation
> Of pecan trees edging the bottom
> Of his herb garden [15–20].

One of the liberties Scarbrough took with Han-Shan was assigning the Cold Mountain poet a sexual identity. Most critics mention that Han-Shan had a male companion, and some also suggest that Han-Shan chose Shi-te in his later years as the substitute for his own wife and children. Scarbrough allowed Han-Shan to be gay so that he could examine his own sexuality. When asked about the issue of sexuality, Scarbrough wrote:

> All my poems are gay poems, all my religion has been gay religion, every breath I've ever drawn has been a gay breath. You see, I understand gayness as genetic in origin. I am that I am. No reviewer of any of my books has mentioned sexual predilection. I'll be doing that in *Poetry* Chicago soon, with a poem that accepts my "gay connection" in a way I've always understood it. I wear the "coat" with pride, though mostly in hurt because of the world's way [Letter November 1, 1996].

What the poet said is very true, and yet none of Scarbrough's hundreds of poems in print, up until "Sunday Shopping," published in the February 1997 issue of *Poetry*, could be labeled a "gay" poem. In this metered and rhymed piece, the speaker laments the absence of the *vox angelica* and the *vox humana*, relating in simple language that a lapse has occurred in a relationship: "The telephone is dead" (2). The central image of the poem is a worn tweed coat that the speaker and his companion purchased while shopping at a local store. The lover left the coat on a bed before departing at the conclusion of a weekend day set aside for the two to be together:

> Sunday became our day — great, soft music,
> Bantering talk and laughter — the more
> Made so because we said love lasted.
> He never left his coat with me before [17–20].

The coat becomes something of a farewell offering, a remnant of what the two had shared. Coupled with the absence of either human or angelic voices, the tone of the poem is one of finality.

"Sunday Shopping" is a very tender poem about human relationships and how they often end abruptly, even those that are well-established to the point of weekly regularity. The poem, as Scarbrough wrote in the letter quoted above, illuminates his acceptance of what being gay is, because it approaches this relationship as utterly and hopelessly human. The only factor that makes it a "gay" poem is that two men are experiencing the closeness of a relationship and the one left behind is suffering the pangs of separation caused by the other's departure.

While "Sunday Shopping" is not, as later work with sexual overtones would become, a Han-Shan poem, it is the first in which Scarbrough revealed his own "sexual predilection" to the public eye. Only a few months later, in the July issue of the same year, *Poetry* published "The Garden," a Han-Shan poem with gay overtones that offers a more expanded view of how Scarbrough felt isolated and misunderstood for his desire to "visit longer with the postman / Without embarrassment" (8–9). Because he is concerned with what his neighbors think of him, Han-Shan manipulates his garden to provide the ultimate cover, or as Scarbrough writes, "Landscaping has become his specialty" (10). In Scarbrough's second published poem with connections to his own sexuality, a notable change has occurred in tone. "The Garden" does not mourn loss but celebrates individuality; the piece has a whimsical nature as Han-Shan plans more gardening techniques to protect himself and please his peers. He considers planting bamboo at the clothesline and between the house and the road to serve the same purpose as the clematis on the fence that shields him "against public derision" (3). And for those curious neighbors who wonder what goes on behind the walls of privacy, Scarbrough leaves a clear message that he is in control. Han-Shan "squats in the peonies by the gate / To relieve an old man's propensities" (12–13) and pretends to be "digging / among the pretty flowers" (15–16) as the neighbor exclaims, "'What a splendid garden you have!'" (19). Through a humorous approach, Scarbrough tells us that he and Han-Shan are comfortable living as individuals often viewed as left of mainstream. In many ways "The Garden" also asserts Scarbrough's acceptance of his gayness, using an amusing scenario to reverse the ridicule of neighbors who, in the blindness of their ignorance, do not see what they think they see.

As a parallel to "Sunday Shopping," another of Scarbrough's published Han-Shan poems deals with the absence of a lover. In "Revenant," Han-Shan finds himself alone, but discovers the apparition of Shi-te around every corner and involved in every menial task. Again, the tenderness is present because Han-Shan would like to "confine his / Lover's absence to the bedroom," but cannot because of the bond between the two men (1–2). The reader gets the sense that this absence is only temporary; it is the fleeting desire to be at all moments with someone you love, but that is made impossible because of the routine demands of the day. Shi-te, in the poem, is only a revenant, but it is not a ghost that causes alarm; these memories bring to Han-Shan that feeling of peace and contentment that only comes in the closest of relationships: your lover's presence is felt even when he is away.

Both poets share a comparable cosmology. While Scarbrough claimed to have no formal cosmology, he admitted that when prodded by a college professor who insisted he find some source for his images, he answered, "I remember telling him that a stick, a stone, a frog, a cow, whatever happened on the landscape was my cosmology" (Interview). These simple images close at hand also form the cosmology of Han-Shan's poems.

"Initial," the third Han-Shan poem published by *Poetry* in the July 2000 issue, connects Scarbrough and the Cold Mountain poet in a different way — through the first letter of their last names. Using very simple metaphors, a "dollar sign without bars" and a "plain double / Clef without benefit of scroll," Scarbrough tells the reader that Han-Shan is just a human being with human limitations (2–4). Even though the "S" in Han's and George's last names may resemble a monetary symbol, they are both penniless; though the "S" may appear to be an altered musical notation, neither can carry a tune, not even with the "aid of a manure / Fork" (10–11). While the curvature of letter does not guarantee Han-Shan a connection with loftier goals — music and money — it does provide a link with the natural world. Scarbrough ends the poem with this scene:

> Yet once, when walking
> In a winter wood, his was the charming
> Gratuity of chancing upon a snake's
> Ivory spine torsioned across
> Old leaves on Christmas morning [12–16].

For Han-Shan and Scarbrough, the pleasure is finding that even the letters of their names are essential to a natural cosmology and a product of that environment.

And in the April 2001 issue of *Poetry*, Scarbrough found another avenue of expression via Han-Shan poems: celebration of his solitary lifestyle and the opportunity not only to revel in its simplicity but point out that it is preferable to those lived by some of the people around him. In "Music," Scarbrough sings of Han-Shan's daily activities and the old poet's sudden realization that his is a good life. Han-Shan spends his day sitting on a flat garden stone and playing the flute, building a trellis for a rose bush, painting his drinking gourds, or papering his ceiling with his "delicate but strong" poems (12) so he "can lie and read / His own masterpieces" (14–15). The poem concludes in happiness and satisfaction: "No man, he avers, can catch / Such fish in one basket" (16–17). This was true, also, of Scarbrough's simple life in a cozy, well-kept house, where he spent his hours enjoyably writing and taking care of daily chores. More than once in his journals Scarbrough stated that, when he was away from Oak Ridge, he longed for his own space and the joy he found at home. In a similar vein, the poem "Catch-All," speaks of these same pleasures. Han-Shan wakes from a nightmare of falling to find the solidity of earth under his feet and the security that firmament provides. Han-Shan is proud that he has been able to "keep a good straw mattress between / Me and elsewhere" (11–12) and goes outside with a basket lined in manuscripts to gather the eggs. The real, again, supersedes the ethereal.

Attention paid to Scarbrough's work, which is discussed in another chapter of this study, did not go unnoticed, and he allowed Han-Shan to comment on what it really meant to him. In "Up Front," Han-Shan calls himself the "year's Poet Laureate" (20) who enjoys the notice he receives in the village and the "light tapping / Of applause" (18–19) when he reads a poem to the "barefoot audience" (13). But he relishes equally the opportunity to have fun with fame, to speak in his poems of "topaz melons," "citron moons," and "virent vinery"— images the peasant listeners may not comprehend. Han-Shan concludes by saying, "Besides, / He enjoys rubbing the country's nose / In the real stuff" (22–24).

And, finally, from the April issue of *Poetry*, Scarbrough made another connection with Han-Shan — the physical. "Preferment" not only laments the loss of youth and the effects of old age, but in the poem Scarbrough gave, for the first time, a detailed, imagined physical description of the Chinese poet. He was, of course, depicting himself; reading the poem is equivalent to looking at previous and current photos of Scarbrough, a before and after rendering. From the standpoint of corporal aspects, Scarbrough painted a portrait of the poet as a young man:

> And he was indeed handsome:
> Forehead as smooth as a garden leaf,
> Eyes dark as charcoal,
> Ears taut and pink as fanshells
> Under hair the color of government ink [12–16].

And just as Han-Shan has lost the beauty of his youth, so had Scarbrough in the final lines of the poem:

> His temples are veined now like spice melons,
> Eyes wan as chestnuts long out of husk,
> Ears like small wilted cabbages.
> And O the nose pitted as honeystone,
> Mouth squashed as mashed mulberries,
> Beard scragged as winter-blow clover [28–33].

Equally important as the physical similarities is the effect: with the loss of youth comes loneliness. Scarbrough wrote that Han-Shan now lives on an unused road and the poem he posts on a dilapidated gate "flutters / Unread in the wind" (26–27).

While sense of place has been discussed at length in another chapter, it is also noteworthy here to establish an additional link between Scarbrough and his alter ego. In his preface to the translations of Han-Shan poems, Snyder makes the point, "When he (Han-Shan) talks about Cold Mountain he means himself, his home, his state of mind" (35). That can be said, too, of Scarbrough on some level. The mythical county he created for the reader is mythical only in the sense that it is re-created in Scarbrough's mind. The people in it, the landscape, the rivers and mountains, the near profligate farmland, are very real, and the bond between the poet and this place was so tightly weaved, the two seem, at times, inseparable. That is the point Snyder makes about Han-Shan; he does not live on Cold Mountain, he is Cold Mountain.

Because of this kinship between man and the earth, a closeness that can not be explained and is difficult to describe, Scarbrough experienced disappointment that others so integrated with a particular place do not feel. In the journals he wrote:

> Yes, I am stuck up to my ears in county mud. My chimney rises from fieldstones stuck in red clay up to where the silver wedding rings of a county culvert begin and continue upward the climb of the blue spiral of smoke, which, below the corrugated steel, wisps out in exhalations from the cracks in the mud.... What you forget is that I am only the image of my native landscape, am smart enough to know that; and despite the birdshit, often glaucous on my cheek, the leaf-fall in my hair, I never let the blue-veined rivers limit my travel, nor the blue mountains get in my light of the world, though I remain, and happily, in place. You have, it would appear, never understood at all [K-271].

The connections between Scarbrough and Han-Shan, then, are profound and unique. As a poet desiring to explore more facets of what makes him human, Scarbrough found a true friend in Han-Shan, a mythical figure who could be shaped according to the poet's whims and behind whom Scarbrough could be more revealing on a personal level. Why did Scarbrough publish only one poem that approached in first person his own sexuality? Perhaps the answer lies in his own statement, "I wear the 'coat' with pride, though mostly in hurt because of the world's way" (Letter November 1, 1996). The poem, "Sunday Shopping," was an exercise in courage that Scarbrough had to face, and did, with clarity and purpose.

Referring to the poem "Scrapbook," in which a scared child holds his mother's hand to walk across a plank bridge on the way to his first day at school, Scarbrough said, "Between the planks, the cracks looked like the Grand Canyon and I was fearful. I've been afraid all my life, afraid of everything. I don't know how I've survived" (Interview). Even in his tenth decade of life, Scarbrough was still dealing with that child-like fear; writing and publishing "Sunday Shopping" was another step across the cracks in the floor of that bridge. Scarbrough reached the other end of the bridge, holding Han-Shan's hand.

The companionship with Han-Shan continued into Scarbrough's final years. In fact, almost all of the later work is centered on fashioning and expanding the Han-Shan myth, even in the journals where Han-Shan and Scarbrough exist side-by-side — to the intimate level of personal exploration, and to the extreme of Scarbrough using Han-Shan as an almost daily vehicle to express his fears, anxieties, and more frequent failures. Both Scarbrough and Han-Shan creep toward decrepitude — their linguistic skills failing — and eventual death:

> In his ninetieth year, Han-Shan's only hope of heaven is that he will be able again to compose simple sentences without insulting the book of grammatical rules. He has, to his dismay, lost his sense of syntactical connections. Is he speaking, he wonders, of subject or object? He wants his words to dance and sing their way along as they did when he was in his primary years. But the easy flow of verbal expression has been interrupted, and his expressions of verbally impaired linkages is not his anymore. Who shot whom is the president's order of the day. Or disorder? And he wonders what is the nature of language since it comes to him repetitively or is given him in distracted runs of sense and nonsense. That is, in jumps and fragments of half remembered sense. The old guy is, in a sense, lost from reason. He does not recognize anymore. His sentences were once his pride and joy. He is no longer at the head of the class.

SEVEN

Myth and Metaphor Out of the Way

Scarbrough's attitude about organized religion might best be summed up in a statement he made to a close friend: that he "got saved" and "joined the church" on numerous occasions—whenever a new, good-looking, young preacher came to town. And while that sardonic sense of humor is often present in the work dealing with church issues, the topic also challenged the poet—in perhaps his best and most serious poems—to use all his skills as a verse maker to tackle the matters of religion, theology, and mythology. The subject matter also elicited a gamut of emotions, from anger to flippancy to confusion, all leading the poet to sober examination.

First, however, the reader needs a grasp of Scarbrough's leanings and a firm hold on the poet's belief system. Instead of subscribing to any particular doctrine or creed preached in a typical, denominational church setting, Scarbrough described himself as an animist, choosing to believe that any God who cared more for humans than other living beings was not to be followed. Iris Press publisher Robert Cumming, in a piece he wrote for the *Nantahala Review* after the poet's death, quoted Scarbrough from a 1999 conversation:

> I don't believe in a Christian God. I don't believe in any power in the universe that has any consideration for humanity, say, any more than it has for a frog, a tree, a blade of grass, whatever ... I am an animist. I believe that everything has a soul. If a man has a soul, a rock has the same electricity or whatever it is [Online].

While animism is not identified as a religion, in Scarbrough's case the belief appeared to take the place of religion, an acceptance that should come as no surprise for an individual whose longest lasting relationship—other than with family—was anchored in the closeness and oneness he felt with the natural world, where all animated, living beings were equally valuable, and the environment from which Scarbrough routinely drew images, thoughts, consolation, and sources. The natural world was Scarbrough's cosmology, as he stated in an interview, and the fount of his spirituality.

However, Scarbrough's description of himself as animist does not mean he was atheist. Many of Scarbrough poems address God, and recognize a supernatural force as being responsible for the creation of the world. But, as with all his attempts at true understanding, Scarbrough enlists language as the proper conduit by which to connect to the divine, as in this undated journal entry:

> The God-seeker need only find the right metaphor to find God. It may be that what we call the universe is only a metaphor for a half-glimpsed greater unity. We know nothing but analogies. What, in our dim but hopeful understanding, equates with something else, is like, will bear a burden of similarity. God, then, may be a metaphor man has to deal with on the most figurative of terms only, despite his yearning for literality. But who will tell the man on the anxious seat that what he is looking for is a figure of speech? The bench he mourns on is a hard fact to his anatomy.

Nor does being an animist suggest that Scarbrough did not need, even crave, the familial atmosphere of church. He attended regularly the Unitarian Universalist Church of Oak Ridge; a quick glance at that particular institution's tenets explain why Scarbrough found the UUC attractive and welcoming. The Oak Ridge church's website explains in eight brief statements their belief system: freedom of religious expression, toleration of religious ideas, authority of reason and conscience, worth and dignity of each human being, ethical application of religion, necessity of the democratic process, importance of a religious community, and — likely the most important for Scarbrough — the motive force of love: "The governing principle in human relationships is the principle of love, which always seeks the welfare of others and never seeks to hurt or destroy."

The UUC, unlike many other religious organizations, is also openly tolerant of gay, lesbian, bisexual, and transgender concerns. The national website for the Unitarian Universalist Association of Congregations (UUAC) has an office committed to acceptance of individuals who might be shunned by more traditional or fundamentalist religious groups. The vision is unusual in that it hopes to find itself obsolete: "The Office is guided by the vision that someday we will be able to put ourselves out of business and that oppression against bisexual, gay, lesbian, and/or transgender people of all ages, abilities, colors, and genders, whether it be overt or subtle, will be a thing of the past."

This willingness on the part of the UUC to accept everyone, regardless of differences, is in direct opposition to the religious upbringing of the poet's youth. Scarbrough discovered the UUC well into his adulthood, and remarked jokingly in one conversation, the "little Unitarian Church down the road will let anyone through the doors."

Several of Scarbrough's mid-career poems reflect his feelings about organized religion, especially his disappointment in the church's tendency to create people of a like mind who are unable to think for themselves or seek spiritual enlightenment in any way other than what the church ordains. In "The Source is Anywhere," from *Summer So-Called*, Scarbrough makes light of people who "have gone searching,/Screaming for their find/With one mind" (1–3). The speaker of the poem is satisfied to "wait here for a miracle/Beside the brook, a revelation/Of time and space they do not know" (4–6). On the bank of the stream the speaker is aware of the cyclical rhythms of nature, that what "the others" run off to discover will, sooner or later, pass where he waits: "When they arrive wherever they are pleased/To name the source,/They will but drink/From the end in the beginning" (17–20). Reading into the poem a religious overtone, with careful attention to such Biblical words as "miracle" and "revelation," the plural searchers — those of "one mind" or of one pre-determined belief system — are looking desperately for meaning, while the speaker knows that anything of value will come to him as long as he maintains the inherent closeness to nature he feels on an intrinsic level: "I wait at any point along the brink/For what they seek to come to me" (23–24).

The failure of religion — or more specifically, the words of a minister delivering a eulogy — to bring Scarbrough closer to God is explored in "Church Funeral" (*New and Selected Poems*). The preacher in the poem relies on broad language and worthless commentary to avoid saying, in the speaker's estimation, what should be said. Scarbrough describes the minister's words as "incredible platitude, mosquito net to keep out the sharp-/pointed rain! Damn it, Man, say something simple/... And great-souled, like 'Cancer is no golden joy'" (33–36). The speaker accuses the preacher of delivering drivel as "glaucous as birdshit on the windowpane" (40), rather than accurately describing the pain of the deceased, rather than providing phrases that would accurately describe the personality of the man who has died. The distance between the funeral sermon and the actuality of the situation leave the speaker feeling even more separated from the God who could be a source of comfort for those people left behind. Scarbrough sums up the degree of separation in one of the two-lined stanzas: "I keep reaching, God, but you always bound away,/Some mutual unattraction keeping the distance always the same between" (15–16). Instead of suffering through the religious service, the speaker "must get up and out of here" (45), and in doing so, turns to nature for solace: butterflies, chipmunks, crow, waving wheat. In a nearby field the speaker discovers the divine, and the antidote for his sadness: "In that field I'll find me a god-filled pool/And wash these glittering blood-drops from my eyes" (50–51).

Disenchantment and the confirmed fear that misplaced religious ardor always fails are evident in "Noon Baptism." In this poem, also from *New and Selected*, the speaker's father, obviously never before a religious zealot, has agreed to be baptized. The son witnesses the physical act of immersion, and "stood close to see/The miracle worked on him, but was blind/As usual to the musculature of faith" (34–36). The father returns "in a few days to himself,/Despite my mother, God, and any light,/River or cloud, or of my mother's eyes" (37–39). The failed conversion—the baptism without effect—is reassuring to the son who was "happy ... to hear his words again/Damning the landscape of our paltry peace!" (40–41). In a rare moment of solidarity—for son and father in the poem, and for Scarbrough and his real father in life—the speaker is drawn closer in the paternal equation because the father's inability or refusal to change is precisely what the son expected: "for I am his son twice over" (43). What religion offers both the younger boy and older man makes no permanent difference whatsoever, but does confirm the speaker's expectations.

Sarcasm returns in one of Scarbrough's longest poems, "Madness Maddened." In this autobiographical piece from *New and Selected Poems*, the speaker has recently undergone abdominal surgery in which the young surgeon opened him up "from testicle to tit" (441) and removed a large portion of intestine. Scarbrough underwent such a procedure and found himself in the throes of a drug-induced and prolonged mental fog. The operation and ensuring pain have left the speaker in a funk, not quite himself, an existence made worse by the nosy and condescending mailman who makes fun of the poet's effeminacy and quotes St. Paul, the apostle, as a verbal confirmation of his superiority. The daily visit by the postman sends the speaker into a diatribe against St. Paul, "that mouthing, dysenteric,/winding dustball roadrunner/of a charlatan/who renounced the world on the road/to fabulous silken things/and excellent cuisines" (125–130) instead of at a more appropriate "crossroads/where there are, at least,/directions to be taken,/one road to be discontinued,/another to be chosen" (135–139). The speaker despises St. Paul for not being honest enough to present himself for what he truly was: "that sublimated homo,/supreme Master Baiter,/with his sadistic turn of mind/because he could not love women/and scorned his love of men" (533–537). Perhaps the greatest sin, says the poem's speaker, is St. Paul's hierarchy of "decency and order of things/in a chaotic world —/putting poetry last" (539–540). The poet feels disowned by the apostle who disdained "ecstatic tongues," interpreted by the speaker as verse itself, "the everlasting clamor of poets" (543). The mailman is of the same caliber, a religious fake who makes fun of the poet because of his differences, and is intolerant of what he fails to understand, though the postman's "name shines brightly/on the deacons' roster" at his church.

Scarbrough felt most god-like, more in touch with the divine, when he was involved directly in the creation of poems. One of the poet's most uplifting spiritual poems is "Dream," relating just that: an imagined long journey that returns him home to find "six beautiful sons" waiting for him with acceptance and loving hugs (*New and Selected Poems*). These children are his poems — the work started and yet to be completed. The smallest of the children leaps into the speaker's arms, "his cold hands grapple at my throat" — the source of language (69). The poet's reaction is both ethereal and concrete. Rediscovering his sons is an emotional, religious experience that guarantees his offspring (poems) will grant him perpetuity: "Love bursts my vessels./My human mix pours towards eternity./What I have made cannot be finished./That is the true father-art./I feel the consuming pride of God" (70–74).

A later poem draws together all of Scarbrough's feelings about religion, the afterlife, his belief that all living creatures exist on equal terms, and his level of comfort in a personal theology crafted and honed through many years of living. "Though I Do Not Belive," one of the final poems in his last collection, *Invitation to Kim*, is a creation of eighty short lines in one stanza, devoid of punctuation, signaling a stream of consciousness connection not only with the world around him, but with the divine through a close association with nature. The poet says plainly — without compunction — that he does not believe in the holy trinity of "God the Father/God the Father's Son/Nor that other Emissary" (3–5). In keeping with animist thought, and in the same breath expressing his doubt about a Christian-envisioned afterlife, Scarbrough writes that he does "not expect/To be lifted up/From the floor of being/Any further than/A mouse is" (7–11), and that the idea of being no more important than the lowliest of creatures does not cause him fear. "I am not afraid/I am not afraid,"

Scarbrough repeats at two different points in the poem for emphasis and effect (12–13, 32–33).

Despite having been baptized as a youth into the Christian faith in the "river/Where the dusty earth/Was once exclaimed/From my timorous soul" (28–31), the poet chooses instead of the promise of eternity the excitement and joys of life in the present where "The dance is exquisite/The skip is exquisite/The leap is exquisite" (36–39). For Scarbrough the truly ecstatic is found in "The glaze of lilies/The gloze of wheat/The fire of onions" (56–57), earthy symbols that spring actually and figuratively from the ground. The animist—not atheist—gives God credit as being the divine source, and expresses his appreciation for these fecund treasures "for understood reasons/Thou It of Things" (69–70).

That Scarbrough's most fully-realized poem deals with religious issues should come as no surprise to his readers. "Good Friday, New Mexico, 1955" marks a mid-career turning point for Scarbrough in several ways: in terms of technique, in an attempt to push the limits of poetry's capabilities, and as a test of his own abilities as a verse maker. A decade earlier, in an unusual statement of frustration in a moment of despair, Scarbrough composed the following brief. What makes the note even more unusual is it was handwritten, and never typed into his permanent daily journal, where ideas were often stated, later revised, and finally fleshed out:

> I dislike writing a poem. I trouble and torment over the inadequacy of English as I know it; I fret, fume, even swear at the clumsy words. But I know the face is only to be called from the stone. And I know I must keep calling. As yet I have said nothing I might say; but some time I shall say sufficiently. That is why I keep trying. To feel like God is to find in words a way straight to the heart of poetry, as did Theocritus in his verse on the urn. What is wrong with me? Was I born into the wrong place and at an ill time to produce the perfect poem on the inevitable theme? To leave one, only one, perfect poem behind me is my desire.

Perhaps "Good Friday" was that poem, or as near perfection as Scarbrough was able. Written, rewritten, and finally completed over several years in the 1960s, the poem was published in 1967 in the *Sewanee Review*, under the editorship of Andrew Lytle, who once remarked, Scarbrough recalled, that "Good Friday" was "among the great poems of the last half of the century." Correspondence between Lytle and Scarbrough indicates that the *Sewanee Review* editor first saw "Good Friday" four year earlier, in the Fall of 1963, and made considered comments and suggestions.

Part blank verse, part dramatic dialogue, "Good Friday" is one of

Scarbrough's longest poems, and recounts an actual camping and sightseeing trip the poet took with one of his high school students, Larry, to New Mexico in 1955. Photos archived at Sewanee provide a visual history of the expedition to the arid U.S. Southwest. The photos show a middle-aged Scarbrough and the teenager at various locations, including cityscapes and the expansive desert — the setting for the poem.

But "Good Friday" is not a travelogue; the poem takes advantage of the desolation to explore mythology — both Christian and Native American — and the failure of either myth to provide sustenance in an environment that is beautiful during the day but foreboding after nightfall. In the end, myth fails and only love is a sustaining force.

"Good Friday" is also one of the few poems about which Scarbrough wrote extensively in his journals. Following is a long, undated entry (likely from the mid–1990s) sparked by commentary from critic Jim Britt, in which the poet surveys not only his intent in the poem, but judges the success with which he was able to accurately present those ideas:

> The myth of the boy and the man is entrapped in the greater myth of Christianity, whose central aim is to be interpretive of all other myths that have gone before and those still to come. Free from school for the summer, the travelers, student and mentor, have come west to a strange, dry land on a journey of search and enlightenment, only to be dazed by a place that, in its barren waste, reminds the mentor of some Dantean Hell, with its blasted landscape and the dark terrors of the flat western earth after the sun has plummeted out of sight and the darkness surges up from the earth to cover all day things.
>
> The man and the boy seek cover in an abandoned house on the edge of the arroyo in whose potholes of water they have gone fishing. Between the failure of light and the uprushing darkness, they have an instantaneous glimpse of a bright-skinned antelope leaping across a still-lit corridor of light, and fleeing away. The man thinks of the myth of the father, the son, and the holy ghost. Whatever the boy surmises in terms of myth, he says nothing. The knife in his hand, however, in the startlement of the wisdom, moves and pierces his palm. The aloneness, the darkness, the sickle moon over a butte only confuses the issue further, for the man. Some beast is howling in the darkness. Coyote, the man says. Myth fails as a shield against the terror and nothingness of sudden night. The man kisses the child's hand in grief as he tries to staunch the hand's wound. Love, he knows, is the only answer available to him and his ward. In the bleakness of the place, all reference to myth fails except the myth of love. Neither the Indian myth nor the white man's myth stand up to comfort. They no longer fit the circumstance, no longer offer a mythic comfort. Redemption is not in chant or other ritual.

> Together, they sleep in the abandoned house, whose windowpanes have so recently flooded with the glares of sundown, and are not indiscernible in the darkness. They sleep on the rim of the arroyo, on the edge of explanation. Far away, high on a hill, they can see, still faintly illuminated, a tamarisk tree. Under Jim's persuasive reading, I could see quite plainly, again, that only human love is redemptive in whatever time or place. Under whatever kind of tree.

A brief journal entry, again undated, perhaps sheds light on the successful methodology of "Good Friday." Scarbrough wrote: "Each word has always seemed a poem to me. But I could never be the poet I wanted to be. Metaphor always got in the way." Metaphor does not "get in the way" in this poem. In fact, Scarbrough's use of metaphor and simile is negligible. Instead of relying on the two most common figures of speech to create images, "Good Friday" is redolent with symbolism, a higher, more strenuous form of analogy. Symbol provides the mechanism through which Scarbrough is able to create a new anti-mythology powered by love that trumps the Christian and Native American myths reliant on faith. Consider this entry from Scarbrough's journal:

> Faith is for God; trust and confidence for man. Love is for man, not for God. One does not love the unknown; he fears that. He has faith in that. He loves what he sees, hears, touches, smells, and tastes. He has confidence in these things, he trusts them. They are not matters of faith. Faith and love are incompatible. Trust and confidence may suffer setbacks. A loved companion may betray. Clear water may poison. The apple rots. But these betrayals, these failures, belong to the natural world of wary trust and confidence, of experiential knowing. Faith and fear are bedfellows; fear and faith, rather. Neither can have anything to do with love. How confused the preacher is! He cannot trust and confidence man, but he can love God! Was that what Jesus meant by his examples? I had rather thought his preachments began and ended with man, with God always and only the summation of man's compassion and mercy for his fellow.

To discount the notion that faith in a mythical construct will sustain and save the poem's characters made disconsolate by their harsh surroundings, two symbols in "Good Friday" are of particular importance: the antelope and the tamarisk tree—the first denoting a Native American myth, the second a Christian legend.

According to several sources, the antelope, which is an antlered animal, is a totem link to the Third Eye, or the Crown Chakras. Individuals akin to this totem have exceptional intuition, are capable of great insight, and rely on meditation to tap the subconscious and open pathways to intellectual endeavors and knowledge. Through intellect the believer is able to tap into the spiritual realm.

The tamarisk tree, which appears in several books of the Old Testament, is believed by some scholars to be the tree that provided manna to the Israelites during their Diaspora in the desert. The manna, attributed in the book of Exodus to divine intervention, saved the Israelites from starvation. Manna is still collected in the Middle East, a byproduct of a small, sap-sucking insect which produces a honey-like substance that falls to the ground under the tamarisk tree. The tree also serves as an offering when, in Genesis, Abraham plants a tamarisk at Beersheba to honor God and invoke His name. Some modern scholars still refer to the tamarisk as a "tree of life."

For an animist like Scarbrough, these two living creatures should have immense value, but that is not the case. Neither the antelope nor the tamarisk provide comfort or consolation. In "Good Friday," the antelope appears at an opportune time, an almost expected fulfilling of the trinity: father, son, and the pronghorn as a symbol of the Holy Spirit. But its presence is transitory, drawing the son toward a statement of abandonment: "Why have you forsaken me,/Animal with the feet rare as rain?" (129–130). The father's truthful prediction, "The antelope will not come again" (149), is met with disbelief by the boy whose fear escalates in the knowledge that the animal appeared momentarily, offering a fleeting hope, but then disappeared just as mysteriously. The man and boy are once again left alone in the absence of the sacred, the full realization of God failing mathematically. As a symbol of Native American totem — and simultaneously, the missing third part of the Christian trinity — the antelope does not produce in its viewers an increased knowledge; the son, especially, is rendered confused. The father's statement at the end of the stanza likewise offers no hope: "For each man holds the death of his vision/In a dirty hand:/No washing will obscure it,/No praise or prayer cure it:/The antelope will not come again" (186–190).

The tamarisk tree, beside the abandoned house where the father and son seek refuge and safety, is described variously in the poem. Early in the piece, the tamarisk "plumes kept the creaking wind/In a stage of music" (38–39), but later — as darkness consumes their surroundings — the tree is more ominous, is no longer capable of "affect[ing] its music" (156). Under the tamarisk tree the bloody knife that wounded the son is washed. Even the language changes as the tree is described: from "subtle music" to "heaves soundlessly" to the sound of "whips" punishing the dwelling. The poet says, "Under the tamarisk tree is no heaven" (206), and during the long hours between sundown and sunrise, when "the gulch darkens to obsidian," the tree "bruised the house/With windy music all night" (234–235) and its plumes — so beautiful in the light of day — pile in a corner of the house and make a "distance for the heart to fall in" (238).

Why, then, do the tamarisk and antelope collapse as sources of reprieve? The animist would argue that true spirituality is found in the natural world, that these living things — an animal and a tree — have value. The problem is that both have been elevated to the status of myth: the antelope as a Native American symbol of knowledge, the tamarisk as a holy, Christian relic. Neither is any longer what it truly was because each has been infected, in Scarbrough's estimation, by false faith.

In this void created by the failure of myth, only one recourse applies. The father obviously cares for the son; the man takes the boy's bleeding hand in his own and cursed the knife, then kissed the "welling wound to make/It well again" (89–90) without apology, "I am not sorry, Son, I loved you" (91). As Scarbrough wrote in his journal, "Human love, not only for ourselves but for all the living and non-living earth, is all we have down here. God grows like a tree in such soil."

Eight

Scarbrough's Critics

The life's work of George Scarbrough has met with little or no negative criticism. In a career that spanned most of the twentieth century, and was still moving forward in new directions at the beginning of the Twenty-First, one must wonder why he was not a more popular artist, why Scarbrough is still not listed among the elite group of writers whose names are known outside tight literary circles. At times others have made the same observations. Consider these quotes from a number of well-respected critics:

In the *Black Warrior Review*, Rodney Jones commented in his review of *New and Selected Poems*: "These poems, among the finest written in the South in past few decades, are a direct chronicle of the development of a poetic style so individual that it invites comparison with Hopkins or Thomas.... As fastidious as they are powerful, his poems are major by any standard that I know, and deserve our closest reading" (104, 108).

Of *Invitation to Kim*, Phillip Balla wrote of the first sixty-three pages, the portion of the book he felt was strongest: "Those first 63 pages recall the very best poems of Robert Penn Warren ... of James Agee's 'Knoxville Summer, 1915'.... They recall the searing layerings of Thomas Wolfe's best prose, the lyrical heights of the West Virginia epiphany at the end of Eudora Welty's *The Optimist's Daughter*.... If only those 63 pages could stand on their own, Appalachian poetry would, finally, be on the map. Everybody knows, who knows, that Jeff Daniel Marion has charm, that Robert Morgan has exquisite loveliness, and that Jim Wayne Miller has integrity and sauciness to boot. For better or worse, they are our benchmarks. But George Scarbrough is better" (80).

Also in a review of the book nominated for the Pulitzer, David Rogers writes, "In his *Invitation to Kim*, George Scarbrough give us, through fierce love and loyalty, the textures of a life so brutally American it can stand as a living image of our cultural experience.... Scarbrough is, as he says in 'Thomas Jefferson,' 'A prince of fashion in a strange land.' He is a major artist and *Invitation to Kim* is a fine book" (1, 5).

In a *Poetry Daily* prose feature, R.T. Smith listed Scarbrough as one of the many reasons he chose to teach a course in Appalachian literature at Washington and Lee University. Naming Scarbrough as one of several artists who form the "bedrock" of Appalachian letters, Smith praises the poet as resilient and vigilant, and his verse an "astonishing lyric resource." Smith goes on to say, "The variety of tones, images, forms and information demonstrate just how fluid and flexible the American vernacular can be under the touch of a poet whose simple allegiance is to the sounds of the spirit crying in the wilderness."

And in the most recent criticism of Scarbrough's work, Daniel Cross Turner, in *Southern Literary Review*, explores the role of nostalgia in Southern literature, focusing not only on Scarbrough but also on Henry Taylor and Donald Justice. Turner makes a careful, considered assessment of Scarbrough's reliance on nostalgia, and in doing so illustrates a new, important revelation about the poet's work. Turner argues that Scarbrough routinely and unabashedly returns to nostalgic memory as a source of imagery, theme, even motivation, but that the poet does so with a full awareness of the lurking danger of being labeled old-fashioned, romantic, or worse—sentimental. Turner states, "Though Scarbrough writes something more than mere 'regional pabulum,' this may not absolve him of all charges of using nostalgia as a cultural palliative. His work typically engages the restorative dimension of the southern past, cloaking it in a redemptive pastoralism, yet his self-deprecating awareness of his own tendencies toward excessive nostalgia counts in his favor." In other words, Scarbrough embraces his personal nostalgia, and in doing so, escapes the traps of sentimentality. Memory for Scarbrough is not always pastoral and calming, but can be the lens through which he sees clearly a past marked by beauty and ugliness alike — both the balm of redemption and the abrasion of reality.

Despite these accolades Scarbrough was always a virtually unrecognized poet, at least outside the region considered "the South." What recent adoration and appreciation his poetry received was, unfortunately, late. Keith Flynn, who chose to include Scarbrough in the "Ten Great Neglected Poets of the 20th Century" millennial issue of the *Asheville Poetry Review*, attempted to correct this wrong, this oversight on the part of the *literate*. Speaking of Scarbrough's inclusion, Flynn writes, "His poetry comes at you from every angle, like a flock of pigeons exploding from the rooftop only to turn and circle in a single motion, like a muscular regiment perfectly in sync landing gracefully back where it began" (x). Flynn, also in the introduction to that issue, remarks that many poets are neglected because they are not part of the "booming incestuous MFA programs carving cookie cutter mannequins beneath a billowing canopy of competence" (vii).

Flynn may have hit the proverbial nail on the head with his burning commentary, at least in one respect, when it comes to Scarbrough's poetry. George Scarbrough was never part of those literary circles that promote their own. His stint at the Writers' Workshop in Iowa can not be considered productive, and the resulting attitude about workshop settings and production is evidence that this environment did not work for him. If anything, his experience drove him home to his "county" with a new resolve to redefine the limits of poetry and find an even more distinctive voice. Rodney Jones, in *Black Warrior Review*, explains:

> The contemporary poetry scene which de-emphasizes the individual and lauds the great collective effort has not ignored George Scarbrough as much as he has ignored it, pausing to swat at it occasionally like a great, lazy bluefly. And he has earned the right, paid the full fee of his exile [108].

The exile Jones labels was self-imposed. The same shortcomings that resulted from his clannish family spilled into the personal adult life and professional life that Scarbrough claimed as his own. Not only was he far removed from the necessary literary circles that might have worked all these years to further his career, his social cir-

Scarbrough with his dictionary and portrait, at his Oak Ridge home, 2000 (author's collection).

cles were even more closely knit. The bane of the artistic — a life devoted to creating poetry, or painting, or sculpture pleasing to one mind, one eye, or one person's sense of space — trapped Scarbrough in his own world. He did not like to give readings, he was uncomfortable before crowds — large or small — and in his latter years was unable, physically, to meet the demands of a book tour.

This hermetic existence was no accident. In an important essay, "I Yam what I Yam," published in *Touchstone*, Scarbrough explained his solitary life:

> By the time I reached college by dint of hard work and scholarships.... I was a confirmed loner, not joining nor being asked to join. I went my own way, as I have always, for most part friendless, though often yearning for what I could never conceive of as becoming real — a comrade who would silently understand.... There was, and is, a sense of comfort and security to be found in my own company. I had books, my imagination, and my dreams. I had been forced to become self-sufficient, almost.... My early years unfitted me for any part of family, immediate or extended, personal or professional. Yet those years equipped me for the only kind of life I can now see as possible: that of a perennial, closeted student, cogitator, bookman, writer, even poet, as some have said [8].

In "Small Poem," Scarbrough revealed what he hoped this solitary life would one day accomplish, perhaps after he had left this world, but left behind an impressive body of work:

> Walking
> the paths of his own
> premise
> fixing the right word
> daily nail-like into
> its post
> speaking exactly
> crossbar and
> beam
> living with
> utmost precision
> a man could
> eventually go away
> without leaving.

As so many artists before him, Scarbrough struggled daily to create. And consistent with his life-long effort to be an artist, George Scarbrough always walked the "paths of his own premise."

Part II

Selected Unpublished Poems, Letters and Conversations

Nine

A Selection of Previously Unpublished Verse and "Good Friday, New Mexico, 1955"

Han-Shan at Home

Han-Shan likes coziness.
His house is small, even as small houses go.
He raises a window without getting out of bed.
And from his chair, stirs a fire on the hearth.
But it is his kitchen that is so snugly convenient.
There, he stands in the middle of the floor
And spins like a lazy Susan along both
His cooking and his serving.
A little man in a small house living
A large life, is how he views himself.
When he gets dizzy turning his cakes,
He blames his giddiness on his ears.

Odd One In

Han-Shan says:
"My father called me Kai-te's boy,
And I was glad to be so identified,
Being too much like her not to be.

When he spoke of me to others
There was a note of caution in his voice.
But I grew to fill his house.

Cowbird in cuckoo's nest,
Dislodging all the others,
Until I became the oldest child

In the county. It was clear
That I had become famous for
My juvenile delinquency.

Even my mother looked ashamed
When the other children came home
And asked about their famous brother.

'He's somewhere about reading a book,'
My father said. 'He's somewhere about
Looking for stolen nests,' my mother opined.

'The cat has shat in the flax,'
My elder brother said. 'You'll never
Get him off your hands.'

I went to all the funerals.
I avoided all the churches.
Stayed out of all processions,"

Han-Shan says.
"I always stayed at home,
Or walked my father's fields alone.

Now I live where I was born,
Liege lord of all I survey
By right of occupancy."

Upon Opening His Gifts on Christmas Eve

"Look!" Han-Shan cries to the balanced cock
Peering in at the window. "Instead of reams
Of foolscap and quantums of onion-skin,
Here is a traveling case of embossed
Leather and a pocket compass
For finding my way about the garden!

Instead of stout needles and drums
Of mercerized thread, not to mention buttons
Of polished shell to hold my coat together,
I receive a brush for my bald head!

To what grand reception for my poems
Shall I wear this mock-gold chain
With the imperial image stamped
On the clasp as if I were still
Included in the royal favor?

And here, God be adored, is
An alarm clock. O, great snowbird

Nine. Unpublished Verse and "Good Friday, New Mexico, 1955"

Teetering on the windowsill, what
Gross insult to your clarion call!

My new poems will again have
To be written over last year's pages
And, what is worse, with ruined pens!
Quadruplicate on triplicate on duplicate!

Already lines show through themselves
Like ancient palimpsests badly scumbled:
Fore- and back- shadowed adumbrations
Of financially-estranged genius!

"This," Han-Shan roundly declares,
"Is the saddest day of the year:
O, most disobliging, most melancholy,
Most sinistrously deplorable
Day of the year!"

Such words recover the old poet's sense
Of humor: Han-Shan is beginning to smile.
From where his house is on the edge
Of the crag, he can see far out and below,
The golden town most goldenly glowing.

"I can manage," he reassures himself.
"Weevils in the rice-sack are of little moment.
Things will improve when spring comes,
And Shi-te returns, bringing
In abundance all things we need."

Generations

"I'm going to build a kite
Big enough to carry us all over
The mountain," young Han-Shan
Says to his father
Because it is Sunday morning.

Because it is Sunday morning,
Old Han-Shan, knowing nothing
Of the Icarian fall,
Answers his son: "You," he says
"Are going to shit
And fall back in it,"

Thus giving his hopeful heir
The best lesson in synonymy
Any father not born to the classics
Could ever have offered his son.

Chromatics

Han-Shan loves the multifarious
Bindings on his bookshelves:
"My library," he says, "is no
Country attorney's closet.
I read for style."

Yet when he goes to town,
The famous yellow coat that brought
Him to the final orgasm
Of his public self
Remains in the house behind him.

The rowdies roiling past on
The other side of the street
Allow him to go by in peace:
Chromatics rule even in
A colorless kingdom.

When April comes to Exile Mountain,
And Han-Shan hangs his loud investments
Outdoors to freshen in the sun,
Not even the garden crow is disturbed
At his task of picking early peas.

Newscast

Han-Shan listens indignantly
To the latest news from the capital:
Legislators there have voted to do away
With the Man in the Moon, and the Speaker
Of the House is roundly declaring
That Humpty-Dumpty is no longer of use
To the people.

"Soon," Han murmurs sadly,
"Old King Cole will be deposed and Jack
Horner's Corner will be pronounced off-limits
To children under thirteen unless accompanied
By their parents. Old Mother Hubbard
Will be caught stock-piling bones and Betty Blue
Hauled off to court for wearing one shoe."

Any day now Han expects a runner
To come announcing at his door
That the law protecting little boys
Under the haystacks has been repealed
And Old Mother Goose herself
Put in a government nursing home

Where she is kept under strict surveillance.
Furthermore, anyone found in possession
Of her politically incorrect Book
Will be brought to justice.

Foreseeing all this,
Han-Shan keeps his copy under the sticks
In his woodbox. "No one," he thinks, "will think
Of looking there even though tinder
Attracts fire." The old poet is delighted
With his metaphor.

Each night, after he has condoled
With Lucy Lockett over losing her pocket
And complimented Kitty Fisher on returning it
With its ribbon still around it,
Han hides his Book under the carelessly
Arranged woodpile and goes to bed, happily
Saying, "It takes a poet to fox the Grinch's men."

Ministroke

Han-Shan's face burns like the look
Of electricity on a stove's eye:
Then the heat turns to gray ash
On a dead burner.

He tries his hand to see,
But his hand is blind.

How quiet the world grows, he thinks,
Watching an ant's progress
Across the arctic expanse of the cabinet door
Above his head.

He names the insect *Ross* after a man in a book
He once read about death in a white place.

By and by, the ant reaches a crack in the door
And tumbles down the crevasse.
Only then does Han-Shan crawl to his feet
And try to act as if nothing has happened.

On Exile Mountain

When Han-Shan heard of his own death
From a passing traveler, he prepared
From the fruits of his garden
A sumptuous meal, of which he ate
Much of each fine dish to celebrate

His own aliveness, and nearly
Died of flatulence before morning.

At Home

Before going into the village,
Han-Shan washes and mends
His good, gray clothes
To wear among the citizenry,
Liking to think himself invisible
As a monk girded in the drabness
Of his faith.

Home again, in his garden,
He goes pantless among his rows:
Below his belted shirt, his brown
Legs become balletic. Under
A pavilion-wide hat, weeding leeks,
Melons, and sunflowers, he has all
The aspects of an ambulatory toadstool.
He is a different man.

Indoors, he draws all curtains,
Scours himself with aromatic rushes,
Rubs down with imported oils,
And, wearing an embroidered garnet gown,
Moves along the shelves of prized volumes
Before he returns to the old story
Of a foreign boy who dared to go
Among his hostile brothers
Drest in a coat of costly
Divisive colors.

Flowerchild

Convinced that somewhere he wore
A sign of his lineage, Han-Shan
Looked himself up and down for years
Before finding the small, brown rose
With the aid of a handmirror.

Lessons

Remembering his schooldays
With their rotes and yammering expectations,
Han-Shan laughs contemptuously:
"How fine it would be," he declares,

"To have my old masters here
Walking with me this fine fall morning

Under tossing pines,
Without the dinning and drumming,
And with only the cold mountain wind

In their open mouths.
How I would examine them
In my hand-me-down clothes."

Endowment

Han-Shan is not indifferent to fame.
Often he imagines himself winner
Of the literary competition held each
Year at the capital, to which end
He stores his poems in the family's
Ivory ringbox, ready for transport
Should the invitation come.

Ah, he thinks, at fall festival to stand
Among the great bards of the province!

What troubles him is that he has no robe
Fit to wear in such company nor any way
To arrive at the august presentation
Except on foot. No one he knows
Owns a mule he might borrow
For a trip to town.

Then there are those scandalous reports
He hears of what the judges demand
For a favorable decision.
A coupling for a couplet!
What, Han-Shan wonders, would a villanelle
Cost him by way of quittance.

Each year, on the night of funding,
He sits at the crag's lip reading his pieces
Toward town in his loudest voice,
But no runner comes upmountain
To announce the good news.

So he adds another season's worth
Of poems to his already brimming box

And plants another garden in the purlieus
Of summer, telling himself that in all reason
He should have been a ringmaker
Like his father.

The Mountain

Han-Shan says:
"I have traveled lightly back
To this mountain.
The few things I brought in my case
Have fallen out on the way.
Behind me along the road
Strangers pick up the curious flotsam
Of my journey saying:
'Who in his right mind
Could ever have valued this?'
When they find the empty box,
They will be even more bewildered.
But I have reached the mountain,
The high face under a coronal of cloud.
How unchanged it is:
How incredible still its autumn color:
How purple the shivering sedge
Among the gray headstones.
The church is like an October cloud
Dropped to the foot of the mountain.
Everything turns simple again:
Leaf-shape, mountain-shape, stone-shape,
The shape of the beholder's face
Lifted simply into the simple air
In beautiful seeming.
If I were to look back,
I could see down the red road
A bright scrap of blue
Bouncing in the wind.
But I can only stare, entranced,
At the great mantled capstone of the county,
As fabulously whispering now
In the autumn wind
As in yesteryear
Before the angry, purposeful dream
Came true."

Invitation

Han-Shan says:
"Among peacocks sparrows don't count.
I've a taste for the flamboyant,
For dyed-in-the-wool folk
Whose appearance makes a shout

On the quiet mountain,
Even among autumn trees.
Come to see me if you have
Something startling to wear
Or a poem in your head.
I don't much care for visitors
Too pallid to stain the mist."

The Poet

Late, the time of ready acceptance
Of the exceptional man in the mirror:
"Yes," Han-Shan says, "I was born to be a poet
And love flowers.
What else was there for me to become,
Ashamed as I was of my cousins
As they were ashamed of me,

Yodeling on the hilltop,
Unable to change my image?

True, my double-mindedness
Drove people to go
And make unexpected visits.
Whatever I said
My feelings were human.

In careful families mutations
Are also needed lest they become
Unvaried in their ways.

So come and visit me here
In my small, prefabricated house
At the end of a lane
In a faded, government suburb

Where I raise lettuce and roses,
Can in pretty Mason jars
My home-grown tomatoes,
And on my old Remington upright
Hunt out my marginal poems."

The Kitchen

Broad planks laid on the raw clay
Composed the floor. Some had cupped
At edges, others at ends, so one made
A higgledy-piggledy journey from stove
To table. The butter-churn walked
The jigging timbers, and I passed and

Repassed the cynosure of the room:
Herself seated shelling aprons of peas.
Ah, that trundling jar scudding yellow
Gold in spits and jots and tittles, frog-
Eggs of savoury oil gathering slowly
Into summer islands. She saved for me,
Knowing that in my going I came again.

Neighbors

"Whoa
There,
Noah,"
The neighbors came yammering
At the old man for keeping them awake
All night with his hammering.
They groused: "That flood
'S getting to be old stuff, Bud.
You got water on the brain.
Besides, it ain't gonna rain,
And if it did, that boat
Wouldn't float,
You obstreperous old goat."
And went back to bed.

And one said, yawnin'
Through a window, "Stop
All that fuss, Pop,
And take two of these
And call us in the mawnin,
For Gawd's sake, please."
And tossed him seedcake.
But Noah'd done supped,
And he just upped
And kept on sawin'
And figurin'
While the neighbors kept
On jawin' and sniggerin.'
Till the rains came.

And then, Lawd God Amighty,
They laid on his name,
But Noah wasn't havin'
Any of their society,
And, clamping on his hat,
Said, "Back 'er up, boys,
And head for old Ararat.
I just cain't stand this noise."

And away they sailed in the rain,
Loaded to the gunwales, twain
By twain, until they came
To dry Ararat,
And Noah took off his hat
And stood listenin' for his name.
And the Lawd said,
"Whoa,
Noah."

Two Climbers on a Mountain

I have, it may be,
One of the few vulnerable cheeks
Left in the American crowd.

It is a high cheek,
Full of the blood of my Indian father
And perpetually unblushed

Because of its born color.
So you will not know how hot my face
Grows on the cold mountain
When, forgetting he must enter
My mind before he enters my body, the poet,
In the heat of his own

Disowned genius,
Exclaims in his opening line: "Fuck you,
My brother!"

I can read no further.
The gray mackerel sky, the thick, dull
Horizon's sullen blue are more

To my liking. Besides,
There are other matters to be considered.
Behind me, the hugely

Anatomized cliff of the over—
Look is itself a weepy ejaculation.
Examining the stunning

Graphicity of the pictures,
I think: *If they last a thousand years*
In the weather of this rock-gap,
What will the reader think
Then who comes to this mountain: that
We were no better in our final

Convictions than ithyphallic
Dancers proceeding upmountain at the behest
Of some hard old god?

Not, please understand,
That I object to the human body. We are not,
In any event, likely to be encased

In anything more spectacular
Than our own smooth skins. Nor do I hedge
At honest exclamation.

But, may I ask, what trope,
What turn of truth is so highly exclamatic
As to be so ejaculatory,

Though we shout repeatedly
"O!" in the act of discovery? Neither, may I
add, is shit subtle. It hardly

Scans even in the loosest meter,
Though of much marvelous stuff are we all
Too consciously made. A more artful

Knowledge is needed. Let
Us forget, at least for a little while,
The pink and brown dichotomy of

The human ass, gorgeous as
It may be. The earth, the world we make
Upon it are capable still

Of other miracles. On
The way up, in a stand of young hickories,
I found new buds as thick

As a man's thumb. There was
Also a vine beginning to spread its purple
Web over a stairway of rock,

And in another place
Under rotten stems of old ice, the curly
Scrollwork of pale ferns.

Now, below me, another
Climber ascends through the bare hardwoods.
It is cold on the mountain,

But it is April,
And he picks up a sudden halo of sun,
As snarled black branches,

Steep plane of earth, early
Morning light construe a natural wonder.
Where I am, there is only

The peacock green of hemlocks
Starred with gold and purple and blue finches.
It is a good place to wait.

With luck, the other climber
May be someone coming with a poem of apology.
Let me breathe. I tire so quickly now.

The Visit

I stop and whisper softly "Damn!"
Because I don't know where I am.
The only certain thing I know
Is that I'm either in Monroe

Or Polk, and all about are trees
With differences as slight as these:
A little wind, no wind at all,
A stoop, a standing clear and tall,

A bluer moss, a barer bole:
And north and south is all I'm told.
But since the line runs east and west,
Just what I'm north of is the test

Of what I'm south of, or the other
Way around. The wood's a smother,
A rank, a file, a crowd: confusion
Too great to come to a conclusion

And know which county I am in
On my way to see my kin.
I think it odd that living trees
Should bound human civilities

And odder that a tree of girth
Itself grows in divided earth
Where civil entities construct
Imaginary usufruct

And cut a splendid oak in two
As in the wood I'm going through.
The thought bemuses for a mile
Of hogback and a swale. Meanwhile

The sun becomes as lost as I
In a similar tree-grown sky
And I'm startled by a breath
Of wings as quiet as sleep or death —

Which may be how the end may be
With line's demise, neutrality
Of here and yon, a merging scene
Of all into one desmene

Of here and here. The only hope
I have between Monroe and Polk

That I have not advanced (so far)
Into a place where boundaries are

No longer drawn, 's a rattlesnake,
A glittering autumnal fright,
A sudden papillary ache,
That brings my nerve-ends into sight

And lets me know, in ice sun-kissed,
That boundary lines do still exist
(Though questionably for my sake)
and tells me that, in sun-killed ice,

I'd better do some thinking twice.
He gives me from his narrow ledge
The right amount of body edge
To hurry onward in the trees,

A bit uncertain in the knees
And still not knowing where I am
And still inclined to whisper "Damn!"
Though for a different reason now,

To similar trunk and similar bough,
Hogback and swale and twisted sky
Where the sun's as mazed as I:
For nothing matters now except

The glittering step I never stepped
And happiness, pure happiness,
Happiness directionless
That through the mazes comes to bless

As my folks, to hell and gone,
Like a lodestar draw me on.

Eden

As children we fought
    under the orchard
        trees,

Among the apples,
    while the wind from
        the wood

Tossed down gifts
    to us more culpable
        in the ways

Of offense than the slit
    cheek, the bruised
        offending

Eye. We shouted up to
>   the clouds the glad
>   dicta
Of our wrath, and stoned
>   the blackbird there
>   with
The blunted fragments
>   of our words, furious
>   with syllables.
We danced on the grass
>   those rings that bespoke
>   fairies
And ran to treeholes
>   the paths that taught
>   trolls.
Under bells like apples
>   knocked together through
>   silk,
We trod the measures
>   of happy war. And the
>   blackbird
Came with its quaint eye
>   to see the dance, and
>   the clouds
Raised up as if buoyed by
>   our breath, and the wind
>   rustled
Suavely as if something secret
>   had just passed by
>   in the grasses.

Good Friday, New Mexico, 1955

The fish leaped toward the hand in lightness
And finished in dark, wet splendor
The little journey:
Sudden deep dark took the house from the land,
The willow from the waterhole:
There was nothing in the steep ditch
But a voice, wondering,
And a step seeking reassurance
Among stones: then he came to me,
Bringing the bright fish conquered in darkness,
The cold hand, the turned face, startled by sunset,

The swift faring in this day-dead land.
Are you there?
He said, beside me, the wet fish at my neck
As he found an answer in the thin curve
Of his arm, as his hands
Throttled the head once source of all the world.

I am here, I said, myself wondering
Where here was.

But the fish, dead already in the searing air,
Stenched at my nostrils, and over his
Shoulder I gagged at the new moon:
In the dark, his smile murmured
At this small devilry, but his hands held,
And his face, over the thin tree of his neck,
Had silver in it, as I held him,
Fish-forced in knowledge:

Here was now, New Mexico, 1955,
And spring turned odd, out of its context coming.

Only the new moon above the tamarisk in the bare yard
Rose equably: the moon that awed him,
The house he would not enter,
And the tree whose plumes kept the creaking wind
In a stage of music.

My poem begins with Larry:
A dry month in a dry country spent
With a loving child;
Begins here, now, at dark this evening,
On this prairie in a steep ditch,
Important as transfiguration,
Under a new moon.

It is no mere matter of speech,
The world is shaking: under
The skin of things a motion flicks
Mightily at the outside,
A streaking surge fulminating in the willows,
A flurry arising in the immediate darkness.

Yet the house incorporates the swell,
The tamarisk does not affect its music,
And no rock falls.
We have been dashed together in another land
Where earthquake eyes precipitate a landscape:
No tremor here unless the grouse, bellowing,
Are seismic counters of world's malaise.

Nine. Unpublished Verse and "Good Friday, New Mexico, 1955"

II

Look, Larry, the new moon,
Lighter than wood made in the light west,
Is thinner than a tree-ring in a dry year.
We will make a torque of it for the doe
Your heart owns as of this evening, a light torque
That will lean upon her neck
Without breaking the finest hair,
Even on the aghasting leap in the red
Ditch your blood ran shame to when the eyes
Looked beyond the knife's periphery
And the hand received.

How your blood dropped, Son,
In the crucible of my hands holding
Your hand!
How the bright wetness sang
In the sand between us,
I cursing the knife,
You praising the deer with your eyes,
While the hot sand sang
Of usual crucifixions, the wind
Blew in the ditch and a scrap
Of weed bounced towards the mountains.

Larry, forgive me if I saw the face
Of love and fury wedded in the west,
Kissing the welling wound to make
It well again.
I am not sorry, Son, I loved you.

But we will make a halter of the moon
To lead the calf by in those arroyos
Where your young heart will now be finding her forever:
Make it with our words now
Under the tamarisk tree while we wash
The bloody knife in water.

Come to the basin in the hollow stone,
Son, the font where love's faith
Will cleanse the instrument of love's disloyalty:
Dip the knife in the cloudy stream
A scarlet second in the stream's hour,
Son, Son, my Son, O Larry!
The sediment darkens and sinks away
In the gray face below the stone
That is not either of our faces,
But a third face drinking the sweetened

Flow. See it going, parabled,
Down among the sediments and fishes
Drowning its own poor lightning in less light!
The trinity has fed again!

The art is over, and the glimmering blade
Dries in the dead air. Clean, clean
Is the footed nail under the cactus hill,
The spiked knoll of evening glowing anguish
Where the light is. The wind stirs
The tamarisk tree to subtle music, your eyes,

Grayer than the fruits of wind, look
Beyond me, higher than the sun, to
The sunrays, pass to the peak,
Then to the mesa where the priest fell
Down hard walls to soften anger.
The art is done, Larry, I see again that I am alone.

Son: speaking:
Why have you forsaken me,
Animal with the feet rare as rain?
The wind blows in the red ditch;
The tamarisk heaves soundlessly;
But the dry well,
The house leans, one-eyed, on the land:
There is no vision left
After the wild earnest leaping.
Why have you forsaken me?

Father: answering:
Beware the vision repeated, Son!
Made plural, it decorates odd houses
Whose disciples, tying your dream
To a drift of their exploded stars,
Compose strange letters to the folks at home.
Look at me now:
I sit at your feet, not to correct your vision,
But to follow it.
The antelope will not come again.

Son: in bewilderment:
Not come again!
Animal with the teasing feet
And the shinbone round as a branch of broom,
Not come again!
In the evening when the light,
Going west like stars,
Hangs in the wake of your flying feet,
Not come again!

Nine. Unpublished Verse and "Good Friday, New Mexico, 1955"

Father: in pain:
I have washed your hands, Larry.
I would wash your feet as readily
To prompt the vision, once again
Raising the bright accidents of fortune
To the reach of both of us.
I would do this, knowing better.
But the antelope will not come again,
Not for a year of summer only,
Not for a day of only morning:
Not come again.

Son: not believing:
Not come again, Father?
Say, not come again?

Father: determined:
Though you give the knife away,
Though you throw in the rocks
The knife you love, the six-inch lover
Against your loin, the white steel
Gleaming in its deerhide cover,
Tipped with a doe's heel,
The antelope will not come again!
Not come again to heart's flurry,
Or hand's hurt in this tamarisk land,
For each man holds the death of his vision
In a dirty hand:
No washing will obscure it,
No praise or prayer cure it:
The antelope will not come again.

Son: in desperation:
She went with the light, Father,
And the light will come again.

Father: finally:
Son, the gulch darkens to obsidian:
In blood is the color of darkness,
The rich blackness of dry love.
The land leans over the rainpool;
In sweet, heavy water a fish leaps
But not for lovely leaping: the clean
Coolness of night air
Calls him from the gathered tilth
Into the living open.
But it is not so for us.
Under the tamarisk tree is no heaven,
By the rainpool is no harbor

But of ghosts, and of one
Ever so lightly, gravely leaping.
Let us go, Larry, into the house
Where we shall find such blessings
As are granted us. Goodnight
To the whole round question growing
In the dark, the huge, the houseless.
In the house we shall find protection
From the painful interest of love
Which the antelope flees now
In the cracks of the hills.
She too is the death of her vision,
We too are the death of our vision,
As God was, at the murder of His.
There is nothing left but a corner,
A low corner in an old house,
Where love combats the source of its healing.
And always a tree somewhere crowning
The slope of a hill.
Somewhere, Son, always a tree.

III

Total darkness, like total war,
Aimed at the house its black fallacies,
Or dark modes of truth, where
Interpretation slept in its half-rounds:
The tamarisk bruised the house
With windy music all night,
Letting the smother of plumes
Into the low corner, making
A distance for the heart to fall in;
And, stung by strident plumes,
Pelted by peacock color, the heart
Rolled the hours forward
In the beginning:
To invarious midnight,
To wayward two o'clock in the morning:
Arch time when between
The object and its art is a gulf
Too monstrous for conception,
Arroyo beyond which, in the icy world,
Goes the last fable;
To the hour when the pool settles
In cavern blackness, and the heart,
Like a blind fish, nosing its way through the night,

Rests. In total darkness. In total peace.
No longer breaking for a hand,
In the androgynous peace of worms,
The heart rests in the great
Solitariness of night.

In a gust of sleep forgiven.

Night. Unprevious night. When man
And boy slept in a small place
Under the whips of the tamarisk tree,
And small crucifixions kept their times
On the little trees of memory,
Until a deer, returning, drank from a bright pool
And the dream failed,
In a gust of sleep forgiven.

Ten

A Selection of Scarbrough's Letters

Letters to Marion

The following letters are from the private collection of poet Jeff Daniel Marion, and included here with his permission. With one exception — the first letter from the early 1960s — the correspondence occurred during a period from 1975 to 1980 when Marion edited and published the literary magazine, *The Small Farm*. When possible, specific dates are provided but Scarbrough did not include dates on some of the letters, though he did make creative suggestions about the applicable months. In most cases, the following quotes are excerpts only.

July 2, 1963

Miss Sally Cupp — now there's a name for a story — writes me that you are compiling a book of Tennessee verse — now there's an ambitious project, since an anthology, with its garden implications, necessitates more weeding than gathering flowers. But am happy to be considered ... I do not write much any more. Teaching is too exhausting, and every moment I am allowed I like to vegetate ... I am only a small fish in the pond, forming a smaller O than once with my goldfishy wonder. A poet, to paraphrase, love his loiny old heart, Ben Franklin, like a fish, stinks after three days. Anyway, Danny, if in Oak Ridge come by to see me. You will be welcome.

After the noon of June

Days ago I sent you a manuscript by way — to the post office — of a 70-year-old neighbor, whose memory is shorter than my most prized possession and who imbibes freely of that which I indulge in only occasionally in the company of a rare soul. You can judge of the frequency by the dearth of rare souls. If I continue my practice, I'll never get hooked, that's for damned certain. The draft of "The Small Farm" [note: a poem Scarbrough composed for Marion's magazine] was the first draft, which has been revised, reconstituted, made more tightly logical, and is twice the poem of your copy. Now, if you received the poem, and should be even remotely interested in publishing it, please let me know and I'll send along the fair copy. In any event, let me know. I slipped into Leonard's car, while he wasn't looking, to see if his big butt had squashed the envelope down under the seat. I didn't find it, but still rest an uneasy head because he tells me I may ride to town with him and five minutes later he drives off without a thought of me in his head! What I'm saying is, he'd forget his noggin if it came unlatched.

June, when if ever some perfect days

Time is wasting. Getting up this morning feeling a little better, after I had cooked, cleaned, bathed my mother, washed the clothes, etc. I wrote "The Small Farm" just for you. It may be nothing. My critical sense has been so dulled by drugs I cannot make evaluations. But you can. The two prose poems I cut from a manuscript of prose poems. I like them. But again, yours is the evaluation. If these won't serve, I'll have time, if I have the mind, to try again. The doctor gives me twelve months more to be normal again.

July 2

Here is "The Small Farm" once more. Plus another poem, "Breakfast." If you want both, one, or neither, please let me know at once. Another magazine has asked for copy, including *The Sewanee Review* and *The Green River Review*, and I've nothing much that has not been published somewhere. If you do keep "Breakfast," please mimeograph or Zerox a copy and send it back to me. This is the only copy in existence. Sure, I'm crazy.

July 28, 1975

May I please call you Danny in exchange for George? I'd like to know you much better than "Mr." will allow. I like your style, the man of you which comes through to me from what you write. As a teacher of composition, I think I could tell more about each student from the papers he wrote for me than any action of his ever exposed. And speaking of teaching, I did not mean any denigration to you, please believe me, when I spoke of Carson-Newman. I suffered hell at a small religious institution in this area, every idea I broached in class questioned, even gravity—that being countered by "walking on the water." Bless my soul, I got around the origin of languages question by bringing in Breughel's "Tower of Babel," and another art work, postcard size, whose artist I've forgotten and *then* slyly insinuating possibilities of man's having first imitated birds and a wondrous lot of other ideas, some of them, quite frankly, ridiculous, just to see what I could get away with. I had to "git" with it to get a dictionary into the hands of each "compo" student, and fight like hell to over-rule objections, among the students this time, to the teaching of Greek mythology via Edith Hamilton because "it conflicted with the Christian Idea"! Oh, it was rough — the division not for emphasis but because of a worn out typewriter which has been hell beaten out of it for sixteen years.

Thanks for the acceptances. I'm glad to be with you as I am glad to be appearing soon in *Poetry Now*. I think I told you about the Who's Who in America invitation, didn't I? I'm a little dizzy about it all, but not too dizzy to can tomatoes, make applesauce, apple butter, cucumber pickles, and fried apple for the winter. I'm an apple man and quite a farmer this summer. I didn't get to the blackberry patch because I must remain with my mother at all times. Thanks for the concern about my health. That's rough, too. I'm walking with a stick today but hope to be more balanced later. When I try to be dapper with my cane, I fall off the sidewalk. Please, let's be friends, shall we?

Undated

Couldn't agree with you more. I could have sent you many another piece from cold storage, like the one appearing currently in No. 18, I believe, in *Wind*, and the two in the fall issue of *Sewanee Review*. "The Small Farm" was an occasional piece, and so, like most of these, not up to erectable standards. There is a whole of shit in it. I admire all shit but human shit, and that I can't take! Like fools, I can't suffer the humanly excrementitious gladly. Besides, I had just revised the mule stanza anyhow: the lines now read:

> what farm can be considered whole
> without the presence of that hybrid soul?

A mule is not a eunuch. He hasn't lost his nuts, as you well know. He just doesn't have any workable nuts available. Then he doesn't have the passivity either eunuchs are supposed to suffer.

November 6

The Small Farm is a beautiful little magazine. More than most. I have time now for reading nothing but my own contributions, one of which, "Tropic of Cancer," I am sorry to note, had its two closing lines in the middle of the poem. Perhaps you can say something to that effect in the next issue. I know how these things happen, Danny, and have had to be forgiven myself several times when I was proof reader for *The Sewanee Review*. Do hope you see my poems therein for this autumn. I think the reason my sails were windless at the typo was that another editor had just referred to me as one of "the top U.S. poets," and another as "the leading living Southern poet." You see how a man's vanity runs? God knows I've waited long enough for even that much recognition. Will read in Oak Ridge on Sunday at the Unitarian Church should you be passing this way. Herewith a long poem that says several things about the human condition. Hope you can use it. My next door neighbor just died, and I am all shook up and full of tranquilizers. Please forgive.

Undated

I am right now doing a cold turkey withdrawal from drugs I became too used to during and after a colectomy, and the resulting state of mind is a bit of hell. "The Small Farm" sounds right, and I'd like to contribute, but until I am a little less shaky, more able to write, and certainly more self-critical, I'd be afraid to make a move. In the meantime, much success on the magazine. By October, or before, maybe I'll feel better.

Undated

Again, the idea of the small farm delights me. May be I'm just a bit envious. A small snug house on my own land! The sharecropper in me won't stop stinging! Confucious say: "Man who farm other man's land always have other man's shit under his fingernails." So much for my barnyard wisdom.

"A Death in the Family" makes me nervous. Please, Danny, as busy as you are, would you alter two more stanzas a little bit: make these little rooms a bit more comfortable? 13 should read as it stands:

> Now!
> Brother he was on other days
>   of heavy glass marbles: cat's-eyes, blueyes,
>   milkys, water-clear bubbles
> and 14:
>   twisted with cables of yellow,
>   red, blue, green, and pokeberry purple
>   flaring from pole to pole.
> And 32:
>   thunderous roar, until he grew
>   out of my slower ken, which never included
>   a gun.

I am sorry, but the poem just won't settle down into sensible lines. Do this for me, I'll not ask for wine.

Undated

Brother, I tell no lie. The cure is sometimes worse than the disease. Sitting on tables, bureaus, shelves, even chairs, there were twenty clocks around the room. As I stared from one to another, the numbers fell off the clock faces, sifted down like black dust on the floor. I awakened, came to, regained consciousness — whatever the phrase is for a return to knowing — to find myself in my own front room, with only one clock ticking away on the mantel. I am like a drunk, wanting another drink. There is a cold spot between my shoulder blades. My muscles and bones grind together. My mouth is crumby with dried saliva. I roll it off my lips with a sleeve. God, how I need another Triavil!

******

Danny, yesterday in a mad hour I offered you the indignity of a card. My apology. If the explanation of the wrong word "now" in stanza 37 — stanza 37? O migod! — is not clear, it should be supplanted by the word "since," as I wish to introduce two "times" at once — the before and after: the one long but short; the other short but incredible long. If that poem itself is too long, Danny, don't use it, please, I do not wish to pester you, dear Brother, but I am coming off Triavil — or trying to — and am a bit mad in between, wishing rationally to attain in the quiet excellence of your poems, not the tearing drama which always seems necessary to me.... Off now to Knoxville to see my dear Mother. I love few people, Danny. Myself not at all. A day at the nursing home re-acquaints me with the nature of my love. I never loved anyone for his humanity; only in spite of it.

Undated

Apparently "sense" made no sense to the young lady, but it rarely does to anybody, whatever the sex. I'd much rather you printed the whole poem with explanation but you will have the final "druthers." The reading received mucho praise, although I distrust praise. Wish you had been there, not just to hear me read, but to meet you. I'd like that, Danny. There's no hard feeling here, depend on it. *Spirit* left off the entire last stanza of my very, very, very long poem in its latest issue — a stanza which, like the two lines in "Tropic of Cancer," had to be in place for the entire poem to make sense. Alack and welladay! Who is Robert Morgan? Sorry, I am so ignorant. We get so little poetry at the *Times* nowadays that we will review, I am beginning to wonder whether my next book, when and if, will even be reviewed.... That sounds like a persecution complex showing.

April 30, 1977

The poem moved me deeply. I shall always treasure it. Thank you.

The reading at Carson-Newman was an experience of good, warm-hearted people whom I liked and who, in some small measure perhaps, liked me. That is the beauty of words among us, that they promote the human feeling. As I age, Danny, human touch becomes more and more important, possibly because as the dark comes I take on more and more the coloration of MacLeish's "J.B." All we have is the feeling we have for one another. Someone said that was too weakly humanistic a theme for the poem to labor by. But to paraphrase Margaret Fuller, "I accept humanity." And to paraphrase Carlyle's response to that bumptious, female assertion: "By god, I'd better."

Ten. A Selection of Scarbrough's Letters

July 13, 1977

Until lately, when I almost lost my youngest brother, I had never quite known what the depth of meaning in the word "brother" can be. Truly, out of all my brothers, I have only one. You met him, I think, at the Bookstore Party. I call him Kim. Thanks for letting me have another brother, Danny....

Anything I send to you unasked for, Danny, is for your reading. The two poems, not finished, were in progress and I thought to delectate you with "Communion" anyway. If you have not been jacked off in the grass down by the riverside by a good minister, dear brother, you haven't had the religious insights I've had and could find the poem offensive, even repulsive. And if you haven't watched him do the job for himself—a second coming—why, then—as we used to say—you ain't been there!!! Am I being irreverent, Danny? Did it come to you as a surprise that the minister had clutches of hair in an inverted triangle from armpits to crotch like other men? God, how, when, and if do we learn! I know now that angels are not codling moths busy among apples signed in paradise. I don't write to other people, Danny, in such a heathenish fashion. That I write to you suchly, please, does not mean that it takes one "heathern" to know another "heathern." It took longer to straighten out that word than "sistern" because there was a well of water—if not a well, a depository—by that name. Any kind of word play helped mnemonically. Speaking of word plays, why do Frenchmen eat only one egg? Give up? In France one egg is an eouf. Do you know why there are no whores in Germany? Why, in Germany oars are for boatin'! I'm going to let you figure that one out....

So if this horseshit isn't the answer, Danny, forgive me. You sound so tense and worried I was bound to try.

Another little unfinished poem for your reading:

>"By George"
>Even though life has become
>"Warfare on a grand scale,"
>And "the best poem by the best poet"
>A plated chariot racing by the land
>It can never quite by-pass,
>This afternoon,
>Spreading manure on lonely ground
>Between the river and the mountain,
>I meditate on Rome, Virgil,
>And the statesman-patron's wishes
>That the art of spreading manure
>On lonely ground be revived,
>While, distance knotted in their voices,
>Wood doves are calling still
>All over my county.

It isn't finished, Danny, and I doubt it will be....

I'm off now to begin my own series of cardiac tests, Danny. Of such is life beginning to be complexed. How I wish we might have remained in the age when a cardiac arrest was no more than the knave of hearts being apprehended for apprehending tarts. Would I had never learned that tarts can also be accosted.

Letters to Mobbs and Others

The letters that follow are from two sources: Rebecca Mobbs, the recipient of one correspondence and the short piece from one of Scarbrough's non-archived journal entries, and the rest from papers secured by literary executor Mobbs at Scarbrough's home during the latter years and following the poet's death. The letters to former *Poetry* editor Joseph Parisi, Seton Hall Professor David Rogers, and *Shenandoah* editor R.T. Smith were never mailed.

To: Rebecca Mobbs, 30 August 2004

The Monastery

Uphill from Town and across from the River

Dearest Rebecca,

As we wrote in those penny-postcard days, I take my typewriter — read cedar — hemlock? — tasting pencil in hand to drop you a few lines. Not plowlines, as one humorist wrote to me in the thick and deep of County Daze — God how formal we were in those days, without have heard of formalism, and the Model T of the maleman came, trailing clouds of dusty glory along roads that turned mud in winter, and we — I — plodded and splashed along to the "mailbox" to see what the Lord had wrought — I almost said "wroughten" in someone's rough hand. How we chewed on the pencil trying to think what to say to our correspondent, but what we wrote didn't matter because no question had been asked and, so, to be answered.

I'm writing in a room whose corners are filled with Stygian darkness because all the bulbs are low and not made to illuminate Black Oak mountainside. Just had a good breakfast, such as it was, and such as it was, bears no repetition. The apple sauce was good on my neighbor's homemade bread. She is the lady who cuts the grass, and works to keep her three sons at the University, all at one time. Her husband is bandmaster at school. She does a good job of cutting the grass and hauling away all trash and trimmings to the city dump. A most competent lady, she. Thanks, thanks, Rebecca. Over and over again, thanks. The old homestead on the Clinch is beginning to look itself, after my long absence from home.

Today, Margaret is mailing the latest batch of "journals" to the Sewanee archives, where my friend, Annie Armour, will stash them away for futurity, if there is to be any. Athens has prevailed. The God has come down from the Mountain for the quatrain competition. I can't see my page. So I make for you a poem, dear heart.

> For Rebecca
> I'd never thought I'd take the tack
> That ancient Greeks were mostly black,
> But after having seen the Show,
> I do not have to Think. I Know.
> And curiously the privilege
> Did not seem a sacrilege.
> White and yellow, black and brown,
> They all came down to Athens Town
> And took the chance of stand or fall
> With skill and grace: Athenians all.
> Though some indeed begrudged the gold
> And left the record halfway told.

Margaret and I turned the house inside out, looking for the Cold Mountain explique but found it not. I recall giving it back to Margaret the day she brought it to me. I'm so sorry, dear one. I know you love books, and I apologize. I'm sending you an Audubon guide to say I love you. If you were here I'd gift you with several great volumes. With you they could find a home.

To: Rebecca Mobbs, undated, from the journal

Rebecca,

I love the old County crowd. How mysterious that we all came together at the end of the road — poor wayworn travelers. I know the County by heart. Fact is strange. Good literature is made for wonder. I recall that once upon a time I made and entwined a wreth — wrath — wreath for my own head, and took a book of poems down by the hog pen, for reading out-loud among fumes of pickled corn. Give my affection and respect to all those we know, half-know, and confess to late-ly out of compassion for our and their ignorance. I'd like to see the little farm some more. Give the good master of the house my respect. And keep my love close, dear friend and daughter of our mutual great friend, Ruth, who enabled me in so many ways, as all good friends do. Thanks and thanks. Ye olde handes are wearing.

To: Joseph Parisi, 20 January 2003

Dearest Joe:

Today is the first day in a while I'm able to attempt a letter. Arthritis is burning and raging, especially in my fingertips. Otherwise, I'm in fine fettle and hope you are up and running. I'm sending along four shorter poems for your consideration, in the hope that I've not made a mess of them as I'm doing with this letter. I hate to whine, Joe, but Old Arthurities, as we said in the County, makes a bad bed-fellow. I made my 87th birthday wearing a great sausage-like catheter in my pants. I'd never had such full pants in my life.

Which brings me to the little news I have. In April, the Knoxville Writers Guild will give me their Lifetime Achievement Award. Friends will pick me up, as they did for the new governor's reception, and return me to my little home on the mountainside, where I abide in splendid aloneness, most of the time. I was so delighted to hear of the Award of good CASH made to POETRY recently. Luck, Joe, acclaim and happiness. Give Stephen my thanks and gratitude. The Anthology was stout and handsome. And wonderful to have. There they all were! The local paper, *The Oak Ridger*, gave it, and me, a three-quarter page spread, with photo of the book. We are deep in hinterland here, Joe. But now and then a scrap of old newspaper blows over the mountain. I've lived in a vacuum most of my life, Joe, a stranger among strangers, even at home, but the going has been good at times. Wonderful people from all over are now my friends. David Rogers, professor of English at Seton-Hall University, wrote a scolding letter, saying "Why, oh why, did you kill him?" I didn't. I just left him [Han-Shan] on the mountainside trying to get home through the snow. I just hinted, as did the Man Araby in his great short story from *The Dubliners*. God, what a man Jimmy was!

I listen to music a great part of the time now. Go to dinner with friends now and again. I even went to a country church with my wonderful neighbors recently and had a good feed. They were my people, Joe, of earth the saving salt. Outside snow patches "leprify" the mountainside. The community is silent now, after a row of fire engines and an ambulance. Migrating starlings and other somber birds pick in the dead grass. A sense of abandonment, not abandon, haunts Black Oak Mountain. But I'm safe inside my cabin, looking out at the American holly tree and a flag drooping dispiritedly on its staff. Glory, glory, hallelujah!

Thanks for everything, for all things, Joe.

Next morning, January 21, 2003

Dear Joe, there is nothing but story. I never wrote anything but story, it being my conclusion that a single word is story. At the moment, I feel somewhat like a spider who has run out of spinning material. An old word-lover who is running out of ink. I still write with dead fingertips, but I mistake in every sentence. Please forgive me that proneness to error. All of which is to say that I'm becoming an old man and wish to offer you necessary parts of the Han-Shan story before I run out of mind. Some of these pages have been duplicated, since I can't make a fair page anymore. I use endless trials to no avail. Bob, beloved friend, and my "typist," was one of the two dearest men on my earth murdered by their house guest. "The Invited Guest" is about that unholy event. So I come to my question: Would you, would POETRY, accept the complete manuscript of *Under the Lemon Tree* as a gift of appreciation for all the great things you've done for me? I've no one here to leave it to. Do with it anything you wish, or archive it for preservation. Give it a home, if possible. A home for it is what I'm looking for at the moment, since old man Altzheimer seems to be knocking at my door. You've much of it already in your possession — dearest friend — and I'd like you to have the rest. It's a heavy book, Joe, perhaps, for what it's worth.

The *Knoxville News-Sentinel* just called, asking for pictures and an interview about the Lifetime Achievement Award tomorrow (at one past noon). I feel rather sad about it — the word "lifetime" sounds so final. But, I'm heading towards 88, dear Joe. I didn't mind being a sexygenerian, Joe. What, O what, does one do at ninety, become a none-a-generian? I want none of nothing. I'm still a happy man, Joe. But can a man live on happiness?

Please pardon me, all around, Joe. You are one of the few trees in my wood that stand tall.

To: David Rogers, undated

Dear David,

Sorry to be so behind with this project. My eye has not healed as yet. New glasses will be ordered in a few weeks. I still can't see well enough to handle this machine.

But here are the poems, many too many of them: out of voice. Those that are handicapped there might be gathered together under a general caption of "Han-Shan Says." When I began all this, I wasn't planning a book, just writing because I had to write. As I do still, old as I'm becoming. Writing has been one of the two major passions of my life. No, the other isn't sex. It is devotion to family and those I call my own. Teaching might well be a third passion. The elimination of illiteracy in East Tennessee has also the potential of being a passion. For that devotion I was awarded an honorary degree in letters last Saturday by Lincoln Memorial University, an astonishing school compared to what it was when I attended that school for my Bachelor's Degree in 1946–1947. I was much pleased by the award. Saw again the Outdoor Theater where I starred as King Oberon in the spring I graduated. I still know by heart some of the lines of *A Mid-summer's Night Dream*. Hell, I've forgotten the title. I was a passion in run-down hose and a bathrobe! I felt more like the player in the Ass's head. I'm working my balls off in order to get the manuscript in the mail. It's too long, too disjointed, too informed or not at all. Of course, Han-Shan is a mask, a persona, about whom as little is known me, its pretender. But I wanted to give Han-Shan and Shi-Te some kind of recognizable existence outside the poems, which are strong and beautiful, what there is of them. I love what I know of ancient China. Of course what I done is figmental and fanciful. Yesterday, under the persona of Han- I wrote of my own love of trains, equating a train with Dark Pony, about whom which I read a story in my first owned book, a primer with that first metaphor for darkness I ever recognized as analogy.

Included, David, money for the return, which, by all means, do if you don't handle the bundle. It won't affect our relationship, which I treasure, in my way whatsoever. Dark was a little pony who came galloping by after sunset. O god! Buddy, we were young once. Take good care of yourself, David. My friends are most gone now, having passed the vanishing point.

Please keep in touch when you come home.

To: R.T. Smith, 13 August 2004

My dear R.T.:

I, too, have been through hell these last two years In addition to four surgeries, one of them heart, loneliness had driven me almost mad with ineptness from the stroke that robbed me of most of memory for a while, including using the typewriter for months — you'll note that I can't write a fair sentence even now. I've delayed answering your request because of all these matters and a few more personals thrown in. Now an arthritic arm and right shoulder are giving me hell. Both of us outrun poor old Socrates who said before they killed him, "I've prayed enough." Read "prayed" as "suffered." This note is an unholy mess. Forgive me my insufficiencies, dear friend.

If nothing here is sufficient, toss this group [of poems] and ask for more. I am so tired, inept, and bone-weary, dear Heart, it's hard to keep living. I know you live in hell, too. Keep in touch, Buddy. As they say in England, "Keep your pecker up." All my love and support, R.T. Thanks for asking. My arm is hurting like hell, as we say here in Tennessee.

Letters to Mother, Hitt, and Oprah

A number of letters — such as the ones that follow — offer a closer glimpse at Scarbrough's personality and writing skills: his concern with family issues in the first of two long missives to his mother, and his ability at creating detailed prose in the second when Scabrough describes his passage to Europe, and his experiences in France when he was sent to teach for the military in 1952. The final two letters tap into the poet's sense of humor through peculiar manipulation of language. The correspondence with Jack Hitt was in response to a request from *Harper's* Senior Editor to "numerous speakers of the English language to coin a new word for a meaning they thought was missing from everyone's desktop *Webster's*." Scarbrough apparently took the idea as a challenge. The letter to Oprah Winfrey was in response to her television show, but again exhibits rhetoric tested to its limits.

Ten. A Selection of Scarbrough's Letters

******

May 12, 1943 [University of the South, Sewanee]
Dearest Mother,

    This finds me in a very undecided frame of mind. I don't know what to do, or where to turn. For some time, I have been trying to land a job, teaching; but as yet have had no success. And I wonder if I should be satisfied, if I did. You see, if I drop the scholarship here [Sewanee], there is no indication that I will ever get it back again. And in case I did drop it, I'd hardly earn the thousand dollars they're giving me here. I wonder about going to school in the summer. I could get a half-year from July to the first of November, as we are running full-time now; and if by that time, things are no better I would drop out and find a job. Now is an opportunity, an opportunity when I would not be able to do a lot of hard work, and taking it would mean a lot, but I want Kim to have his opportunity also. Mother, tell me honestly, will it be possible for Kim to start high school if I don't get a job this summer? Now you can say what you think—you know that. There is no one whose interest is more mine than Luppy's and Kim's. They are my boys, and I am only trying to accomplish more for their sake, whatever the rest of the family think. With a degree, I could settle down to college teaching, and send them on. I wouldn't get rich, of course, but it would be a fairly steady and comfortable living. But I'd much rather stop now and go to work—and I shall—if Kim cannot start his high school in September. This is why I want to know. Tell me, Mom, if you have ever spoken frankly; for I would hate to get in the middle of another semester and have to stop, because Kim did not go when school opened. He has to go. I can always come back. I can graduate in three summer school sessions. And you know how most of the family have been. A little delay, and no go. A year lost for Kim might mean his whole education lost. If I could get him into St. Andrews, a prep school two miles from me, free of charge, might I have him up here on the Mountain, I could see him every other day, he would be taken care of by the fatherly men of the church, would get some excellent training, and on the whole the associations with the boys would be good. Do tell me these things. Because you know I love him and Luppy, and want to have the best for them; even tho it may seem I am trying to get ahead myself. Of course, I know you and Dad understand. But judging from a letter I had from Pete, he doesn't. He says to "Tell Bill to look out for Dad and Mom and the boys. I suppose you will be going to school all the time. You know I can't do two things at one time." That hurt a little, perhaps because I know I had not done anything for you and Pop. God knows, I am trying; if it is too late when I arrived, there will be small comfort in the fact that I stuck.

    Lyle says to stay here, the boys say to stay here if possible, the professors say the same. One of the instructors suggested that I borrow the money to keep Kim in school for next year, saying that such a procedure would be wisest. I can't ask Pleasant to buy his books, or clothes; I couldn't ask Pete, as someone suggested. That would be a confession on my part, so far as they are concerned, of the failure of all this schooling. I might say that if the breaks had been with me, I should have finished long ago, but that is not true. The breaks have been with me. I have been extremely fortunate. Not long ago, I had *Thomas Wolfe's Letter to His Mother*, a book which you must read when I get home, for review, and I feel the frustration that he felt, when he stood up and tried for self-justification against circumstances and the members of his family who criticized him for the money he spent, when they themselves had had no chance at an education. But I suppose a man must make his own decisions, though I don't seem to be having much of success at doing so.

When you answer this letter, read it carefully, answering every question I have asked, Mom. For I must have answers, answers, answers. Don't start a new letter, as if I had never written one. Ask Dad what he thinks. Though he must have given my case up long ago, not understanding this long wait before I accomplish anything. I wish I might be there and talk face to face with you; we get more done that way. Whatever your decision, Mom, you and Dad, remember I am perfectly willing to abide by it, without reluctance. Kim and Luppy are my main interests here. I have the foundation; theirs must not be neglected.

Sunday, a friend, Maury Eby, and I are going to hold an old-fashioned sing for the colored people at St. Mark's Church. We are singing "Love Lifted Me," "When the Roll Is Called Up Yonder," "In the Garden," "Swing Low Sweet Chariot," etc. Songs that the negro heart loves; not the stilted, awful things the Episcopal Church terms hymns. For some reason, I am reminded of Mindy, who stood up for a hymnal one day in church at Muddy Ford! Poor old Mindy! I wonder if she's still alive.

Sunday last, Jimmy Sherrill, a young thirteen year old from the Village, and a very dear child to me, and I went hiking. Along with us, went Edward Hawkins, another thirteen year old who loves snakes, eats rattlesnakes. That's the kind of men we grow — when we bite a rattlesnake, he dies! Anyway, we had a wonderful time, though I was exhausted. We found a yellow lady-slipper, or moccasin flower, the first I had ever seen. It was like a spot of gold against the green. It was alone. No others grew near it. In the top of the flower was an opening, like the opening into a Dutch shoe, exactly. I could readily see why it was called a lady-slipper. There are more of the pink variety than of the yellow; though the mountain people, here as elsewhere, have almost destroyed it entirely by careless picking. It will not stand being pulled. Trailing arbutus is very rare also.

I have a close friend, Edward Peebles, who is a bird lover, and he and I have many pleasant hours together. He paints, loves good music, etc.

Is a rather amazing person altogether. The other night something strange and exciting happened. You remember the cocoon we took away from the jay-bird last year? Well, it lay around all year on my windowsill; and though I inspected him occasionally, he didn't seem to be coming on. He did grow more defined and darker, however. Well, night before last, I got to bed late, being rather tired after my hike. About four o'clock in the morning, I heard a frenzied beating of wings in the room. Ha, I thought, my bug is out. I got up, turned on the light, looked behind a photograph to see if he really had. An there he was, wet and wrinkled, hanging to the support of the picture. But it was not he who was making the noise. Four other huge cecropias were beating themselves to pieces trying to get in at the window. It was a strange sight. I opened my window and in they came, paying not one bit of attention to the wet one on the photo, but flying around the room frantically, in a constant beating and wearing of themselves against the walls. It was all probably a part of the mating instinct, or possibly group instinct. I don't know. And I haven't had a chance to ask Dr. McCrady, the biology teacher here, about them yet. Anyway I went upstairs and asked Ed if he wanted to see something strange. He hopped out of bed instantly and came down. We sat up until seven, watching the antics of these night creatures. They lit on our heads, on our clothes, and one even stayed on my nose for a long, ticklish time. I wish you could have seen it. After a bit, the visitors flew out doors and away, and we put the wet one on a limb outside the window, where he was still sitting at eight that night. I never suspected that rescuing a dinner from a jay would result in such a display of the mysterious forces at work in nature, forces right under our noses and of which we are tremendously unaware.

Letters have gone to Spencer, to Pleasant, and to others. Writing is something I am not so hot at, but I manage to keep a few on the wing.

Answer when you have time, and be sure to give me what I asked for.

Lovingly,

George

******

September 5, 1952

My dearest Mother,

At last I have found a machine on which to write you in detail of the adventure thus far: When Bill left me at the train in Athens, I found that it would be some two hours late, and that did not seem to be too auspicious a beginning. But not being a man who believes too much in signs, I took it rather equably. Had I known a little of that which was to follow, I perhaps had not been so complacent about signs. The trip to Memphis was tame, passing without mishap. I arrived there at 8:30 in the morning, went directly to Mallory at 3300 Jackson, was processed and sworn in. Then I picked up my bags at the train station, called Jess Perkinson, this Memphis friend of mine whom you know about, checked in at the YMCA, and went out to Jess' house for a good supper and fun with the kids. I must tell you about his little Lula who is two years old another time. About ten o'clock, Jess took me back to the YMCA, and from there I went by limousine to the airport which is located some distance out in the country. At 12:20, we were airborne for Washington, New York, and Springfield, Massachusetts. Washington, New York, and Springfield happened without any unusual incidents. I refused breakfast on the plane, thinking, in my Scotch way, that I would have to pay extra. I was chagrined when I found out later that it was included with fare. Anyway, I had breakfast in New York, because alarmed about my baggage when the porter told me it had missed the plane; later, however, I found that it had been put aboard the Springfield plane, having been marked for shipment all the way. Then on to Bradley Field outside Springfield by bus, we went to Westover Air Base. And There!

No passport for any teacher. We waited without anything to do for days on end before Washington discovered that eight teachers' passports had been sent to Travis Field in California. We waited again. The eight came. Mine was not among them. The eight lucky teachers flew. Two others and I waited. Finally Washington found ours in Fort Hamilton, New York, long after I had begun to suspect that the government was not going to allow me to leave the dear old USA. But days later, our passports came, and we too started to Europe.

Flying is wonderful the first one hundred hours; after that, there comes a lull in the loving. We flew to the Azores — islands of the hawks — in twelve hours, landed there in Mae Wests — life jackets in case the plane has to ditch — take the water, since the runway is so close that the moment the plane leaves the strip it is over the ocean, and the critical time in flying is landing and take-off; anything can happen to the engines. These mid–Atlantic islands were viewed only briefly, as we landed at night and left in the early morning; it was easy to see that the sea around them is rough; it is filled with barracuda, sharks, too, and the passengers were given packages of shark-repeller, in case we were dumped in the ocean. The barracuda can take off a man's leg at one bite! A colored soldier told us all about it, had made the lad who was going to the Azores to work so nervous he was biting his fingers. Me? I wasn't nervous. I just screamed a couple of times, and called it laughing. Nothing happened though; we landed and took off safely, so far as I could see; though someone said later we had a gasoline leak clear across the Atlantic. The Portuguese inhabitants in the Azores are very dark and dangerous-looking people. My Southern background at work again, no doubt. We suspect everybody who doesn't look and act as we do.

From the Azores, we flew directly to Frankfurt, Germany, coming in over the coast of France, the most beautiful country I have ever seen.

Ten. A Selection of Scarbrough's Letters

Below us the farms looked like immaculate gardens, each farm having its well-defined and colorful patches, bordered by the famous hedges the French maintain around their plots. The highways and rivers were like ribbons across the countryside. It was beautiful. Germany came next with her well-kept farms, but no hedges; the country was lovely, too, but barer. The forests were in large tracts that stood out from the naked countryside with a blackness that called to mind the Schwarzwald , the famous German Black Forest. On the ground, I could see that these forests were as well-kept as parks, and that every odd, untilled acre was planted to little forests, some of the young trees still only about six inches high. As yet I have not seen a French woodland up close. We landed at Rhein-Main, went by truck into Frankfurt, after I found out from American authorities that I had no business in Germany, having no visa for visiting that country; but they turned me in anyway. Washington balling things up again. Luckily nobody asked me for my passport, or I would have been jailed and deported! The worst they could have done would have been to turn me over to American military authorities, and it was the Americans who had turned me in! Frankfurt was interesting, about half in ruins from the last war; the countryside smelled of rotten cabbage, the people smelled of beer and fat sausages and looked moping melancholy mad. GI's were on the Saturday night rampage, obscenities were flying, as they always do in the vicinity of American GI's, whether they are in Frankfurt, Paris, or New York, and the Germans were using choice American phrases the meaning of which, I am sure, was entirely lost to them.

Incidentally, I made something of an ass of myself too. When the porter carted our luggage across the street to the hotel where we were to spend the night, he dumped mine, and mine only, three times in the muck and mire. He would load them up, push three yards, and dump them again. My best bag was already ruined anyhow, and he wasn't helping it any. It has a hole clear through to the lining now. Anyhow, a German hausfrau stopped to laugh rather spitefully I thought at the high and mighty American who was angry because his expensive luggage was being maltreated. I tipped the old boy fifty cents, though, saying he shouldn't have anything, wherein I made an ass of myself. I don't like tipping; that is what hurts. But the truth is that here such people as waiters, porters, ushers in movies, et cetera, do not get any salary; they live entirely off what foreigners mostly will give them for the services they do. In America, of course, things are vastly different; it is not so necessary to tip, since our people in the same situation have a small salary anyway.

He finally got my bags to the hotel, as I said, and that was that. Mazie, the Michigan country girl who came in on the plane with me, and I decided to see a bit of Frankfurt. We walked several blocks, but when a sotted GI embraced her in the street, I thought it time to take Mazie home. I saw very little of Germany, for I left the next day, the officials getting me out as fast as they could for fear some question would be raised concerning the legality of my being in that country. We flew to Paris Sunday evening, getting into Orly Field about nine o'clock. We had seen Paris from the air by daylight, and now we saw it at night; the town lovely both ways. The military took us to the Hotel Littre in Paris where we were to be quartered until processed and told where to go. Monday was Labor Day, and all offices at Orly were closed. I took the day in Paris. Astounding city, loveliest I know; filled with trees, ablaze with flowers, spacious with broad boulevards, statue-filled, scattered with parks, arches, and the world's most beautiful bridges over the Seine. I visited the Arc de Triomphe, where France's unknown soldier lies flower-surrounded, guarded by a gendarme, and lighted with an open flame that is never allowed to die; then I went down the Champs de Elysees, Paris' most famous street, to the Tuileries, breath-taking gardens, to the Louvre, famous art gallery and museum. On the way I had stopped to see Pont Alexander III, a beautiful bridge, and had seen the Eiffel Tower, a regular monstrosity towering over Paris. Why the city doesn't tear it down, I'll never know. The Louvre is housed in the palace of Marie Antoinette, famous French queen. I saw the Regent Diamond and da Vinci's "Mona Lisa" among a million other things. Wonderful, wonderful. Then home to bed. Tuesday I went out to Orly Field again — this was September 3, I had been there early Monday morning too, but got no help. Tuesday I was told to report to Number 17 Rue de La Perousse to be directed. Back to Paris I went, and to Rue la Perousse. There I was told that I was to be sent to Nancy, an old town in northeast France to organize a grammar school. I objected, saying that I was hired as a high school teacher; Mr. Estop, the director, said it made no difference. So we were slated to start to Nancy the next day, two of us for the school there.

Since I had nothing else to do, and Mr. Estop didn't speak French at all, he asked me to go to number 67 Rue de Tocqueville and have his car repaired. I was to go to an auto garage, find a man, bring him to 67, et cetera. Imagine, I had the French girl in the office asking someone to help me with the car. I know now that I should have said "Voulez-vous reparer ma voiture?" As simple as that. But I didn't know then. I can say now: "Voulez-vous reparer ma pneu avant gauche," which means, Will you repair my left front tire? But I didn't know then. It has been such fun learning. Anyway, I found the garage, made my wishes known, and was immediately taken in hand by the owner who proceeded to teach me the French words for about everything in sight. He and his young assistant, a boy who wore some ballet slippers and moved like a dancer, went with me, removed the tire, which I could have done myself, put on the spare, were paid, and went away. Then I remembered that I should have had the old tube repaired, so Mr. Estop would have a spare. So back I went. Everybody looked surprised. I explained. Everybody looked amused. I said, "Pessez-vous les Americain sont malade a la tete?" Meaning, Do you think Americans are crazy in the head? The owner grinned and said, "Oui, oui," meaning Yes, Yes! Anyway, we got the pneu-pardonnez-moi, mama. I mean tire fixed, and the owner took me to café and bought me a small glass of cognac, which kicks like a mule. Wow! Anyway, I spent six hundred francs — about two dollars — of Mr. Estop's money, including tips. Too much, I guess, though he didn't say anything. I had made another ass of myself, this time with the French. They not only thought I was giddy, but rich, and terribly American, I'm afraid.

I took dinner with Mr. Estop and had a wonderful time in his apartment. He drove me home later to the Hotel Littre. And so to bed.

We left Paris the next day. Everything was in such an uproar, taxi arriving, tipping which has to be figured for the lad who insists on carrying the bags, etc., that I forgot to pay my bill. The third ass I made of myself, this time with the American military. I owe them two dollars, or 700 francs which is the same thing. I shall be sent to Siberia, doubtless.

When we arrived in the communist-ridden, god-forsaken French city of Toul, there was no one to meet us. En route, though, we had come across another of our teachers who could speak fair French, and she went into the station and called the Air Base, and was told that the representative was twenty-five miles away in Nancy, waiting for us. O me! The base sent another driver for us, and we were away again over the countryside, the poorest section, however, we had to turn in the old tickets we had purchased in Paris. In France you get off the train inside a high-fenced, well-guarded area, and you are kept there until the tickets are produced. Luckily, I hadn't thrown ours away — I usually do. The big iron gate swung back and we were free, or some thought. Reminds me of the 200 francs I paid for a book of tickets in Paris, used one, and threw the others away. I should have had twenty rides; instead, out of ignorance, I got one. O well. I know better the next time. You simply have to learn by doing. And we have been left a great deal to do for ourselves, which has helped me immensely in controlling the situation. I wouldn't take anything for the experiences. On the street-bus in Paris, however, two housewives who looked upon me as an innocent foreign lamb, jumped the conductor when he charged me three hundred instead of two hundred francs, smiled, patted me almost, and told me to beware. C'est deux cent francs! It is only two hundred francs!

Most amazing thing in Paris is, that despite Pasteur, the French have seemingly never heard of germs. They go about the streets using their long loaves of bread something like walking canes. They don't deliberately touch it to the ground, but wouldn't mind if they did. Funny sight: a young boy riding his bicycle with two huge collars of bread stuck one on each handle-bar, brown, delicious-looking, and unwrapped. Of course, it is the most delicious bread in the world. People eat plain bread on the streets. The young university student, French, who shared our compartment on the train when we came to Nancy, ate only a large chunk of bread for her lunch. We Americans went forward to the expensive dining car for a wonderful French meal, poached eggs and rice — oeuf poche de l'indiene — some kind of meat, wonderful potatoes cooked with garlic, lettuce delicious with sauce, cheese, coffee, large bunches of grapes. The French really know how to eat.

Well, we got to Nancy to find that as high school teachers they did not want us; they wanted grammar school instructors. We are still here, waiting to find what is to become with us. Maybe we'll be sent to Germany, England, or even back home. The truth of the matter is that somebody hired far too many teachers for this area, and we were told yesterday that somebody would have to be sent home. Who will be, nobody knows. Meantime, we draw a good salary and are having a nice vacation. I think we'll be placed somewhere, because the government is very embarrassed by the situation it has got itself into. We may not be moved for days yet though. It wouldn't be so bad to be returned to the states. We'd get a long vacation in Europe for nothing, being paid all the time as well. Who could ask for anything better. As I said, I don't think the government will send us back, though I may go to England. At least, I have asked to be transferred there, if possible.

Mother, this machine is no good. Perhaps you can read this. Anyway, please keep the record. I'll need it later. Our contracts here are only for the school year. So it looks like I'll be back in the states about the time I usually get out of school. I'll be sending you some money the first check, Mother, which should come at the beginning of the week. You need a stove; start paying on one. I'll be able to send about $150 perhaps. Keep fifty for yourself, put fifty on part-time payment for a stove, and have Bill pay fifty on the note at the bank. We'll make it all right, I guess, when we get started, though prices here in France are ridiculous. Prices are one reason I should like to get out of here. Germany is very inexpensive.

Kiss all my boys and girls, especially my boy. God bless him. To see little French boys and girls here makes me know that we are all indeed no more or less than humanity. Little French boys particularly amuse me. They seem to be eight, nine, ten years of age, maybe older, and they hold Mama's hand and nuzzle her shoulders with affectionate nose right on the street. They are lovely little fellows.

Don't write me here, as I may be moved to England.

All my love,

George

******

February 24, 1991
Dear Mr. Hitt:

Your letter pleased me since it was right up my valley. I'm a word-person incurably, and my books, so far, have been serious books. There is not one neologism in my latest, *Invitation to Kim*, Pulitzer nomination in verse for 1990. But, for all the seriousness, I like to off-color in my verbal games. This is not to say that my journals, already in place at the Memphis publisher's establishment, are not filled with inventions. They are but are not immediately available to me. So, foot in mouth, I jot down a few I've contrived within the past forty-eight hours, in hope you will find some of them amusing if none of them usable. Remember, I'm from East Tennessee, and keep in mind that if anything here pleases, I'll be glad to send you a further batch.

Grooms' Wedding — no derivation needed: the wedding of two males. It was the most manly grooms' wedding to date — not a female in sight.
Pristine Christine — an old maid virgin: no obsolete. Poor Pristine Christine — looks so forlorn at her friend's prenuptial shower.
Auto-de-fay — a limp-wristed car salesman. I bought my Chevy from auto-de-fay.
Prickly Pear — gay couple. I met this wonderful prickly pear at the concert last night. (Male obviously.)
Arrow Smith — penile surgeon. I went to this arrow smith who thought he might be able to take the crook out of things.
Hell-Spouter — fundamentalist preacher. Make your own sentence.
Homofactualist — Kinsey. No sentence necessary.
Twig-Bender — Madame's fastest moneymaker. As soon as her man's inclined, the twig is bent.
Limber-Member — an older man. He's the only limber-member in our club.
Sad Sadie — a real bust but not breastwise. No sentence necessary.
Breast-Wise — knows where his mouth is; a nipple-nibbler.
Body merchants — see dictators, presidents, madams, and undertakers.
Spigot-bigot — a male chauvinist.
Mow-Mow — a two-faced person. She's president of the mow-mow club.
Janus syndrome — afflicted by a two-way game; two-faced.
Stem-Stasis — impotence. I hear he suffers from stem-statis.
Ripped rivet — loose connection. The man has a ripped rivet or I miss my guess.
Run in the sock — varicose veins. She has too many runs in the sock for my taste.
Sad Sexualist — a mournful fucker. No sentence necessary.
Defrank — to make sex change; emasculate. We call him Frances now that he's been defranked.
Bussboy — ass kisser. He's bussboyed his way to the top in his firm. (I like the hint of levitation here.)
Letterhead — an intolerable academic, as in any university department. Choose your favorite.
Dematurate — to render childish. One drink dematurates him to gooing and gurgling.

Irrespond — to respond irresponsibly. Youth nowadays is not irresponding, only responding as it has to.
Root-Ruckus — sex orgy. We had a real root ruckus this past weekend.
Cod-Curdler — an ugly woman. No sentence necessary.
Turd-Head — One who can't think for shit.
Turd-Cake — supremest confection of its kind. He's the perfect recipe for a turd-cake.
Idolized — to render impotent. She's had three husbands and idolized them all.
Tongue and Tassel — lingus and lingam. Yes, I protested the measure and shall continue protesting as long as I have tongue and tassel. (The courage of one's convictions.)
Cap of the Turd Stack — top dog in the corporation. My grandfather's expression.
Ferk — a fucking jerk. Polite usage.
Minimock — an imitation meant to amuse not hurt. He made me a minimock.
Maximock — an apeing intended to devastate. Sentence likewise.
Helevate — opposite of elevate. Helevation is something the preacher is good at.
Nipple-Pivoter — a titty-twirler. No sentence needed.

I won't apologize for this crud. When your letter came, I was "off my typewriter," and unhappy about it, and glad to have this opportunity to vent the spleen that often backs up to my Adam's apple. As you see I've no great respect for the human species, of which some allow I make one. Others disqualify me without reservation. My family's genius lay in puns and rhymes. My brother's bawdy taught me more about "poetry" than any master of the subject at the university. Seventeenth Century England, Scotland, and Ireland furnished our basic speech and speech-appreciation.

If any of this stuff is less than nauseating, and you wish another batch, as I've said, let me know. Glad to know you're there.

Cordially,

George Scarbrough

******

October 1, 1990
My dear Oprah,

I enjoy your show but am occasionally infuriated by it, particularly on those days when the old man-woman tussle is being discussed. May I say that women who drain a man physically, financially, morally, and spiritually, cast him off (all the while howling for child support from the poor devil), and put themselves up as being personally superior to all things male should be deprived of the children and sterilized forthwith to prevent the same old tired cycle from being run again?

Reading a book I've just bought on the subject of reptiles, I find that some lizards are parthenogenetic, producing viable offspring from eggs unfertilized by males, and think, ah ha, that would solve the old male-female bickering and put an end to the Oprah Show. And, of course, to all the soaps, and possibly to the human race as well, which event, as I see it, would be no great catastrophe to the world. Unisexuality is an interesting topic, and one that prompts theories as to the manner in which it may have begun, including the rather edenic one that all female forms arise by way of mutation. That over the protests of women, of course. But perhaps not. In most cases, however they got here, a high percentage of women might prefer having their own children without male interference, particularly if virgin birth were subsidized. Ah, there's the rub, the one great argument against unisexuality. Men have always brought home the dinosaur bacon for the family, up to now. The times they are a-changing, however. The conditions and prospects for parthenogenesis are looking up. A brighter future for us males may be predicted, and so double the fun, with each other of course. Who says there are no solutions?

Good health to you, Oprah. You've aired a few closets for us all.

Very cordially,

George

(I am a writer, Oprah. My last book, *Invitation to Kim*, was a Pulitzer Prize nomination for 1990. This is to let you know I am not a "nut" from the atomic piles of this city.)

Eleven

A Selection of Letters to Scarbrough

Spanning four decades, the following correspondence is a sampling of the many literary greats with whom George Scarbrough communicated over the years. In some instances, the entire letters — which are housed in the archives at the University of the South's duPont Library — are reprinted here; in other cases, only excerpts of pertinent commentary. The correspondence included was penned by William Alexander Percy, John Crowe Ransom, Jesse Stuart, former *Sewanee Review* editor William Knickerbocker, William Goyen, Andrew Lytle, James Dickey, Wendell Berry, Allen Tate, Charles Edward Eaton, and Marilou Awiakta. The texts, aside from grouping according to authorship in multiple letters, are presented in chronological order.

June 23, 1941
Dear Mr. Scarbrough:
    You are very kind to have written me so cordially about my *Lanterns on the Levee* and I am glad you found some merit in it.
    I shall look forward to receiving your poems. As I wrote Mr. Kilvington, the first batch I saw in the *Sewanee Review* impressed me very much.
    Your interest in my religious chapter encourages me. I certainly didn't want to shake anyone's faith when it's fixed, no matter what it is, but I hope this chapter might help those whose ideas were in flux and flow at least to escape atheism.
    I'm delighted you are going to Sewanee and hope you are not disappointed. If I am on the Mountain during term time, I shall certainly try to find you. If successful, I hope you will correct me on anything I might have said about sharecroppers and sharecropping system. I spoke truthfully and accurately as far as I know the facts, but those facts were probably only true in the Delta and of negro sharecroppers. The whole

problem of land tenure is a very troublesome one and I'm not completely satisfied with my own conclusions and would welcome any light I can get on the subject.

More power to you and don't bother about being too honest. The only person you have to live with all your life is yourself, a pretty bum companion without honesty.

Sincerely,

W.A. Percy

******

December 7, 1943

Dear Mr. Scarbrough:

Please do not think my terrible procrastination in acknowledging these poems has any critical significance. I apologize most sincerely.

Poems like these are the hardest to deal with. They rate some careful critical remarks. They are almost what one wants to publish. You have advanced very far from the point where you began in poetry, if I am not mistaken; and way so very far indeed. But I don't think you need advice, or that I have any. I'd just like to see you continue advancing, by ways which I won't try to predict.

Sincerely yours,

John C. Ransom

******

February 27 (year not noted)

Dear Mr. Scarbrough:

I think you've come a long way. The Unicorn poem is a pretty good metaphysical one though not as homely and specific in its action and detail as the 17th C. people had it. The Strict Hunt one is good and seems too much like an attempt at murder TV movie. The Death of Lovely Humans is a good application of Dylan Thomas' fine oral methods. The Mississippi Romantic is a character sketch, keen. The Pictures one quite good.

In general, you seem to me a romantic, and that connotes a little of logical vagueness, and making a Greek exhibition of a special personal effect in some way. I believe you've got to subdue the romantic a good deal further. It's a matter of themes and of treatment too. But you have really acquired a lot of technical power.

Maybe this doesn't reach you, it's poorly said. But your reader feels, I think, that a sensibility behind these poems quivers too much; that it is not toughened and matured.

I wish you all the best in your very actual and serious progress with this difficult art.

Sincerely,

John C. Ransom

******

January 9, 1941

Dear George Scarbrough:

Just one more thing I want to mention to you. You are an Agrarian in practice. You are truly an Agrarian. You are not an Agrarian of "sweet theory," not one that talks it and doesn't know anything about making a living from the soil. You are the true Agrarian that knows the earth, seedtime, growth and harvest. I hope you never lose this firm foundation.

And strange to say that one Agrarian I know (Agrarian so called — in sweet theory and practice) would dismiss your poetry. It's wouldn't be poetry to him. How metaphysical (so called) poetry and Agrarianism can go together, I cannot understand. Nor can I understand how any honest-to-goodness man of the soil would give a damn about metaphysical poetry.

I hope you continue to write, that you write poems like "Dark Hester"— poems with a piece of the heart in them as you promise to write in the future. You can judge poets by the type of poetry they write. When it comes to farmers writing metaphysical poetry, I have to laugh and laugh damned loud.

My best wishes to you always. I hope to hear plenty about you in the future.

Yours very sincerely,

Jesse Stuart

******

March 26, 1941

Dear George Scarbrough:

I am glad you liked *Men of the Mountains*. I would love to see your review. I have not seen a single review of that book. You know from Feb. 6 until March 9 I was on the road. I traveled with my wife 4,000 miles — gave eight talks. Four were given at the University of Miami Florida — then we drove on down to Key West — over 146 miles of highway that separates the Gulf of Mexico and the Atlantic Ocean. It was a highway that went from Key to Key — from island to island. After this trip we were so tired out; yet I had about an eight hundred mile trip and three talks to make and six days for the trip. I took my typewriter and wrote three articles and two short stories and one poem and gave the three talks. Now I am back home working on the farm. We don't have a radio; we don't take a newspaper. On this trip I had forgotten that my book was published and was reminded at Heidelberg College the evening I gave a talk there that was its publication date and they had copies for sale which I autographed.

Now *Beyond Dark Hills* was written for a term paper at Vanderbilt. I never passed the course. I don't know what to tell you about college. You perhaps will like it and it will be good for you. But I don't know where to tell you to go. Just don't accept too much of the University's polish and so on if you want to write. You don't get material at college. You get it right there in those Tennessee mountains and in your struggle with the elements to make your bread to eat. You get life by living life and don't let anyone tell you differently. College instructors may help you go put your work in shape and tell you where to send it. I got a lot of help in college. Now you make your own decision.

Another thing George Scarbrough, you keep your feet on the ground and always keep a reserve in the back of your head that others don't know about. Never let them know it. Keep something for yourself. Don't be shoved around and don't be a joiner of clubs and so on. I can give you this information because I know. Be yourself always and whatever there is in you will gradually find its way. Instead of your pulling to the others let them pull to you. You may join this and that and later kick over the trace-chains. Now for the tea, if it is well made I can drink guzzle it. I can really put it away. But the trouble is so many women don't know how to make it. It takes the English to make tea. I usually drank sixteen cups of tea per day in England. You can't get coffee over there that is any good and the tobacco is rotten.

Keep your poetry close to the earth too for you belong there. Let it be soil poetry for you are a man of the soil. And if your MS [manuscript] is turned down — well, what of it? You won't be the first man that ever had a MS turned down. I never give advice but you are so damn close to my own situation I have just said these things to you. Love people but, damn it, you be leery. You watch your step for many a young author with great possibilities has been ruined by the damned so-called elite — people that dilly-dally before a comfortable fire and discuss democracy — afraid to dirty their own soft hands and they don't know what Democracy is all about. Put them out to work and they would faint in their tracks. All for this time. Send me that review. Many thanks. And write me when the spirit moves you.

Sincerely,

Jesse Stuart

******

November 24, 1947

Dear George:

You will hear from Duttons. You will also get a contract to sign. I can almost tell you in advance about the contract. They will ask you for an option on your next three books. And, of course, they are interested in a novel. If you write a novel, they will be pleased. Again, if you write a novel, I would try to have it written so it could be published in 1949 so there won't be too long a lapse between the publication of your poetry and novel. This is just a suggestion.

Now about something else. You said in your letter "even if it were published in autumn of 1948," meaning that was a long way off. Let me tell you something. Duttons publishes two books of poems each year. That in 1948. Another thing, it was a year or longer after *Bull-Tongue Plow* was accepted before it was published. And you are fortunate to get it published within one year after acceptance. That is certainly true with Duttons for they have books accepted and ready for publication from the present until 1951. Many magazines are made up six months in advance. I wanted to tell you these things for this publishing game is a very strange one. It is a very difficult one now. It is really something to get a book of poetry accepted. Remember one thing, it has to be good, have plenty of merit and show promise. So, this to you George, should be a consolation.

I had three meetings with Duttons editors and the publisher. I can't tell you all that happened. Not until I see you again. Then I will tell you in detail the whole process. Louise Townsend Nicholl (she had had four books of poetry published and is a Dutton editor) and I battled for this book's acceptance and for its publication in 1948. They wanted to publish it in 1949. Your poems are excellent, George. And acceptance couldn't have come in a better time when you, Glennis, your brother and friends were altogether in Oak Ridge. I sent you one letter that was returned to me. I sent it again but to Glennis at LMU to forward on to you. I didn't know she was down there at the time.

Among the poems was the one about the man who owned the land. His returning. Skillfully done. Beautiful. The poem to me, I appreciate. Duttons wanted to use that in front of the book but I objected. I said leave it over in the book. I was afraid of reviewers. Reviewers can be a little prone to connect a young author with an older one. I wanted this book to be accepted on its own merit, reviewed on its own merit. Because this book can and will stand alone. I wouldn't write a forward for the same reason. For when I wrote the forward for Byron Reece's book, several reviewers reviewed me instead of Byron Reece. So, I didn't want this to happen again. But I had a feeling after I had met you and asked you to send me these poems, Glennis suggested it too, that I would take them directly to a publisher myself. If Duttons hadn't taken them I would have gone to Scribners. I told them so. I had the feeling they would be accepted. So it happened. And this is something, believe me! I am glad you rejoiced. You should. It's perfectly normal to rejoice when something like this happens. Glennis will be home this week and I'll get the details of what happened in Oak Ridge and I will tell her what happened in New York. Best of luck, George. Oh yes, if you do more good poems between now and publication send them to Duttons too and let them be included in the collection. Your title is not a good one nor the right one. But this is a simple matter. A title can be found.

Sincerely,

Jesse Stuart

******

Eleven. A Selection of Letters to Scarbrough

September 3, 1942
Dear George:

Thanks for your kind letter of August 25 which I shall preserve as a relic of the last vivid reminder of the Sewanee phase of my life — a place of strain, sacrifice, humiliation, and long-suffering. I never thought of you as you signed yourself at the end of your letter — namely, as my "hopelessly incompetent office boy." While you stood by nobly and helped out in a dreadful year, I wanted you to regard your assignment in my office as a "token" — to use one of the over-used words of Mr. Guerry.

All this was in my mind during our brief year together as friends in Sewanee. I am sorry that it was so but I was helpless. You recall that when we were cleaning up the office you announced you would not return to Sewanee: I urged you to revise your decision and to return: I am happy to know that you will return and breathe again the clean, pure spiritual atmosphere of a place which not even Mr. Guerry can dispel. The place needs a poet: and you are he. You have a pure heart, you have not lifted up your eyes to vanity, nor sworn deceitfully. Keep your vision clear, fulfill the thrust of your genius, listen to what others may say about your art, but remain strong in your faith in your own gift and bravely stalk the highlands of your soul knowing that you must, in the last analysis, do what you — and you alone — think is right.

I had heard that you had a heart attack during the summer but you did not mention this in your letter. I could not write you because I was too mentally disturbed by Mr. Guerry's cruel treatment of me. I have written to no one at Sewanee since I left; and I should not be writing this had you not written me in so friendly and kind a spirit. I was deeply touched by your words. When I learned that you had been stricken, my emotions were too strong: I felt that you knew I admire you and your work and that, even if I did not write, my thoughts were upon you. This you will please remember. Among all the unseen readers of your verse you may can always count me, for I shall follow the unfolding of your heart in words as they appear in print, and will find in them fertilizing power for my own life.

I am glad you are returning to Sewanee. Sewanee has deep secrets which only the poetic could may discern. You will find them in the landscape of the plateau there and in the hearts of truly dedicated souls there. I am sorry not to be with you there next year but some time, some where, we will be seeing each other again. God bless and reward you for your faithfulness to your vision.

Cordially yours,
William Knickerbocker

******

September 1, 1955
Dear George Scarbrough:

 Thank you for the cheerful letter and I meant long since to answer it, but a rather disastrous summer has demolished my sense of time and incident. Will it ever end, summer? I hold this one no love anyway. I was grateful for your letter and was sorry we missed meeting. I had, I guess, just left for this city where I anticipated a number of good things and found few or none. I wish you had met Ted and Sylvia Brown, or had come a few days earlier. It will happen again.

 I'm glad about what you say about my work, glad to have your friendship. I'm learning more, forgetting less, and not content. The more you have to say, the harder it is to say it, later a time maybe to be lucid gasps of awe and astonishment, or just of laughter — or pain. Anyway — let me hear sometime again; I'm here and there, but use Random House's address — that's more permanent (or is it?) — a serious writer is a hound on the road these days. I still don't care. But I care about hearing from my friends and I'm glad you're one. I'll look for your poems. Please send me the new volume, won't you? Good luck and pleasure in your teaching. Is it? I believe you are a good one. I wish you good work and happiness — and thanks again for writing.

Cordially,

Bill Goyen

******

November 12, 1959
Dear Mr. Scarbrough —

 A knot head then, a knot head now. I still profess to profess at dear Old Rutgers. And still profess that 5 good poets is a better audience than 5,000 school teachers. I fact I've spoken to at least 20,000 teachers and 20 poets in the last four months, and swear the ratio holds.

 This one poet, at least, is more grateful than any 1,000 teachers for "Cradle Gift." I'm delighted to have it for SR [*Saturday Review*]. Sometime in the next 47 months our creaking routines will get it into print and you will then receive a pittance for it.

Yours,

John Ciardi

******

September 3, 1963
Dear Scarbrough:

 I really think you are a new voice, as far as verse is concerned. I can't publish everything you send me, but I am going to do my best to publish a lot of it. I don't believe "Die Brader Grimm" is in its final version, so I am returning it. I like "Good Friday" very much. You have two images of immortality or the divine: the fish and the doe. And you also have the antelope, which, so far as I know, has no such mythological meaning as the doe. Very likely, since the poem is done in New Mexico, it does have for the Indians. I am not quite sure that you unite, in the structure of the father-son relationship, these three parallel images. Let me think about it, and will you also look that over?

It may be the holiday confusion; but in Part II, Stanza 1 (the first part of which is magnificent), I am a little confused about the boy's blood and the doe. I think, without losing anything, you can make clearer what happens here. The relationship between father and son is very private. No matter how consciously or unconsciously the father hides something, nevertheless, it is in his head somewhere to withhold it from the reader. It's not quite fair. Would you tell me what you meant there, if you feel I am reading badly here. I would like to read it again if you feel like paraphrasing for me the various myths involved here. Of course I understand most of this, but I feel a lack of a ring through which they may all be pulled and connected.

Again, in "Summer Revival," do the dull children who become the militant, creative children, by analogy infer actual children? I think this is a strange and almost terrifying poem. You are probably working too much alone. In an effort to increase the tension of the verse, you may be neglecting certain superficial, outward parts of structure.

I give you this for what it's worth. I would like to publish "Good Friday." I certainly think it is a poem. No more for now.

Sincerely yours,

Andrew Lytle

Editor, *Sewanee Review*

******

July 20, 1964

Dear Mr. Scarbrough:

I've been meaning to write you for a long time, but you can understand that there was a lot of work to catch up on. Also, it takes time to recover from a major operation so that I'm not at the top of my form. You understand how well we like your verse, and I want to print it right along. I hope to have some out in the winter issue.

I hope that you have found a job that is less of a strain, and I of course am delighted that your illness took no sinister turn. I wonder if you would like to do an omnibus review of verse for us. If this would appeal to you, I'll send you six or eight current books we have on hand. I hope sometime to engage you in a long conversation, but for the moment this will have to serve.

I've read "Nocturne: Springtime." I'll put it away to read again. Thank you for sending it.

Sincerely yours,

Andrew Lytle

Editor, *Sewanee Review*

******

March 28, 1965
Dear George Scarbrough:

    I was passing through a bookstore at UCLA, and happened to pick up a copy of the *Sewanee Review* with your review of *Two Poems of the Air*. Please allow me to say how much I appreciated what you say about the poems, and also about the makeup of the book itself, which I know the designer-editor-calligrapher-publisher, a student at Reed, where I was teaching when the book was conceived of, will appreciate as well. After all, there are not many schools where a student will take on herself a senior thesis subject where $1,500 is a required part of the enterprise. It could have failed drastically, lost money, been a bum thesis, and the rest of it, but as it is the small first printing has sold out and the girl even made fifty or sixty bucks out of it, as well as graduating in pretty good shape. But I was full of guilt about the thing, and allowing her to do it. Now I can heave a sigh of relief, and send the words that come after it in your direction, telling you how heartening it is to read comments like yours. Robert Duncan had what seemed to me a very dense article about the poems in *Poetry*, full of his own absurd theories of poetry, but otherwise the little book hasn't got much attention, though a few people whom I respect seem to like it. But your comments are so close to what I thought I was saying — and was afraid I didn't' really say — that I am persuaded that maybe I did say what I thought, or almost, anyway. The kind of poem in *Two Poems* is the kind I've been wanting to write for years, but I had no clear idea of how to go about it. Now, thanks largely to your remarks, I am emboldened to try some other things with the same approach. In the words of Blind Gary Davis, a folk singer I very much admire, "I done come this far! I don't find no fault! Lord, I feel just like going on!"

    I'll be coming to Kentucky next spring at the invitation of Wendell Berry, to read some things at the University of Kentucky. Would that enable us to get together? I very much hope it will; I'd like that.

Sincerely yours,
James Dickey

******

February 14, 1969
Dear Mr. Scarbrough,

    I thank you for your kind and intelligent review of my poems in the *Chattanooga Times*. I learned something about my book from reading what you had to say — which is to say that I am grateful for more than your praise. I do still think of it as a moral ideal that man should become what he is and not more, and I think what he is would be God's plenty if he would be satisfied with it. The rest of your reservations I take to heart.

Yours sincerely,
Wendell Berry

Eleven. A Selection of Letters to Scarbrough

******

April 5, 1976

Dear George:

You may send to your publisher the following for quotation:

In my opinion George Scarbrough is one of the few genuine poetic talents to appear in the South in the past generation. I hope his work gets the attention it deserves.

Best wishes.

Ever yours,

Allen Tate

******

March 28, 1963

Dear George,

Your splendid letter reached me at time when I was in bed with a persistent virus, and it did me more good than the medicine the doctor was prescribing. I am up and about now, and I am grateful to have you as a friend. Why is it that those of us who have so much in common have to be struck around here and there in this big country, so far away from each other? There ought to be a national map of poets, and at least we could pull it out once in a while and see where our friends are. I think the country then might appear to have more character than it sometimes does. One good poet is radiant enough to charge a large section of the mass with life!

I liked everything you had to say about "Countermoves." To use your words, I am trying to write poems that are "modern but not modern," trying to draw on the history of man and not just his present, which has some aspects of an unholy mess. I do not see much point in breaking off abruptly from the best that has gone before since to deny the past is in the long run to deny one's present which will all too soon be past.

Chapel Hill is ablaze with flowering Judas, dogwood, and it sounds with the music of spring in every corner. I can only repeat with Rilke, "Never forget that life is a glory."

We turn northward in a few weeks. Do you ever get to Connecticut? Woodbury is my name-place on that mythical map I was talking about. How about bringing yourself there one day and making the little New England town vibrate with the presence of two poets instead of one?

With affectionate regards,

Charles [Edward Eaton}

******

June 6, 1977

Dear George,

I don't know when I have felt as remiss with anyone as you, but, as they say, there have been "attenuating circumstances." First, your very beautiful book, and generous gift, must have remained here for weeks, perhaps months, while we were in Chapel Hill — in fact until your publisher wrote asking if I were interested in reviewing it somewhere. I wrote her immediately saying that I would be delighted to do so in some appropriate place — preferably *Sewanee Review*— but since I was leaving for Woodbury in two weeks he had better let the book stay safely there since it sometimes takes the better part of a month for a forwarded book to reach me.

George, the publishing scene changes so rapidly these days that I sometimes find it difficult to adjust to it. I think the day of belles-lettres is just about over. When everybody has to be lumped together, the good, the bad, the indifferent, in an "annual" review.

As to the book itself, you have every reason to be immensely proud of it. The Iris Press has done a superb job of bookmaking, and you must be delighted with the beautiful presentation.

So far, with the Mountain still above me, I have had time to read only the prose pieces at the beginning and the new poems which make a fabulous book in themselves. Nearly all of these were new to me and will stay new for a long, long time. The prose sketches — and I wish there were more of them — are sensitive, strong, and very moving, and a perfect introduction to the poems themselves. The poems themselves, of course, are some of the best being written today, putting to shame most of the cheap stuff that is coming out in book and magazine these days. I don't know of anyone who has worked from quite your vantage point and stuck to it so faithfully.

The South, in which the poems are so warmly and deeply rooted, becomes a universal. Local color is one thing, but George Scarbrough's poems are another. I find your scenes and your people unforgettable. They are almost everything much modern poetry has forgotten about: warm, witty, tender, wise — something indeed for the humanities. I am proud to be a friend of the author.

You have given me a book to carry me through the summer, and I shall be reading it for some time to come. Many of the earlier poems are familiar to me, but I am sure I will find many new favorites. This book has a life's work plainly in view, and I very much hope that it will get the recognition and serious consideration that it deserves.

With best wishes,

Charles [Edward Eaton}

******

August 4, 1977
Dear George,

I thought you would like to know that George Core [*Sewanee Review* editor] backtracked several weeks ago and asked me to do "a short review" after all. He said your books came back from the reviewer, along with a great many others because it "did not fit into the pattern" the reviewer had in mind — whatever that means. Perhaps nothing more, in your case, if the reviewer is Paul Ramsey, than that he plans to review it elsewhere. I think you mentioned he might review it at another magazine.

In any case, I got busy and did the review. George Core allowed me only 800 words, but I brimmed over as much as I dared anyway, and he has written me that he is delighted with the review and will print it in spite of the fact that it was longer than he suggested. I think the man actually sat down and counted the words! I wish it could have been at least twice as long, but Core is not a man to be tampered with, and I am relieved he liked the review so well. He hopes, as he said, "to squeeze it into the Autumn issue." If not — the Winter issue.

I am still down on my hands and knees in the garden, but that is not an altogether bad place to be these days. Otherwise, the summer goes well.

I hope your book is making a fine impression everywhere. I am enclosing an announcement of my own book since I do not know whether the publisher sent you one. If so, do give it to a friend who might be interested.

All good wishes,

Charles [Edward Eaton}

******

May 17, 1978
Dear George,

This is my first opportunity to write since my last card which was sent at a time when I was unable to write anything longer. I was sick all winter and spring, and went through an incredible number of tests, including manometry, endoscopy, the treadmill test for my heart, to name just a few — all very wearing and costly. They did not find anything definitive, and, slowly, I have begun to feel better on my own. It was maddening, though, to have the doctors to prescribe nothing but aspirin for a variety of pains and aches which I will not bore you with here. It may be nothing but the attrition of trying to finish three books in three years. Oh, this business of trying to be a poet!

When we get back out here in the country, my nerves seem to quiet down somewhat. Chapel Hill is a lovely place but high-paced these days as most of the rest of the country seems to be. I get much of my strength from nature, and it is all around me here in the most pleasant and beautiful way. It is good for such "grievous wounds" as we poets seem constantly to take. I look forward to a long, deep summer of work as I, hopefully, begin to feel better.

I appreciated your sending me the brochure on the Cumberland Writers Conference, and I am sure you will be an adornment to their meetings. It is very nice of you to want to discuss some of my poems, and I wish I could hear your remarks.

One bright spot — my third collection of short stories, *The Case of the Missing Photographs*, will be published by A.S. Barnes in a few weeks. The title story is taken from *The Sewanee Review*.

I hope you are getting many good reviews on your fine book. I was glad of the opportunity to register my admiration for it.

Take care of yourself. You are one of our national treasures, and should be carefully conserved.

With best wishes,

Charles [Edward Eaton]

******

July 7, 1977

Dear Mr. Scarbrough,

What a rare treat it was to have a visit with you "in the middle of the day." Both Phyllis and I felt it to be one of the best times we've had.

I am looking forward to reading your book. When I read the poem about wine-making, I immediately thought about what Margaret Mitchell said about reading Stephen Vincent Benet while she was at work on her manuscript — she found it so much more beautiful than her own work that she became depressed and didn't write any more for several months! So, lest my "literary remains" amount to nothing, I have laid your book in a special place — to be eagerly taken up when I write "end" to my manuscript — which, you will be glad to know (since you have so graciously offered to read it) in no way resembles *Gone With the Wind*. Can you imagine the size of that manuscript bundle — it would be like a mountain falling on you! Also, I would not put myself in the same league as Margaret Mitchell except as regards her response to excellence.

I really appreciate your offering to read my manuscript — it will make a slender book of about three dozen poems, which I hope do contain some new ideas. Preparing my mind to do it has taken over twenty years, so I have been as wary as the wariest of my mountain kin about whose hand should touch it. From all I know of you — your reputation and work, your conversation and manner — you seem a just man, as well as a fine poet. So, I feel very much at peace sending you the manuscript. Whether the criticism is positive or negative, I know it will be thoughtful and fair, and I will welcome it.

I hope your mother and your brother are doing well. His picture that you showed us is very beautiful — such a spirit in it. And I am very glad that you and Phyllis have begun some discussion about the possibility of using some of his work in my book.

Again, it was a great pleasure to be with you in June. I hope your summer is happy and full of new poems.

Sincerely,

Marilou Thompson [Awiakta]

Twelve

"Something of a Bio and an Itinerary"

(BY GEORGE SCARBROUGH)

September 13, 1992

As sharecroppers we were always in transit in the county. Here is an itinerary for the years between 1915, the year of my birth, and 1941, the date of my entering the University of the South. I reconstruct this from memory, using farms and birthdates to establish succession. I think there is no error. The years are split due to the autumn movings. Almost always we wintered at the new place.

1915–1918, the John Harrison Place. I, third child in the family, was born here in October, 1915, and my next brother in line, Charles Spencer, in August, 1918. Here, there was a cedar tree, a yellow rose, a cardinal flower, and a great roan bull, whose massive masculinity was set ajoggle when he set forth to comfort the cows. "Heere there were wild beestes." My mother read to me the "Cubby Bear" stories from *Comfort Magazine, the Key to Happiness in a Million Farm Homes.*

1918–1919, the Spencer McClary Place, owned by the doctor who had delivered Spencer and for whom the boy was named. Heere, there was a kitchen with loose plank flooring laid directly on the clay, and a tub full of cold catfish fresh from the river, sunflowers, a crimson-gold cock who tolled my mother's hens to his owner's barn to the decrement of our egg supply and who was cautiously killed and tossed into a wheat field uphill from our house, causing the neighbor much puzzlement and us much quietness. Here, too, because of my mother's great illness, I was sent back over the river to sleep for a summer with "Brother John," the sight of whom in his nightshirt, otherwise naked, taught me the similarity between men and bulls. Heere, too, was the train, running as it had always run since the birth of my consciousness. Heere, I read "Dark Pony" in my brother's primer, and spelled out black-letter words from the newspapered walls.

1919–1920, the Walt Harrison Place. Heere, proximity of the mountain which had always lain at the edge of my vision and mind; a great double spring of purest water; an abandoned apple orchard high on the piedmont, where my father and I stealthily stole apples; an apple tree of our own in the meadow and a cow who had to be bested in order for us to have the windfalls. Heere, too, was the swamp with calamus, which mother dug for its roots to palliate stomach distress. And later, in my more literary years, to assume significance of a vastly different kind.

1920–1921, the Charlie Moore Place. Heere, there were autumn cosmos flaring over the earthen cellar in the front yard, a garden still brilliant with red and yellow peppers, a great stock pond in the depths of a circular hollow in the meadow, the birth of my next brother, William Athol, in March, 1921, and "Ike" who first taught me the Elusinian mysteries of sex in a cotton shed. Heere, too, was "Luke," a red-haired young man whose brain had been damaged in a fall from a merry-go-round. Luke has haunted me all my life.

1921–1923, the John Lillard Place. Heere, was a two-story house, with empty rooms to dream in, a wrap-around porch, an orchard with plums and peaches, apricots, apples, and pears. Heere, were old books abandoned by the landlord, whose home the house had been: a thick book of Bible stories which I, to my later good fortune, battened on, and, here, a grapevine and a cistern, a pasture pine tree clambered over with muscadine whose leathery fruit was a household delicacy. Heere was Rhats Chapel, where I saw my first Christmas tree.

1923–1925, the Jay Cloud Place. Heere, my brother Blaine Pleasant was born in November, 1923. Heere were storm-driven oaks and acres of roadside longleaf pines who soughed constantly day and night and were never still. Heere, a royal Paulownia tree by the well, with its scented purple flowers. Too, chestnut hunting on cold Fall mornings. I liked this best of all. But for the mountain, which rose to its near triangular peak two miles away from our house, beautiful in all weathers but enthralling in autumn color and under winter snow. This mountain, called the High Peak, with its coronal of white cliffs and dominated by memories of all places and times. Mohammed had come to his mountain.

1925–1928, the Bobbie Harrison Place. Heere, we were even closer to the mountain, with its wintry blues, cold cobalt, and summer grays under the rains sweeping up from the south and concealing it altogether. On this farm was a creek with fishes in it. Heere, I caught the celebrated sunfish, lazily finning. Heere, the body of Franklin, naked in the barn, stunned me with beauty and a prescience of art. Heere, were fields of dewberries, that fantastic fruit. A haunted house, an abandoned cabin in the pinewood with books scattered on the floor. And here were Byron and Earl and Haskell and Rassie.

1928–1929. Again the John Lillard Place. Heere, was Miss Woodson, my fifth grade teacher, whom I would not have missed for worlds—for worlds are what she gave me. And words and books and a love of writing. All of them worlds, too. Along with cocoons and a love of all wild things. I remember her as the first in a series of "mothers" other than my own. Heere, for the first time, were books enough to read during the school months. And the foretold orchard. And the muscadine pine. My oldest brother's marriage. And my first torturing love affair. Ah, Stonewall, how little you knew. Writing this, I recall Colin from *The Secret Garden*, whom I loved too as Miss Woodson read to us that fabulous story. And the best, last: here was born my beloved youngest brother Kim, in December, 1928. By name, Joseph Kenneth Scarbrough. By love-name, Kim.

1929–1931, the Coop Biggs Place. Heere was near-starvation, the down-rushing Depression, which reduced us all. Heere, a dearth of books. Of magazines except for the *Saturday Evening Post*, lent to me by my eighth-grade teacher, who was handsome and kind and who persuaded me to "join the church," which I did because I was in love with him. Is there, was there ever, a better reason? My affiliation with the church was tenuous. I rarely attended except when a good-looking preacher came down the railroad track to get me "revived." It was a glorious if slightly less than heavenly time. Heere, at Coop's place, my nephew Lupton was born, his mother having separated from her "worthless husband." And here was R.L., dearest of lovers up to that time. I remember the starvation most vividly, however. It was the direst time of our lives.

1931–1935, the Boyd Mason Place. Heere, for four years, there was more starvation and desperate, drudging work. Heere, happened the loves of my high school years. Heere, violence from my father, whose sense of outrage was always near the surface of his volatile moods. Heere, the closeness to my mother deepened, and I was referred to by my father as "Belle's Boy," and when he was speaking to her, as "Your Son." Heere, in school, I won my first prizes in life: competitions sponsored by *The Open Road, The American Boy,* and *Senior Scholastic*. During these years I began my study of foreign languages, thus implementing my already passionate love for my own tongue. Heere, I began to dream seriously of going to the university by some hook or crook. Getting through high school had been a major accomplishment in my family, and I could not see any limitations beyond. I would get a Ph.D. for myself and my mother. Ah, those were dreamy years. Again, I remember mostly the starvation. I was approaching 20 when I finished high school.

1935–1936, the Luther Mason Place. Heere, a terrible wreck of a house, open to the weather. My family moved the fall I was away at the university, and I came home at Christmas time to an appalling situation. My mother had taken burlap sacking and stuffed the gaping cracks in the floors to keep out the raw wind. Half-finished upstairs room let in the arctic air. In Spring when I came home again the screenless windows and doors let in multitudes of flies, which I find now in my dreams cluttering the windowsills in my house. I wake with revulsion, hating fiercely the landlords who regarded their tenants as no better than cows in stalls or the pigs in their pens. The summer at the second Mason place was a nightmare. That summer I was left pretty much to myself by the young people in the community. I was suspect. That much was clear. What they suspected me of, they never said. But I could surmise. I didn't fit into their country company of walking out with a member of the so-called opposite sex. I stayed at home and re-read all the books I had won in high school competitions, and wrote poetry. Or walked the ridges in search of plants and flowers. That area of the county was a rich botanical garden, and much of my time away from farming and gardening was spent gathering wild fruits and naming the bloodroot, anemones, violets, wake robins, etc., native to the district.

1936–1938, the Taylor Dill Place. Just a half-mile down the road from the previous farm. I had no way of attending the university for a second year, so I settled in to helping my father farm and to reading and writing and tramping the hills and coves in my spare time. I began writing poetry in earnest now, keeping Miss Mayme Johnston's praise in mind. I had studied composition under the lady at the university and found her a great lover of literature as well as a superb teacher. A sonnet about my brother Kim, written for her class, elicited warm words of appreciation. Years later she would write that she had kept the poem about for all her succeeding classes to show that a college freshman could write a real poem. At the Dill place I began the serious study of birds and insects that I've pursued lifelong. Again, the place was idyllic for nature study, with hill and meadow, creek and woodland, empty backcountry fields fit for a naturalist's wandering and pleasure. I learned much about the natural world that year with the few guidebooks I had at hand, mostly the inexpensive Golden Book Series. That year, in the late autumn, I fell heir to the teacher's position at Horns Creek through the incumbent's default. The following months were among the happiest of my life, among the simple, sweet children of the region, which, in spring, flowered profusely with trees and plants of all description. The wild crabapple could be scented for miles, and whole hillsides were quilted with bird's foot violets. Natives making whiskey carried their sacks of sugar and corn under the window of the schoolhouse on their way to clear-running streams below. In a sense, it was a new kind of life. But life, I find, always renews itself. It has for me. In that, perhaps, I am lucky.

1938–1940, the Chestnut Farm, McMinn County. Heere was another kind of life — that of a great dairy farm whose management my father had secured. He was field and crop overseer. The dairy was the sphere of another family. The work was hard but was paid for in cash, and for the first time in our lives we had money to spend for necessities. When we crossed the Hiwassee River, going north out of Polk County, we changed worlds. The old land between the rivers was gone forever, or so it seemed to a young man, with a taste of the university, who had come close to a college town — Athens was only nine miles away — and to landlords — landladies, in this case — who not only read books but had their own library. Misses Nan and Grace Chestnut were gentility, humanists of a sort I had not known in Polk County, where kindness existed but not in their quality nor to their degree. While living on this farm I made many literate acquaintances in Athens, and began reviewing books for the *Chattanooga Times* under the aegis of Gilbert Govan, the upshot of which was the literary fellowship given by *The Sewanee Review* under the then editor Dr. William S. Knickerbocker. That would be in 1941, after poems of mine had appeared not only in *The Sewanee Review* but in *The Atlantic* and *Harper's* as well. Among my new friends instrumental in my securing the fellowship, Robert Clayton and Lyle Kilvington deserve notice. Life was looking up for us all by then.

1940–1941, the Barnett Place. We were not yet out of the woods, however. The ruined house in which we lived was again open to all weathers in the second story, whose windows lacked panes. In a deep valley, the environs of the house were beautiful and conducive to an imaginative young man's ponderings. That summer, in an accident, Dad's back was broken. I deliberated whether to forego the fellowship to Sewanee but was urged to accept by my mother, who assured me such fortune would not come again. I felt as though I were running out, and in a sense I was. My brother Blaine bore the brunt of brutal work, my mother helping outside as much as she could, her major task being to care for my querulous father, who lay on a broad board on a bed in the living room. Blaine and mother gathered the crops and moved again, this time to a hut of a house with too little room for decent living. My family had so little money that year my mother asked me to buy my youngest brother shoes, which I did with the money I had received from *The Atlantic Monthly*. I was happy to do that little. In the meantime I studied, was rejected for military service on the grounds of both physical and psychological unfitness, and completed my first year at Sewanee with strong grades.

1941–1943, the Croft Place. As foretold, the house was so small the family could not have visitors. Nonetheless, we survived inside its claustrophobic dimensions. The land was poor and again we had little to do with. Water had to be carried either from a spring at the foot of the ridge or from the landlord's house across the field. I came home from Sewanee for the summer, suffering from a panic induced by Dr. Spencer McClary — the doctor in the first segment of this chronology — who said I might drop dead any moment from a defective heart. How wrong he proved to be. But that summer was a horror for me. As it was for mother, who worried herself into a heart attack over my own illness. That summer both my father and I were knocked unconscious by a bolt of lightning that struck the hay-filled barn just over where we were standing in the entry. By the time we struggled to our feet, the flame was blowing like a river just over our heads from the front and of the entry to the back, and I could hear my mother screaming across the meadow. Nonetheless, we managed to flush the four mules from their stalls and escape with them into the yard. In a few minutes the barn was wrapped in flame from its foundation to its ridgepole. By the summer's end I was less panicky and able to return to Sewanee. My second year there was my last because I disputed the chancellor, an angry, spiteful man whose ways and means were brutal, and was denied my fellowship, a denial that both hurt and gladdened, for I could teach in McMinn County and so help my needy parents. At the end of 1943, through money my mother had saved from allotment made her by Spencer and Blaine, both in the U.S. Army, mother was able to buy the old Chastain Place on the outskirts of Etowah — twelve acres with a good frame house, an outhouse for storing and doing laundry, and a small barn at the tope of an orchard. I was teaching at Claxton that year. Life thereafter for my family took a different tack. We had come through to another plane of living, and were fortunate and happy in the prospect.

Thirteen

An Interview

Conducted by Randy Mackin at the writer's home,
100 Darwin Lane, Oak Ridge, Tennessee, 23 February 2000

Tell me about your teaching experience.

The kids seemed to love me and like my teaching and some went on to become PhDs, but I was not given tenure — so the chargers say — because I taught children to think analytically too soon. I remember what John Rice Irwin, who was school superintendent at the time, said. He said, "Seven miles from Oak Ridge, I'd be glad if someone taught my kids to think, anytime."

The principal, who was not all that bad, said, "George, you teach and talk on the college level." So, he gathered together all the college prep kids and put them into my English class, which made the chairman of the department furious. Even her own son left her classroom. And she was, I was told later by a trusted friend, the person who brought the charge of teaching too analytically.

It was true that when her son came into my class, it was near term paper time, and the boy — not a child, he was eighteen, I guess — asked me if he could write a term paper on the premise that God was a mathematical equation. I said, "Harry, if that's what you can present, introduce, expand, conclude, summarize ... that's all I want in a paper." I thought it was a strange request and his mother came to me. I can understand her concern. She apologized for his temerity, and I said, "Don't worry about it." He asked my permission, and I gave my permission, and I shouldn't have said it. But I said if he had tried to prove that God was a hog, and had done it in proper fashion, I would have approved it; but she didn't appreciate that at all. After the charge, I told the principal I couldn't work for him any more and I went to Hiwassee College after that.

Up to that time, something dogged me all the way. I started teaching in 1937, $55 a month. I lost that job because the man, who owned the local grocery store, and was on the local school board — with an IQ of maybe twenty-five — said, "Why aren't you trading with me?" I said, "I can't trade with you when you don't have anything, really, that I want to buy." He said, "Well, I'd hate to cut my own throat."

I taught in Claxton Junior High School in McMinn County for a year. Again, the old complaints of being too liberal, being too forward. I taught history and gave them my own interpretation, which didn't often suit with the textbook. I taught in so many places that, toward the last, it alarmed my would-be employer, because I told him why I got shifted, that I was a horse of a different color.

I think the teaching career was not all a loss. I still get cards and letters from students. I still hear from them. We're all successes in some way.

At the University of the South when I went there in 1941, on a scholarship — the first one ever given, I ran afoul of Dr. Alexander Guerry.

Was it a philosophical difference?

Well, I don't know what it was. I was on the honor roll. I was referred to as a *covite*, someone from the coves. The gentleman harped on his "Sewanee gentleman" until I thought I would vomit, and somebody told him that I didn't much care for his southern gentleman. He invited me out to his house. He said, "You say you don't like my Sewanee gentleman?" and I said, "No, Dr. Guerry, because most of them have more damn money than sense." That was not a politic thing to say. He said, "Next year, Scarbrough, you are going to wait on these boys you pretend to despise." Wait tables, you know, become a boot-lick. And I said, "No, I won't, Dr. Guerry, because I won't be back here next year." And he said, "You, and about twelve others here on campus, ought to put on a dress and enroll in a girl's school."

Those were his words, and when it came out in the *University of Tennessee Alumnus*, two of Dr. Guerry's sons jumped on the editor, saying, "What are you doing printing such scurrilous stuff?" And the lady laughed when she called to tell me. She said, "I told them I was glad we had some scurrility to talk about." That was it. I was always pursued by who I was, what I was, how I was.

Tell me about your early childhood, about growing up in this portion of Eastern Tennessee.

We lived in sixteen houses before I graduated from college, twelve before I graduated from high school, and that was a great worry to me, to see my parents work as hard as they did and have as little as they had. We finally got a little house, bought with very scrupulous savings. We bought a house and twelve acres for $1,600.

Biographically, it was rough. Geographically, it was beautiful, absolutely beautiful. It had its rivers. I refer to the area between the Hiwassee and the Ocoee as my personal Mesopotamia.

(Referring to a photo) It was an earlier time that I lived in that house when the birth of Charles — the brother next to me — almost killed my mother. She got the old fever, and daddy had those two, three including me, and I was probably the one he dreaded most trying to care for, so he sent me back home, or to the place we had moved from. I lived in the house with the man I call Brother John. I was about four. Brother John was, I supposed, forty-five or fifty, but he was unmarried and he took care of me. He and another brother and one sister lived in that house. And Betty, John's sister, became almost a mother to me. He washed, fed me, he dressed me in a blue work shirt, and held me in his arms when I sobbed myself to sleep. That went on for about six weeks, and early winter came. John wanted to adopt me. He called me Little George and all those things, and made me love him, but I didn't hesitate when the day came in November when dad drove the team over, and mama sent me a toboggan which daddy stuck down over my head. He was not a gentle person, and he was mad at mama anyway because she said, "Go bring him home, he doesn't belong over there."

Rejection, the feeling, the sense, the knowledge of rejection, began to sink in then. And I guess, forever after; I still feel rejected. I don't know why. I have all these friends. I feel like the boy in the coat of many colors.

We moved from farm to farm. Here we went traipsing around the landscape, all fourteen or fifteen of us, various houses, various landscapes, various landlords, generally without plough and seed, mule, and all that sort of thing, which reduced daddy's share of whatever was produced to a third. The landlord, on that basis, got two-thirds, and in some of the instances, mama said it wasn't worth carrying home for either of them.

I finally graduated from high school. I was pretty bright. I tried to do well scholastically. I loved to read. I entered some contests sponsored by the *National Scholastic Magazine*, and *Boys Life*, and others. I entered a national reading race in my junior year and won second place. I read sixty-five books and reviewed them in twenty-five words or less. I won Modern Library books, some of which I still have. The man who beat me came from the north — Benny Baker — I remember his name, mostly because he had read 115. I hope it was sheer volume that prejudiced the judges. I remember the principal having me up with all the books, on stage, showing me off, the prize rooster. Like all athletes, my friends among the males couldn't give a damn how many books I read. They didn't read books; they got their girlfriends to read them.

After I graduated I borrowed ten dollars from twelve men, ten each, and started UT in the fall of 1935 with $120. They put me on the National Youth Administration and I made fifteen dollars a month. That helped considerably. After the first quarter, during which I learned to starve to death, I was very visible dragging my sheets and quilts up and down the streets, looking for another and better boarding house, which I never found. Meals, though, at the local boarding houses, were only twenty-five cents, and enough to feed a horse.

My second quarter, since I had made As in English, to the amazement of everybody, including the teacher and superintendent of education way off in Nashville, they moved me to an old dormitory, a self-help, which was run by two senior boys. They bought the food, they collected the rent, as it were. Cora, a black woman, cooked the food. The boys made the menu and planned the meals. We had this dumbwaiter that pulled up by ropes from the bottom, and up would come the feast. They were fairly narrow festivals. There was an apple and good vegetables. Now and then we got dessert. It might be half of a Del Monte peach, but it kept us healthy.

Of course, we swept the house, we made the beds, and cleaned the shower, and we also got quarantined for scarlet fever. For two weeks we weren't allowed outside the house. In the meantime, we all started, if we hadn't started before, collecting soot all over us, in our ears, up our noses. I lived in the basement and it was particularly sooty down there because of the old furnace. And when the doctor came in to give us all a shot, using a nice clean cloth, it came off black. He said, "If you damn boys would take a bath once in a while." People brought assignments and took the assignments back. I guess we made it scholastically as much as we would had we been in class. I didn't learn much of anything in class at UT.

What compelled you to start writing poetry?

Well, that's very easy. I loved reading and I think I knew how to read before I began school. Mother helped me with the alphabet and the walls of the house we lived in were wallpapered with World War I headlines. I read the walls and asked mama what those large black banners said. She pointed out the As, Bs, and Cs, and told me what words meant.

Thirteen. An Interview

We suffered a disastrous in-and-out of school business, because we lost school every time a disease spread — like the fever, small pox, chicken pox — dad would keep us out until all the danger of the epidemic was passed. One time I remember I was out of school for three months.

By the time I got to fifth grade, I chanced upon a marvelous teacher, Eula Woodson. She was one of the most marvelous teachers I've ever known. Greater than the great men at Sewanee, in that she took us into the fields, we gathered cocoons, we planted things in jars, she read to us from *The Secret Garden* if we behaved in the morning. We went to movies for a nickel apiece. They were silent films. Handsome, galloping cowboys, Nelson Eddy singing.

Benton, which was the hub of the universe, never got a theater. Of course, it had a post office and a jail. Those were the necessities. We didn't have anything to fix for lunch, so I generally walked down the hill past the jail house, and I was trying to walk fast because the men inside the jail hollered nasty things at me as I went by: "Oh, I wish I had a twist like that." Well, you couldn't help twisting if you ran. And once a fellow unzipped his pants and hung it out between the bars. It looked like one of those ghastly — not radishes — but whatever they were. And I quit going.

I tried to get to grandmother's house because I knew she always had a pot of brown beans on the stove. Granny had had three husbands. She hadn't married the second, as yet; the first two died. Mother's father was the first one, a McDowell. Grandma was a stern, hard-bitten woman, Scotch-Irish, but she wasn't unkind. And she knew when a boy was hungry. I didn't love her. I couldn't imagine anybody loving Grandma, but I respected her. Of course, respect was that or else. If we offended Grandma, we all got a strapping. She didn't like us laughing, and the more she didn't like it, the louder we laughed. I just couldn't love Grandma. She was out of sympathy with young boys who laughed.

A wonderful old woman. She liked a little totty now and then. I remember one of her grandsons would come down to see Grandma when she was sick and Joe said he had what was Grandma's cure out in the car. Joe said, "I brought in a pint, Grandma took a couple of big swigs, and it wasn't long before she was quite well again." Alcohol seemed to figure largely into the tragedies that happened in my mama's family and my own family.

I loved Miss Woodson. She made us keep a vocabulary book. Every word that we did not understand, she made us put into a notebook, she made us find the definition, she helped us to write a good English sentence using that word. And then, of course, came the test, which the little boy in my first school said, "testes." One day, before tests, he said, "Mr. Scarbrough, are your testes hard?" After class I took him out and told him to say "tests" and "posts." My sister said, "postes." And I explained to him what his testes were.

Miss Woodson was a darling, but if I got to acting smart ass, she put me in the cloak room. One of my failings has been that I'm inclined to be a smart ass. I revere the woman's memory. I used her name in the novel, *A Summer Ago*. She was the grandest person, besides my mother, that ever came into my life. Miss Woodson has been with me all these years, she's never left; my mother has never left, I feel her presence. These women had an immense influence. It started with my mother, who would say, "Look at this, son." She'd pick up a shell or a rock or one of those little polished smooth and beautiful craw things that the hens swallow to cut up their grain. It came out looking like those polished stones you buy, agates and things like that. Mama didn't miss anything she could point out. If anyone else paid attention, I never knew. I tried to do the same with Kim. And I awakened a spark in Kim that was artistic. He was a very gifted man, but he had to feed his family. He had no choice. Let's say Miss Woodson always supplemented mama; she was an addendum to the trees, the water, the minnows, the mountains, the rivers, the bridges.

That bridge got into a poem that was published by *Poetry*. Between the planks, the cracks looked like the Grand Canyon and I was fearful. I've been afraid all my life, afraid of everything. I don't know how I've survived. When I read James Dickey's son's *Summer of Deliverance*, and found out that Jim had been afraid of things all his life, it kind of explained Dickey to me.

Do you remember the first poem you wrote?

Yes. The fourth house we lived in was a two story house owned by Mr. John Lewis, who had built it for himself; and it was really a rather grand house, I thought. John had moved into town to establish Lewis Hardware in Benton. We rented the bottom floor and John Brown, our neighbor who moved when we did, moved into the upstairs. John didn't stay there long, so daddy kept our great big meat box upstairs, which was very salty, smelled of ham. I made that into a desk and borrowed one of our straight chairs. We didn't have too many straight chairs, but mama let me have one, so I would turn the box on its side, stick my feet in there, and I would write poetry.

The first poem was about the orchard. The man had planted a very fine orchard when he had lived there. I wrote a poem about apricots, and plums, peaches and apples. I had read an English poem about an apple orchard in the spring. So, I began to measure my lines by, obviously, the only meter English ever had, and that was iambic. As T.S. Eliot said, "Iambic, in one form or another."

That was it. I think I carried the poem to school and showed it to Miss Woodson, but it was the essay that I wrote about the silent movie on the Canadian Mounties, in which I used every possible word I could get from my notebook, and crammed it into magnificent sentences — that's what I thought writing was, and I'm afraid I kept on thinking that was what writing was through part of my high school.

Eighteen years brought me *Look Homeward Angel*, beautiful as he said it, but he used at least two thirds too many words to tell a story, say, as Stephen Crane would have used. *The Open Boat*, what a classic that is. I was spoiled by Wolfe. I wrote long, freight train sentences. Little by little, that began to be ironed out because in that book contest in my third year of high school, my English teacher supplied me with fine books that were not in the library. One of the loveliest of that bunch of books was Willa Cather's *Death Comes to the Archbishop*. It's absolute marble, it's crystal. And I thought, "Here is another kind of writing." All this time I had been reading the Bible, not for religious purposes, but for purposes of my own writing. I got a lot of interest in poetry from the Bible. I knew it was poetry, though it didn't rhyme. It couldn't have been written in rhyme. So, rhyme is really not poetry. I got the Bible wrapped around my consciousness before I got much of anything else. The primers came along, of course, the Henny Penny's. I always shuddered when the sky fell. And I loved them, too. The flavor and tang of those old stories was wonderful.

Wolfe almost ruined me. Robert Frost helped to turn me around because he's plain. Sometimes he's beautiful. Sometimes he preaches a little. He's got a message, I guess, but he never let the message get too much in sight, particularly in "Home Burial," which I think is classic as anything in literature.

I kept on reading. I read everything I could get my hands on, good or bad. When mama and I couldn't get anything else to read, we read "True Confessions." They were brought to my mother by my Aunt Gertrude, who decided that she liked better the somewhat wilder life of Knoxville, so she left home when she was young and had a rather spotted career, the kind that sorted with "True Confessions," if I may. Anyway, she helped feed me during that first quarter at UT and bought me a very, very much too large gray coat because I didn't have a coat.

In one of those forced absences from teaching, I went to the State University at Iowa. I can't say I studied. I just sat there gasping in amazement at what Paul Engle called teaching. He had long, dark, greasy hair which came way back and he would sit on the desk and his hair would fall forward and he would sling it back. He preened a little for the *Times* photographer who seemed always to be coming to the Writers' Workshop in those days. Nowadays, it doesn't make much noise. I also took fiction. I passed more classes with that one short story. I suppose other people had done it. I was no entrepreneur in the field of writing a paper for one class and using it for another, because I hated to write the damn things. I loved to write, but papers, research? I came back, started teaching again, started staying closer to home because my mother was getting old. I nursed her for fifteen years.

How do you approach a poem, how do you know when that poem is finished, and how do you feel about the finished poem?
When I think a poem is finished, I am very happy, because those are about the happiest times I know now. A poem can start with a word, a remark I hear. It is difficult to get that one opening line that will open all the other lines. For instance, a poem I wrote called "Wardrobe" — I'm still working on it, incidentally — is about Han-Shan and how when he goes to the town he washes and mends his gray clothes because he thinks he's invisible against the weathered walls of the village. Then he comes home and darns, as many Chinese people do, in a long, belted shirt, with nothing below but bare legs. But when he goes into the house, he scrubs himself with aromatic brushes and oils himself with expensive oils, and goes into his library, which has all the many colored bindings. And the poet remarks that Han-Shan's library is no attorney's closet where all the books are colored alike and stand at the same height. But, it's all because he likes to read over and over and over the story of Joseph and his many-colored coat. When I get it through, I hope it reads; it almost reads now.

Of course, Han-Shan never read the Bible. Han-Shan came along before the Bible ever did. Who cares? What difference does it make?

Poor old Han-Shan. I used to walk shrinking against the walls of buildings, and that was after I went to school, until I learned everyone was mortal and in a minute the whole thing could turn around and splash blood to your face. I had a hard time growing up. I haven't grown up yet, and I don't want to, in a sense. For a long, long time, sexually, I wouldn't have anything to do with a grown man. It was unthinkable because a grown man had not been kind to me.

I always tried to be invisible because I didn't think I was anybody, lonely, that I was nobody and I was pleased when somebody spoke to me. But after the great illnesses, smelling myself rotting, I realized it was time to throw some of that junk away, stand up in the world, say what you want to. I never read in public, except in school. It took me six weeks to get used to the kids, as friendly as they were. Once, I was asked to Atlanta to read to six hundred teachers. I couldn't even imagine. Deep down inside I wanted attention, and except for Brother John and whatever mother could give to seven kids, I didn't get it. I spent my holidays, Sundays and weekends, roaming the hills by myself, listening, I'm afraid, for Pan to trill his pipe somewhere. I couldn't get out of that inferiority complex until one of my professors sent word to me, "This is not going to do. Get back in here and let's get this thing straightened out."

Is Han-Shan your alter ego?

He is my alter ego and I'm finding that I can be, well perhaps, more truthful, hiding behind Han-Shan. Han-Shan was an old, very, very ancient poet about whom very little is known. George Ellison brought me to Han-Shan, and I found out as I went that Han-Shan lived with his man, Shi-te. Part of the book deals with Shi-te. Han-Shan stays at home a great deal, but Shi-te likes to step out now and then. I'm using him to cover a lot of things that are written under first person. I get so tired of "I." I get tired of "me," but I get *tireder* of "I." I love old Han-Shan.

It's been a cruel, cruel world, but it's been wonderful, too. I wouldn't have traded it for anything. Han-Shan has come in very handy. Han-Shan, bless his old heart, has stood me in good stead. In that way, he has become a good companion, but I don't talk to Han-Shan because I'd be afraid he would answer.

Do you have any specific theories about poetics?

No. I have met college professors who boasted about their cosmology. I remember one who insisted I must have a cosmology. He said, "What's in your world?" I remember telling him that a stick, a stone, a frog, a cow, whatever happened on the landscape was my cosmology. I have been asked about poetic theory. I have no poetic theory. I'm not sure that I write poetry. I'm not sure that anybody writes poetry, not in the sense of John Donne, or some of things that Keats wrote. I was never sure that Robert Browning was a poet. But, happily, perhaps, or unhappily, the tendency became towards Walt Whitman, who I think is a great fellow. And I am so happy gray Walt came along. But he's no jingler. Whitman's work is worthy of a good American poet. "Song of Myself" is super. I know it's kind of narcissistic, but he didn't claim that just for himself, but for all workmen, for all people, with a spark of something in them that didn't necessarily have to bend itself to the artistic. People attacked him, some still do, because he was gay, but that's the absolute lowest of low points to say about a man of his stature. I adore Whitman. I also adore Emily Dickinson. They comprise for me just about the topmost virtue in American poetry.

Now, Wallace Stevens is a mighty, mighty man. You can't touch the man. I mesmerize myself with Stevens. His poetry does not lend itself to familiarity. Some of his poetry is ethereal. Like cotton candy, you try to bite into it and get a mouthful of nothing.

Tellico Blue was largely rhymed, and I love rhyme. My journals are full of bawdy limericks. I do them because they rhyme and they startle. The sonnets came very easily. I don't think now that I could write a sonnet.

Do you have any regrets as a poet?

I regret certain things have been published. There are two sonnets in *Tellico Blue* that Fred Chappell questioned. He said, "These are not right, and then again, they may be very right."

I wish I hadn't tried to conceal things. I felt so low, so cheap, that I used a woman's name in a poem that was addressed to a man. Shakespeare was luckier. He had a fair man and a dark lady. That's cheap. I was taught to be honest, but I have found that lies can be a man's chief support. I think you'll understand that. A lot of people would try to hold me accountable even when I was trying to avoid unpleasantness, and one time, possibly even death.

I regret my sharpness with my mother; she was the lodgepole of the house. And I regret not being mature enough to understand what drove my father to his brutality he exercised against me. First of all, I didn't respect my father, because I knew that my father was illiterate, I knew that he was arrogant; and, of course, when I was in my teens, I thought I knew everything. I found out later that I knew very little and the older I get the less I claim to know. I regret that.

I regret slapping one of my brothers when he disobeyed me because I thought I was the king of the potato patch and he wasn't building hills right. I regret personal harm because I tried to be boss, and brothers are not going to allow bosses.

Would you comment on the journals?

I wouldn't mind everyone reading the journals right this minute if it wouldn't bear down on some of my people whom I do love. My brother,

Kim, never forgave me for being gay. I found out later that he criticized me sharply to people who knew both of us. He had no capacity to understand the variousness of nature. Who can outguess nature? From a billion-year-old gene pool, what is not likely to occur? My theory is that nature is going back to the sea horse; the male gives birth. I can't see humanity as anything but an experiment that will grow old with age and die. We're showing dreadful signs of age now in the lessening of our feelings for our country, America, and for each other, for God's sake. So, I think we may be going back to primal times and that the human race will eventually fade out, and maybe its fragile bones will last as long as the dinosaurs have, for some weak-eyed, bespectacled, hump-backed, future fellow to bend over and search for clues.

That's why mama said to me once, "I wouldn't have you teach one of my children." A student asked me why the Indians put dead fish under their corn hills, and I said, "It's fertilizer." And before I knew what I was saying to the girl, I said, "You, child, will make fertilizer, too." Come Monday, in charged one of my students who said I was the subject of Sunday School lesson at church. The girl had brought up the fact, in Sunday School class, that people were just fertilizer. He said they went around and around and some of the students defended me.

I love the theory of evolution. I can see how it happened, random, haphazard, kill that guy over there because he has a club foot, rope that one because he thinks too much. I think the common people never did catch on. I think they don't catch on now, with all this fear of public education.

Feelings that seem to be innate — feelings of a greater power when we're helpless — psychology never explained it to me.

Do you consider yourself a religious person?

I'm not religious. I believe everything we do now is based on a mythic past, and I'm not so sure that what we're doing now won't be mythic in a few years. I grew up in a fundamentalist community, hell fire and damnation, even went to a snake handling meeting. I did not participate. I started wondering about the time I was ten or eleven; I saw holes in all these things that were being pitched at me and which I was supposed to take on faith. I am sure that if such a person as Christ ever existed, that he was a sociologist, that he was a man interested in helping people who could not help themselves, but he was a quick-tempered man. He whipped the piss out of that bunch in the temple, but he took pity on poor Mary Magdalene. He was a desert man, far, far away from the privileges and conveniences that

Saint Paul enjoyed. Saint Paul went so far as to really screw the whole damn thing up, that's what Saint Paul did. Poor old Paul didn't know who he was or what he was; he was in the grasp of something bigger than he was.

What dangers do poets face today?

I think poetry has fallen to the level of advertising. I don't see much future for poetry. I've been told there's no hope for me, but I'll do my own hoping. I don't see much hope because people are too realistic to accept metaphor of any sort. What happens when a man says to his sweetheart, "I love you like the devil"? Now, that's a miscarriage if ever I heard one, but you do hear things like that even here. Right across that mountain we have some of the most surprising people, scholars, poets. I wish poetry could go on. I wish we could, as the King James version says, "Speak with the tongues of angels."

Appendix: Publications and Awards

Scarbrough's work has appeared in the following publications.

Magazines, Journals, and Newspapers

Appalachian Journal. Atlantic Monthly, Black Warrior Review, Chattanooga Times (poetry and book reviews), *Chicago Review, Cold Mountain Review, College English, Creeping Bent, Cumberland Poetry Review, Driftwood, Georgia Medical Journal, Green River Review, Harper's, Hearse, Hogshead Review, Houston Post, Iron Mountain Review, Knoxville News-Sentinel, Laurel Review, Monument, Minnesota Quarterly, Mossy Creek Journal, Mississippi Review, National Forum, New Orleans Poetry Journal, New Republic, New York Times Book Review, Old Hickory Review, Pocket Poetry, Poetry* (Chicago), *Poetry Dial, Poetry Now, Polk County News, Progressive Farmer, Quarterly Review of Literature, Sam Houston Literary Review, Saturday Review, Sewanee News, Sewanee Review, Small Farm, Southern Exposure, Southern Fireside, Southern Literary Messenger, Southern Poetry Review, Southwest Review, Spirit, Tennessee Poetry Journal, Touchstone, Unaka Range, Vanderbilt Poetry Review, Versecraft, Virginia Quarterly Review, Voices, Wind, Zone 3.*

Anthologies

Anthology of Magazine Verse and Yearbook of American Poetry. Edited by Alan Pater. Beverly Hills: Monitor, 1981.
Best Poems of 1961. ed. Lionel Stevenson et al. Palo Alto: Pacific Books, 1992.
Contemporary Southern Poetry. Edited by Guy Owen et al. Baton Rouge: Louisiana State Press, 1979.
The Current Voice. Edited by Don L. Cook et al. Englewood Cliffs: Prentice Hall, 1971.
Forever the Land. Edited by Russell and Kate Lord. New York: Harper, 1950.
The Golden Year. Edited by Melville Cane et al. New York: Fine Editions, 1960.
I Have a Place. Edited by Jim Wayne Miller. Pippa Passes, KY: Appalachian Learning Laboratory, Alice Lloyd College, 1961.

In Homage to Priapus. Edited by E. V. Griffith. San Diego: Greenleaf, 1970.
New Ground. Edited by Donald Askins et al. Jenkins, KY: Southern Appalachian Writers' Cooperative, 1977.
New Southern Poets. Edited by Guy Owen and Mary C. Williams. Chapel Hill: University of North Carolina Press, 1974.
Poetry South-East: 1950–1970. Edited by Frank Steele. Martin: University of Tennessee Press at Martin, 1968.
Seven in Tennessee. Edited by Stephen Mooney et al. Martin: University of Tennessee Press at Martin, 1968.
Southern Poetry: The Seventies. Edited by Guy Owen et al. Raleigh: Southern Poetry Review Press, 1977.
Their Country's Pride. ed. Sister M. Pascal Campion, O.S.F. and Sister Bede Donelan, O.S.F. Milwaukee: Bruce, 1948.
Traveling America with Today's Poets. Edited by David Kheridan. New York: McMillan, 1977.
The Various Light. Edited by Leah Bodine Drake et al. Lausanne, Switzerland: Aurora, 1964.

Awards and Prizes

Literary Fellowship, University of the South, Sewanee, 1941–1943.
Carnegie Fund Grant, 1956.
Borestone Mountain Award, 1961.
Mary Rugeley Ferguson Poetry Award, *The Sewanee Review*, 1964.
Carnegie Fund Grant, 1975.
P.E.N. American Branch Grant, 1975.
Authors' League Fund Grant, 1976.
The Sheena Albanese Memorial Prize, *Spirit* Magazine, 1978.
The Governor's Outstanding Tennessee Award in Literature, 1978.
Nominated for the Pulitzer Prize in 1990, for *Invitation to Kim*.
Honoree at "George Scarbrough Literary Festival," held October 21–22, 1999, at Emory and Henry College, Emory, Virginia.
Selected for inclusion in *Asheville Poetry Review*'s special millennial issue on "Ten Great Neglected Poets of the Twentieth Century," published as the Spring–Summer issue 2000, Vol. 7 No. 1.
2001 Hokin Prize from *Poetry* magazine for three Han-Shan poems that appeared in the July 2000 issue.
James Still Award for Writing of the Appalachian South, presented by the Fellowship of Southern Writers at the Biennial Arts and Education Council Conference in Chattanooga, April 2001.
Knoxville Writers' Guild Career Achievement Award, 2003.
Honorary Doctor of Letters, Lincoln Memorial University, 2005.
East Tennessee Writers Hall of Fame induction, October 2008.

Bibliography

Balla, Phillip. "*Invitation to Kim* by George Scarbrough." *Appalachian Journal* 19.1 (1991): 79–86. Review of *Invitation to Kim*.

Brown, Bill. "A Gathering of Light: The Gift of Landscape in the Poetry of George Scarbrough." *Iron Mountain Review* 16 (Spring 2000): 10–13.

Brown, Fred. "Oak Ridge Poet to Be Honored by Knoxville Writers' Club." *Knoxville News Sentinel*, January 26, 2003. www.knoxnews.com/kns/local_news/article/ 0,1406, KNS_347_1699339,00.html (accessed February 18, 2003).

Coffman, Arlena Andis. "A Thank You Long Time Coming." *Elnora Post* 2:10, October 2008, sec. 1:1.

Cumming, Robert B., and George Scarbrough. "A Conversation with George Scarbrough" (recorded at Scarbrough's home, Oak Ridge, TN, November 19 and 21, 1999). *Asheville Poetry Review* 7:1 (Spring–Summer 2000): 122–129.

———. "A Creek Backward Flowing: The Sonorous, Passionate and Enduring Voice of George Scarbrough." *Asheville Poetry Review* 14:1 (December 7, 2009). www.red room.com/articlestory/a-creek-backward-flowing-the-sonorous-passionate-and-enduring-voice-george-scarbrough.

———. "George Scarbrough: Death of an Obscure Giant." *Nantahala Review* 4:1. http:// nantahalareview.org/issue4–1/view4–1/Cumming.html (accessed December 7, 2009).

Davis, Lloyd. "The Southern Renascence and the Writers of Tennessee." *The Literature of Tennessee*. Edited by Ray Wilbanks. Macon, GA: Mercer University Press, 1984, 21–36.

Eaton, Charles Edward. "A Dominion in Tennessee" *Sewanee Review* 86 (Spring 1978): xviii–xx. Review of *New and Selected Poems*.

"ET Writers Hall of Fame Welcomes Four." *Knoxville News Sentinel*, 19 October 2008. www.knoxnews.com/news/2008/oct/19/et—writers-hall-of-fame-welcomes-four/ (accessed January 22, 2009).

Flynn, Keith. "Introduction." *Asheville Poetry Review* 7:1 (Spring–Summer 2000): vii–xi.

Francisco, Edward. "Christ-Hauntedness in George Scarbrough's *Invitation to Kim.*" *Iron Mountain Review* 16 (Spring 2000): 25–30.

———. "Familiarity and Honest Remembrance" *Southern Review* 26.4 (1990): 920–923. Review of *Invitation to Kim*.

Gander, Forrest. "The Inflorescence of Variety: Four Inconoclastic Southern Poets." *New Orleans Review* 22 (Fall–Winter 1996): 105–114.

Garin, Marita, ed. *Southern Appalachian Poetry: An Anthology of 37 Poets.* Jefferson, NC: McFarland, 2008, 183–189.
Glass, Malcolm. "George Scarbrough: A Restrospective." *Spirit* 50 (Fall–Winter 1984): 71–75.
"George Scarbrough Wins the Hoken Prize for His Poetry." *The Oak Ridger,* 15 December 2000. http://oakridger.com/stories/121500/int_12150000.html (accessed January 28, 2003).
Govan, Gilbert E. "When Writers Live Close to Earth." *Chattanooga Times,* November 17, 1940, sec. 3: 5.
Green, Connie. "Mirrored Through Metaphor: Family in George Scarbrough's Poetry." *Iron Mountain Review* 16 (Spring 2000): 20–24.
Hay, Sara Henderson. "Double Meanings and Emotion." *Saturday Review,* July 16, 1949: 38. Review of *Tellico Blue.*
Hayford, Harrison W. "American Literature." *Encyclopaedia Brittanica: Book of the Year.* 1957 ed.
Jones, Rodney. "Entering *Tellico Blue.*" *Tellico Blue.* Oak Ridge, TN: Iris, vii–ix.
_____. "New and Selected Poems." *Black Warrior Review* 5.1 (1978): 104–108.
_____. "Poets After Midcentury." *The History of Southern Literature.* Edited by Louis Rubin, Jr., et al. Baton Rouge: Louisiana State University Press, 1985, 51–52.
Justus, James H. "On Reading Scarbrough." *Invitation to Kim.* Memphis: Iris, 1989, foreword, xv–xvii.
Loest, Judy. Email to the author. February 1, 2010.
Leidig, Dan. "*A Summer Ago* by George Scarbrough." *Appalachian Journal* 14:4 (1987): 384–88. Review of *A Summer Ago.*
Logue, John D. "Books About the South." *Southern Living,* October 1978, 118.
Mackin, Randy. "By Way of the Word." *Iron Mountain Review* 16 (Spring 2000): 14–19.
McMillan, Samuel H. *The Poet in His World: Twelve in Tennessee.* Martin: Tennessee Poetry, 1968.
"McMinn County Farm Youth Gains Fame as Poet of Marked Ability." *Chattanooga Times,* November 22, 1940, 11.
Mobbs, Rebecca. "Is This My Home?" Lecture. Southern Women Writers Conference, Berry College.
"Office of Bisexual, Gay, Lesbian, and Transgender Concerns." Unitarian Universalist Association of Congregations. www.uua.org/aboutus/professionalstaff/identity-basedministries/bisexualgay/index.php (accessed August 25, 2010).
Phillips, Robert L. "George Addison Scarbrough." *Contemporary Poets, Dramatists, Essayists, and Novelists of the South.* Edited by Robert Bain and Joseph M. Flora. Westport, CT: Greenwood, 1994, 418–422.
Ramsey, Paul. "The Truth at the Door: The Poems of George Scarbrough." *Appalachian Journal* 6:1 (1978): 55–61. Review of Scarbrough poems.
Rogers, David. "George Scarbrough and the Language of Love" (review). *Spirit* 55 (Fall/Winter 1990): 1–5. Review of Scarbrough poems.
_____. "George Scarbrough's *A Summer Ago*: The Advent of Love." *Spirit* 52 (1986): 1–7.
Scarbrough, George. "Anachronisms." *Poetry,* July 2000, 208.
_____. "Author's Preface to the Second Edition." *Tellico Blue.* New York: Dutton, 1949. Rpt. Oak Ridge, TN: Iris, 1999.
_____. "Catch-All." *Poetry,* April 2001, 18.
_____. "County Lullabye." *Hogshead Review* 1.1 (1984): 15–16.

_____. *The Course Is Upward.* New York: Dutton, 1951.
_____. "Direction." *Appalachian Journal* 20.4 (1993): 396.
_____. "Experience." *Sewanee Review* 48 (1940): 461.
_____. "Friendship Cemetery in Summer." *Poetry*, September 1997, 322.
_____. "From The Journals." *The Small Farm* 7–8 (Fall 1978): 51–54.
_____. "The Garden." *Poetry*, July 1997, 214.
_____. "Good Friday, New Mexico, 1955." *Sewanee Review* 75.2 (Spring 1967): 232–240.
_____. "The Good Mother." *Poetry*, June 2001, 137–38.
_____. "Ice Storm." *Iron Mountain Review* 16 (Spring 2000): 5.
_____. *"Ice Storm" and Other Poems Read by the Poet.* Memphis: Iris Audio Publications, 1996. Audiotape.
_____. "Initial." *Poetry*, July 2000, 207.
_____. *Invitation to Kim.* Edited by Phyllis Tickle. Memphis: Iris, 1989.
_____. "I Yam What I Yam." *Touchstone Magazine* 8 (Fall 1986): 7–9.
_____. Journals. George Scarbrough Papers. General Inventory. Record Group 39: Series 90. University of the South, Sewanee.
_____. "Lee's Funeral." *Appalachian Journal* 20.2 (1993): 198.
_____. "Lesson." *Southern Review* 36.4 (2000): 849–850.
_____. Letter to the author. 23 September 1994.
_____. Letter to the author. 3 March 1995.
_____. Letter to the author. 1 November 1996.
_____. "Monday." *Appalachian Journal* 20.4 (1993): 397.
_____. "Music." *Poetry*, April 2001, 14.
_____. "My Mother Language, My Father Tongue." *Appalachian Journal* 4.1 (1977): 28–34.
_____. *New and Selected Poems.* Edited by Patricia Wilcox. Binghamton, NY: Iris, 1977.
_____. "One Flew East, One Flew West, One Flew Over the Cuckoo's Nest." *Sewanee Review* 73 (1965): 138–50.
_____. Personal interview. February 23, 2000.
_____. "Preferment." *Poetry*, April 2001, 15.
_____. "Revenant." *Poetry*, July 2000, 207–08.
_____. "Scrapbook." *Poetry*, September 1999, 328.
_____. *A Summer Ago.* Memphis: St. Luke's, 1986.
_____. *Summer So-Called.* New York: Dutton, 1956.
_____. "Sunday Shopping." *Poetry*, February 1997, 283.
_____. *Tellico Blue.* New York: Dutton, 1949. Rpt. Oak Ridge, TN: Iris, 1999.
_____. "Tenant." *Sewanee Review* 49 (1941): 185.
_____. "Three Poets." *Chattanooga Times*, 17 November 1940, sec. 3: 5.
_____. "Up Front." *Poetry*, April 2001, 16.
"Scarbrough, George." www.irisbooks.com/scarbrough/index.htm (accessed November 14, 2000).
"Scarbrough, George (Addison) 1915-." *Contemporary Authors New Revision Series.* Vol. 38. Edited by James G. Lesniak and Susan M. Trosky. Detroit: Gale Research, 1993.
Senn, Dorothy. "Local Poet Recognized as a Major Voice in Poetry." *The Oak Ridger*, November 1, 2002. http://www.oakridger..._DOC_TEXT:YES&CQ_DOC_MARKUP_STYLE=7 (accessed March 4, 2004).
Smith, R. T. "The Appellations Yet Rising: A Birdseye View of Poetry from the

Appalachians." *Poetry Daily Prose Feature*, Summer 2004. www.cstone.net/
~poems/essartsm.htm (accessed June 9, 2009).
Southern Appalachian Writers Cooperative. "Renascence." *Appalachian Journal* 4.1 (1977): 34.
Snyder, Gary. *Riprap and Cold Mountain Poems*. New York: North Point, 1965.
Spirit: A Magazine of Poetry, Rogers, David, ed., Fall–Winter 1984, Vol. L.
"Story of Han-shan and Shi-te." http://wso.williams.edu/~wmanuel/china/hanshan.html (accessed June 4, 2000).
Turner, Daniel Cross. "Restoration, Metanostalgia, and Critical Memory: Forms of Nostalgia in Contemporary Southern Poetry." *Southern Literary Review* 40 (Spring 2008): 182–206.
"USNS General LeRoy Eltinge (T-AP-154)." www.navsource.org/archives/09/22/22154.htm (accessed July 6, 2010).
Warren, John W., and Adrian W. McClaren. *Tennessee Belles-Lettres*. Morristown: Morristown Pub., 1977, 100.
Watson, Burton, ed. "Han-shan." *The Columbia Book of Chinese Poetry*. New York: Columbia University Press, 1984, 259–267.
"What do Unitarian Universalists believe?" Oak Ridge Unitarian Universalist Church. www.oruuc.org/public_html/staticpages/Index.php?page=20061031083329450 (accessed August 25, 2010).
Williamson, Jerry, and George Scarbrough. "The Country and Beyond: A Conversation." *Iron Mountain Review* 16 (Spring 2000): 31–38. Recorded at Appalachian State University, November 18, 1999.

Index

Page numbers in **_bold italics_** indicate illustrations.

agrarian 19, 73–75
"Anachronisms" 104
animism 111

Baker, George 22
Balla, Phillip 121
Berry, Wendell 178
Britt, Jim 117
Brown, Bill 45–46

"Calligraphy" 67
"Catch-All" 108
Chappell, Fred 198
Chattanooga College 31
Chattanooga Times 19–20
"The Christmas Dance" 53
"Church Funeral" 113
Ciardi, John 176
Clinton High School, Tennessee 29, **_31_**
Coffman, Arlena Andis 29–31
"County Lullabye" 60
"The Creek" 77
Cumming, Robert 111

"Daddy, You Bastard" 54
Davis, Lloyd 74
"Death Is a Creek, Backward Flowing" 52
"Death Is a Short Word" 52
Dickey, James 178, 194
Dickinson, Emily 198
"Direction" 58
"Dream" 115

"Eastward in Eastanalle" 76
Eaton, Charles Edward 73, 179–182

Elnora High School, Indiana 30, **_30_**
USNS *Eltinge* 27
Emory and Henry Literary Festival 45, 47
Engle, Paul 37
"Experience" 19

Fellowship of Southern Writers 47–48
Flynn, Keith 122–123
Francisco, Edward 46–47, 62–63
"Friendship Cemetery in Summer" 59

Gander, Forrest 60, 63, 72
"The Garden" 106
"George Scarbrough Day" 48
"The Gift" 33
Glass, Malcolm 2
"Good Friday, New Mexico, 1955" 116–120
"The Good Mother" 58
Govan, Gilbert 19
Goyen, William 176
Green, Connie Jordan 46
Guerry, Alexander 22

Han-Shan 100–102
Hay, Sara Henderson 72
Hayford, Harrison 38
Hitt, Jack 166
Hiwassee College 31
"The House Where Rivers Join: Confluence of Ocoee & Hiwassee" 78–79

"I Yam What I Yam" 124
"Ice Storm" 54

I'll Take My Stand 74
"Impasse" 53
"Implication" 66
"Initial" 107
"Invitation to Kim" 55–56, 66–67
Iowa Writer's Workshop 37

Jones, Rodney 121, 123
Justus, James 62

Knickerbocker, William 21, 175

"The Lark" 76
"Leathers" 53
Leidig, Dan 72, 81
"Lesson" 58
Lincoln Memorial University 23–24, 48
Loest, Judy 26–27, 49–50
Long, Tudor 22
Lytle, Andrew 22, 24–25, 116, 177–178

"Madness Maddened" 114
Marion, Jeff Daniel 148
McDowell, Joseph Leander 67–68, **68**
Miller, Jim Wayne 2
Mobbs, Rebecca 41, 43, 154–155
"Monday" 57
Moreschi, Allesandro 8
"Music" 107
"My Grandfather Said" 61
"My Mother Language, My Father Tongue" 64

Nancy, France 25–26
"Noon Baptism" 114

"Of Classrooms" 35
"One Flew East, One Flew West, One Flew Over the Cuckoo's Nest" 38–39

Parisi, Joseph 155
Passmore, Ruth Haskins 18
Percy, William Alexander 171
Phillips, Robert L. 62, 82
"Ploughing" 65
"Poem for William Oscar" 54
Poetry Anthology: 1912–2002 48
Polk County High School 36, *37*
"Preferment" 108

"The Private Papers of J.L. McDowell" 67–68
Pulitzer Prize nomination 39

Ransom, John Crowe 171
"Return: August Afternoon" 40
"Revenant" 106
Rogers, David 84, 91–92, 121–122, 157
"Room with a View" 34–35

St. Paul 114–115
Scarbrough, Kenneth (Kim) 56, 99
Scarbrough, Lee 55
Scarbrough, Louise Anabel McDowell 15, **40**, 57–58, 95, 159
Scarbrough, William Oscar 15, 51, **52**, 95, 97
"Scrapbook" 110
"Several More Scenes" 64
"Several Scenes from Act One" 63
Sewanee Review 19–22
"Small Poem" 68, 124
Smith, R.T. 122, 158
Snyder, Gary 101, 104, 109
"Sonnet for My Brother Lee" 55
"The Source is Anywhere" 113
Steele, Frank 2
Stevens, Wallace 198
"Story" 77
Stuart, Jesse 172–174
"Summer Revival: Brush Arbor" 66
"Sunday Shopping" 105–106, 109

Tate, Allen 179
"Tenant" 21
"Tenantry" 79
Third Eye, Crown Chakra 118
Thompson, Marilou (Awiakta) 182
Turner, Daniel Cross 122

Under the Lemon Tree 7, 10
Unitarian Universalist Church 112–113
University of Tennessee 17, 23–24
University of the South 20, 24

Watson, Burton 101–102, 104
Whitman, Walt 35, 76, 198–198
Williamson, J.W. (Jerry) 32, 83
Winfrey, Oprah 168
Woodson, Eula 16, 193–194

www.ingramcontent.com/pod-product-compliance
Ingram Content Group UK Ltd.
Pitfield, Milton Keynes, MK11 3LW, UK
UKHW041958140426
5217IPUK00015B/862